‑ ‑ 42

HISTORIC AFFAIRS

Historic Affairs

The Muses of
Sir Arthur Bryant

W. Sydney Robinson

ZULEIKA

First published 2021

by Zuleika Books & Publishing

Thomas House, 84 Eccleston Square
London, SW1V 1PX

Front cover photograph © Alamy

All images reproduced in the photographic
insert, unless otherwise specified, are from
private collections. The publishers will be happy
to correct any errors at the next printing.

British Library Cataloguing in Publication Data

A catalogue record for this book is
available from the British Library

Designed by Euan Monaghan

ISBN: 978-1-8380324-6-3

'The Muse Clio ... like other women desires attention.'

Arthur Bryant, 'The Art of Biography', *London Mercury*, 30 (1934)

'More knowledge may be gained of a man's real character
by a short conversation with one of his servants, than
from a formal and studied narrative, begun with
his pedigree and ended with his funeral.'

Samuel Johnson, *The Rambler*, No. 60 (1750)

Contents

Foreword

By Miranda McCormick

It was my good fortune, as an only child, to inherit a vast quantity of family papers following the deaths of my father, David McCormick, and mother, Pamela Street, in 1997 and 2007 respectively. Much of this material related to the Second World War, when my parents met; both were participating in the war effort, my mother on the home front and my father completing a period of officer training prior to serving in North Africa, where he was captured. By the time they married at the end of the war, both were very changed characters. Deeply moved by these records, I soon felt it incumbent on me to make use of them by way of tribute to their wartime privations and sacrifices. The result was *Farming, Fighting and Family: a Memoir of the Second World War*, published by The History Press in October 2015.

However willingly I embarked on this first task, it was far harder to decide what to do with another huge collection of papers concerning my mother's relationship with the historian Sir Arthur Bryant, which lasted from shortly after my parents parted company in 1970 until Bryant's death in 1985. Having skimmed through the contents, I realised that they could, potentially, be of some historical or literary value, but found the prospect of bringing them to public attention extremely distasteful. I therefore consigned them to my storeroom, where they might well have remained, had not a kind friend of mine alerted me to the publication, in 2014, of a group biography by W. Sydney Robinson entitled *The Last Victorians*, which included a chapter on Bryant.

When I subsequently read his book, I could see that William (as I have come to know the author) had not fully understood the nature of my mother's relationship with Bryant. This was hardly his fault, since one of his main sources was my mother's biography, *Arthur Bryant: Portrait of a Historian*, published in 1979 to coincide with her subject's 80th birthday, which gave little indication of the fact that she was far more to the latter than merely an efficient and loyal secretary. As William's present book makes clear, there were many reasons for this omission, not least the great pains to which Bryant went to keep his private life hidden from the general public. My mother also played her part in this, both as a result of her innate integrity and discretion, as well as her residual affection for a man who could, as occasion demanded, be amusing and personable. Anyone who takes the time to watch the Thames Television interview of Bryant (now uploaded to the internet), first broadcast in the year my mother's biography was published, will recognise that even in his dotage he possessed a certain 'magnetism': what my mother once described, in one of her pocket-diaries, as 'the Pull'. This was not only on a sexual level; Bryant possessed an almost Machiavellian ability to use his connections in the literary world, combined with flattery of her skills as a writer and artist, to appeal to my mother at a time when she was naturally eager for some degree of public recognition.

It was only after contacting William and realising that he had a serious interest in my mother's archive that I decided I should follow suit. And thank heavens I did, otherwise I would never have come across her posthumous instruction to me, leaving it to my judgement as to whether or not to allow publication of what she described as a 'curious' and 'unique' record – a considerable understatement, as readers of the pages to follow will surely agree.

This record has now been greatly enhanced by William's extensive research into the lives of Bryant's other *inamoratas* – or 'muses', as he refers to them, in keeping with the historical theme – and the skilful way he has added their voices to my mother's original narrative. In the ensuing pages, William touches on various aspects of my family history; a few more details, however, might help to explain my mother's complex personality. With the benefit of hindsight, I suspect my parents' marriage was doomed from the very beginning, largely as a result of their differences in background and aspirations.

My paternal grandfather, Edward McCormick, was one of three brothers from an affluent Chicago family sent over to England to be educated at Eton. Having married the sister of a school friend from a well-to-do Yorkshire family, he settled on this side of the Atlantic, never needing to work for a living; instead he enjoyed a sizeable annual income from various family trusts set up by his forebears. These stemmed, ultimately, from the invention of the mechanical reaper, credited to Cyrus Hall McCormick in the early nineteenth century, and the subsequent founding of the highly successful McCormick International Harvester Company.

My mother's father, A. G. Street, coming from an entirely different world to the American McCormicks, had an even stronger, 'hands-on' agricultural connection. A 'humble tenant farmer' (as he later described himself) on the Pembroke Estate in Wilton, near Salisbury, he was constantly staving off bankruptcy during the agricultural depression of the late 1920s and '30s until the surprise success of his seminal work, *Farmer's Glory*, published in early 1932, suddenly transformed the family fortunes. By the time the Second World War broke out, he was already a seasoned writer and broadcaster, and went on to become one of the main voices of agriculture during the war years, and afterwards a regular West Country panellist on 'Any Questions?'

People who knew my mother described her as sweet-natured, self-effacing, timelessly elegant in an understated way, invariably putting others first. It must be admitted, however, that she was not always the most relaxing of companions. In her unpublished autobiography, *Time on My Side*, she explained how she 'absorbed worry', and would invariably make herself 'miserable' by doing what her conscience told her was 'right'. I remember how, during my childhood, she seemed to exude 'angst', the root of which probably lay in her own formative years. An only child, she could hardly have failed to pick up some of the stresses of the father she hero-worshipped as he struggled for financial survival, especially in the late 1920s after his wife, Vera, almost died as a result of a botched stomach operation.

The one 'constant' during my mother's childhood was her much older cousin Violet Boon, daughter of one of my grandmother Street's impoverished sisters. The 'indispensable Vivi' – as my mother later referred to her – was first employed by the Streets to 'help with the baby', gradually assuming the role of cook and housekeeper. Together with a small retinue of other staff, Vivi ensured that the household was well-managed. When my mother later observed that Bryant was similarly dependent on many people, including his ex-wife and a series of past and present 'muses', she reflected that the essential difference was that her father never had any romantic interest in his own helpers.

As with so much about Bryant, his latter life 'ménage' was completely incomprehensible to my mother. Given her conventional, small country town upbringing, she was almost painfully naive about so many aspects of life, particularly the *mores* of people in higher echelons of society. It is obvious from her pocket-diaries, and other writings, how shocked and disappointed she was to discover the full extent of the dichotomy between Bryant's public and private personas. The dedicatory poem that she composed specially for *Portrait of a Historian* – included rather against her subject's wishes – sums up his contradictory character so well that reprinting it below seems a fitting way to end this Foreword. I hope that in so doing, I have completed my mother's posthumous instruction to me in a manner of which she would have approved:

TO MY SUBJECT
Sometimes I thought I knew him well,
Oftentimes not at all;
Save for his work: a Pimpernel
Hidden behind a wall.
'Only portray,' he seemed to say,
'That which outlives life's span;
Leave me alone to write today –
I am a working man.'

— Miranda McCormick, November 2020

Introduction

Biographies, like love affairs, often begin with obsession and end in disillusionment. Such, at least, has been my experience of writing the life of one of the most prolific biographers of the twentieth century, Sir Arthur Bryant (1899–1985).

I can trace the obsession back to my school days, when I used to pass a bust of the eminent historian on my way to and from Dr Tyerman's classroom in the Old Schools at Harrow. Bryant had started at the school nearly a hundred years previously, but I soon found myself absorbed in his numerous books: biographies of military figures (Wellington, Nelson, Alanbrooke); portraits from the seventeenth century (Charles II, Samuel Pepys); and also several multi-volume histories of England. When I later read, in the works of modern-day experts, that these productions were 'less of a joke than a menace' (Simon Schama), and that he himself had been a 'Nazi sympathiser and fascist fellow-traveller … [as well as a] supreme toady, fraudulent scholar and humbug' (Andrew Roberts), I was aghast. Surely a writer who had given me, and countless others, so much pleasure could not be so appalling?

My research into Bryant culminated with a short biography of him in a book I wrote in 2014, *The Last Victorians*. Drawing on several archive collections, as well as a number of academic studies, I tried to provide a more balanced account of his life and work than was generally available. Where his critics had denigrated him as having few credentials as a historian, I pointed out that he had graduated with the highest possible degree in the subject from Oxford (having first turned down a scholarship from Cambridge), and that his controversial wartime activities – which included authorship of an overly sympathetic account of the rise of Nazism, *Unfinished Victory* – were the dying crackles of the doomed appeasement movement on which he had staked his fortunes during the 1930s. Had he been a genuine traitor to his country, as some have supposed, it would be difficult to account for the admiration shown to him by prime ministers as various as Churchill, Baldwin, Attlee, Wilson and Thatcher, to say nothing of his knighthood in 1954.

If there was one aspect of Bryant's life that I had struggled to comprehend, it was his relationships with women. In particular, it struck me as surprising that this staunchly conservative figure had not only supported the introduction of new divorce legislation but had actually made use of such reforms to leave both his wives: firstly, in 1939, Sylvia Shakerley of Somerford Park, Cheshire; and latterly, in 1976, Anne Brooke, whose uncle, Charles Vyner Brooke, was the last 'White Rajah' of Sarawak – a sprawling jungle kingdom on the island of Borneo. Equally at variance with Bryant's public persona were rumours of 'womanising' (A. L. Rowse), which included the courtship of Laura, Duchess of Marlborough, to whom he was briefly engaged in the early 1980s. Perhaps adhering too closely to my subject's advice to 'would-be biographers' (see p. 89 below), I confined myself to a few short paragraphs about these private matters.

Then, some months after the book's publication, I received a large packet of love letters purporting to be between Bryant and one of his secretaries, Pamela Street. Immaculately typed on thin paper, they came from the latter's daughter, Miranda McCormick, who explained, in a covering note, that the documents formed only part of a much larger correspondence. Aware, from my previous research, that Pamela Street had written an affectionate biography of her employer, *Portrait of a Historian*, during the 1970s, I read through the letters with great interest but also a certain sinking feeling. It was clear from their style and content that I had completely misunderstood the personality of Bryant in *The Last Victorians*. Either I would have to overhaul that work or else write it again, in a new and different format.

I owe it to Miranda that I opted for the latter course. Over many months and years, she frequently invited me to her London home to read, photograph and discuss a collection of materials which provide an almost daily account of a love affair between two highly sensitive individuals spanning nearly two decades. As well as four sturdy lever-arch files of typed letters (the originals being in steel containers), there were innumerable other sources: scrapbooks, pocket-diaries, three autobiographical manuscripts of varying length, an unused radio play and even a few published novels – all based, to some extent, on the author's relationship with Bryant.

The most notable of the memoirs, from which I have drawn extensively in the present book, was entitled *The Narrative: Floating Doters, or Mother, Sister, Mistress, Wife*. This vivid account of the first ten years of Pamela Street's relationship with Bryant begins with a four-page explanatory note outlining her reasons for telling her story. 'I wasn't sure about writing this narrative,' she wrote, '… I didn't quite know how to go about it. After all, in every relationship or love affair there are always two sides to the story and ... [this] is naturally mine.' She explained that she had written the account primarily for her own satisfaction, and that she had kept the accompanying letters because of the potential importance of so many 'words by a famous man who was writing for a living.' She concluded her note with the following instruction:

> None of this could, or should, be published – if at all – until after A. B. [as she always referred to Bryant], his ex-wife and several other people are dead. But because I cannot help thinking that it is not only a curious, but also a unique record which might be of value in years to come, I propose to leave it in the hands of my very dear daughter, in whose judgement and capabilities I have implicit faith.

Fortified by this ordinance, as well as Miranda's constant encouragement, I contacted the descendants of various individuals mentioned in the papers. As a result, many kind people have lent me boxes or suitcases of letters relating to the historian, as well as offering their unstinting support. These benefactors, whose names are gratefully listed in the Acknowledgements, include not only relations of Bryant's second wife, Anne, but also the children and literary executors of several of the historian's other 'muses'. The owner of the Laura Marlborough papers, Hugo Vickers, has most generously provided me with his unpublished diaries in addition to the many hundreds of letters that he has so kindly put at my disposal.

As a result of this wealth of materials, *Historic Affairs* is more detailed and even picturesque than is usually possible in a biography;

even one, such as this, which is focused on the subject's final years. Readers will be aware that there are some drawbacks to my approach, including the reality that sometimes the story is told from the perspective of one individual, Pamela Street, and occasionally it may not be obvious where information has originated. However, I think that the first of these points is compensated both by the fact that Pamela Street was a gifted and judicious storyteller, and also by my inclusion of many letters and papers that she did not, or could not, use at the time of composing her *Narrative* at the outset of 1980. Rarely have I found anything in her writings that is flatly contradicted by these additional materials – generally the reality was bleaker than she supposed.

In terms of my use of sources, I have attempted in all cases to base what I have written on actual documents. While a very small degree of artistic licence has been taken in one or two places, the overwhelming majority of details – and certainly quotations – come from the materials listed above. I have not felt it necessary to include footnotes, partly because so few of the papers have been catalogued, and also on account of the fact that the nature of what is being quoted is usually clear.

Only once – the telephone row about tickets for an event at the Albert Hall (p. 50 below) – have I allowed the needs of 'the story' to override the strict rules of Rankean historical method. It is unlikely, though not impossible, that this particular dialogue (from *Portrait of a Historian*, pp. 165–6) took place on Pamela Street's first day working for Bryant, and in one or two places I have embellished the scene slightly – the punchline about 'An Evening with André Previn' is pure invention. I have done this because there seemed no other way of including this valuable piece of reportage, without which the reader would be robbed of a rare glimpse of Bryant 'working from home'. In any case, there is every reason to believe that the historian, at this stage, would have been unfamiliar with the fashionable American conductor: over a decade later, when he met Previn's most celebrated compère, Ernie Wise, at a literary party, it was clear to an observer, Hugo Vickers, that neither man knew who the other was. I hope that this brief explanation of my methods will give some idea of the pains which have been taken to ensure that the text is as accurate and reliable as possible.

It is necessary to emphasise that this book is neither an indictment nor a glorification of Sir Arthur Bryant. His views were reflective of a completely different era, and even during the course of his lifetime much of what he stood for was challenged by a variety of movements. As with many of his contemporaries, it would be depressingly easy to compile a long list of his outdated views on matters such as race, imperialism, sexuality, democracy and the welfare state. His assumption that the women in his life existed largely to facilitate his activities is equally anathema to modern sensibilities, but such attitudes were not exceptional in his day.

The real heroes of this book are the 'muses' themselves – women who would generally, had it not been for the chance survival of their papers, be remembered only as the 'patient amanuenses' that Bryant referred to in the Acknowledgements of his works. It would have been interesting to look back beyond 1966, but the records before the advertisement in *The Lady* (and, I should add, *The Times*), which I have used to begin my secret history, are remarkably thin. One can only guess if the experiences of Bryant's earlier secretaries were anything like those of their successors; but it is worth considering that, after all their years of service, Bryant appears never to have referred to them again.

While it is for each reader to form their own judgement of Bryant, I would like to close this introduction with the verdict of Churchill's former private secretary, Sir John Colville. Thanking him for one of his last books, he reflected that the historian had always seemed to him more of an Elizabethan figure than a 'Regency buck' or a 'Caroline rogue'. This, it seems to me, is particularly germane. By his own lights, Bryant loved the women in his life, and depended almost pathetically on their support and approval; but there was always something missing, something that was merely for show. Like the protagonist of his favourite novel – Samuel Johnson's *Rasselas* – his timeless quest for happiness blinded him to what he already possessed.

Part One: Pamela

1

In October 1966, an advertisement appeared in the columns of *The Lady*. 'Sir Arthur Bryant requires Private Secretary,' it announced, 'permanent, temporary or part-time; state qualifications.'

Though England's football team had recently lifted the Jules Rimet trophy, and a Liverpudlian musician had declared his pop group to surpass Jesus Christ in acclaim, it would hardly be an exaggeration to say that this was the event of the year so far as Sir Arthur Bryant was concerned. Disorganised and muddle-headed to an almost pathological degree, this revered historian and journalist – author of over a dozen books, oracle of the right-wing of the Conservative party and confidant of countless peers, royals and generals – simply could not function without a team of capable women to attend to his professional, domestic and emotional needs. He often said that he fed upon their energy.

He was sixty-seven and lived, most of the time, in his large Regency-style townhouse at Rutland Gate, Knightsbridge. For the past thirty years he had shared his home with a variety of administrative staff who, in addition to his second wife, Anne, were generally assigned their own quarters within the property. While most of these women had enjoyed an entirely professional relationship with their employer, several had been so captivated by his overbearing charm and formidable reputation as to accept invitations to Mayfair restaurants – or even to pass the night in his Jacobean four-poster. At least one such ingénue, a young woman known only as Dinah, had been so carried away by their lovemaking during the Second World War that she believed Bryant would actually propose marriage: 'her life's biggest hope', he supposed. 'She wants children and status and a home,' the historian had candidly written to the future Lady Bryant at the time, 'it is tragic to see her.' After 'very calmly' telling this admirer, during the course of a midnight conversation, that he was going to marry her more socially elevated rival instead, Bryant was distressed to be awoken, early the following morning, by the sound of her 'sobbing in great chokes' over her typewriter. As much as this was the end of the two-year tryst, the historian had no wish to forget his past. 'We shall always love each other,' he rather strangely confided to Anne in the same letter, before going on to reflect: 'I am a queer, lone, wild sort, but I could be so cosy with you.'

To the world at large, these proclivities were completely unknown. In his regular column for the *Illustrated London News*, Bryant bemoaned every social development since the year of his birth, 1899. 'The established certainties of the Victorian era have vanished,' he lamented in a typical contribution, 'and the younger generation is groping for new faith and new certainty.' But those who observed him closely could, on occasion, catch a glimpse of the historian's roving eye. As well as being a long-standing supporter of the divorce legislation that had enabled him to part from his first wife in the 1930s, he had latterly become an improbable champion of the miniskirt – 'at any rate, when hung on the right pair of legs', as he told his readers. In the recent scandal involving the Minister for War, John Profumo, and a London cabaret girl, the veteran journalist had been one of the few commentators to defend the disgraced politician, claiming that any 'condemnation must comprise ourselves and the whole standard of outlook and conduct which now pass for "progressive", "fashionable" and "contemporary".'

It was, then, an incongruous assortment of women who responded to the advertisement in *The Lady*. A considerable number of the three hundred or so applicants were recent public-school leavers who seemed to think that a stint working for an elderly, distinguished historian would be an agreeable prelude to adult life.

'I have no secretarial experience,' admitted one, 'but I have youth, and youth is energy, and energy is work – which is what you want!' Several of these young ladies, as well as many older ones, hinted at impressive social connections. One such applicant, Diana Villiers, although without significant secretarial experience, could trace her ancestry from both the chief minister and the principal mistress of the subject of Bryant's first bestseller, a biography of Charles II. There was also a young lady, Joan Evans, who wrote proudly of working for an American tycoon 'whose interests ranged from the performing arts, to yachting, to horse-breeding and racing, apart from his normal business operations.' Yet another promising candidate, Ann Hibbard, came with a recommendation from the vice-chairman of the Conservative Party, for whom she had been working for the past two years.

All these applicants were added to the shortlist, but Bryant's first choice was a Mrs Trevett, whose situation was even more satisfactory from his point of view. Having been abandoned by her husband during the war, this hard-working matron had struggled against unfair odds to provide for herself and an invalid sister. Her litany of woes included the loss of her late mother's home under the Rent Act, a hysterectomy and maltreatment at the hands of a famous boarding school, which had revoked its offer of a residential position at the eleventh hour. Over the past few years she had supported herself as a secretary; first, at the Royal Society for the Prevention of Accidents, which she had left 'on a matter of principle', and, latterly, for a firm of chartered surveyors, which she had resigned from as a result of finding the work to be lacking in 'administrative and intellectual satisfaction.' Rather despairingly, she expressed a hope that her new employer would redress these issues, and also be 'a pleasant human being'.

'As for the imponderables,' the letter ran on, 'I am socially acceptable and also possess social competence – have a thoroughly sound sense of humour and get on well with my colleagues at all levels. While mature, I am most certainly neither a battleaxe nor a fuddy-duddy; I am personable, well turned out, and have a friendly and confident manner.' A final sentence praising Bryant's books on 'the struggle with Napoleon' and 'my dear Samuel Pepys' assured her of an interview – Sir Arthur underlined the flattering words with approval.

The shortlisted candidates were invited to be interviewed at 18 Rutland Gate on a fixed date towards the end of October. Whatever they were expecting, however, it is clear that many of these women did not relish the experience. 'With reference to my interview with you yesterday evening,' wrote Ann Hibbard baldly, 'I am writing to let you know that I have decided that I no longer wish to be considered for the position as your secretary.' Only Mrs Trevett was prepared to accept the low pay and irregular hours offered by Sir Arthur; but even she made it clear that she could work no more than two days a week for him. The shortfall would be made up by one of the younger and less experienced applicants, Susanna Hoe, who made similar caveats and provisos before accepting the offer of part-time employment. In moments of desperation, the historian feared that his working life would soon break down completely. It was at just such a low ebb that he first heard from Pamela.

———

The letter was brought up to Sir Arthur as he prepared to devour one of his famously large breakfasts. He saw from the postmark that it had come from his beloved Wiltshire, where he had, some years previously, attempted to fulfil a childhood aspiration to become a dairy farmer. Like so many of Bryant's flights of fancy, the enterprise had not been a success and he was now searching for someone to buy his abandoned herd. His first hope was that the letter might come from just such an individual.

A perusal of the document piqued this expectation. It had been sent by the daughter of one of the country's foremost agriculturalists, the late A. G. Street, who had assisted him with his forlorn farming adventure over a decade ago. 'Please will you forgive a letter from a stranger,' his daughter, Pamela McCormick, now wrote, 'although I know that you will remember my late father … One of my greatest treasures is the wonderful tribute you paid him in the *Illustrated London News* of August 13th, 1966.'

Bryant remembered the article. In one of those nostalgic rambles so characteristic of his later journalism, he had recalled how Street's debut publication, *Farmer's Glory*, had reawakened public interest in agriculture 'at the very nadir of British farming between the wars'. Since the book had come out within months of his *Charles II*, Bryant wrote to his fellow author, praising his 'direct Cobbett-like English', and inviting him to lecture on agriculture at the Conservative-backed Bonar Law College, where he was then Educational Adviser. Although Bryant admitted in his article to falling out of touch with Street – 'There is nothing,' he grandly wrote, 'like being ... a "public" man for breaking up old acquaintanceship' – he praised the latter's column in the *Farmer's Weekly*. It was, he proudly noted, a fixture in British journalism equivalent in longevity to his own feature in the *Illustrated London News*, 'Our Notebook', which he had inherited from G. K. Chesterton in 1936.

Pamela had now written a short biography of her father, and, after discussing the matter with her publisher, wondered if Bryant would be willing to contribute a foreword. 'I feel very diffident indeed in approaching you like this,' she wrote, 'as I am not an established author, although I have done some writing in the past (mostly the odd verse in *Punch* and *The Field*) and this biography has had some good readers' reports.' Perhaps she had a presentiment of the historian's personality, or had been appraised of this by her father, as she appeared to add a small dose of flattery to her request. 'If you were able to write anything at all at the beginning of the book, I should consider it the greatest honour,' she continued, before returning to his obituary of her father. 'I marvelled at the insight you had to his character. No one else could have expressed my own feelings about him so beautifully.'

Though scarcely a week passed without such a favour being asked of him, it would have been difficult for Sir Arthur to ignore this particular request. One of his secretaries would later recall that he was generally willing to lend his name to books by novice authors, so long as the writer and subject matter were sufficiently close to his heart. Some idea of the historian's peculiar criteria can be surmised from three other works to receive his imprimatur during these years: an admiring memoir of Field Marshal Douglas Haig by his former chaplain; a collection of rural idylls called *Lovers of the Land* by Lady Louise Stockdale, and a short treatise bearing the intriguing title: *Money: The decisive factor; Britain's handicap in the economic race with Russia*. Pamela's biography of her father fitted well into this broad scheme, and the historian responded to her 'charming letter' with a definite promise of help.

Sir Arthur was honest enough not to overstate the inconvenience of this commitment. 'I would gladly write a foreword,' he wrote in his reply, 'but wonder whether – as I am so terribly pressed for time and in such heavy arrears with my work – we could use the whole or part of my *Illustrated London News* article? Would you very kindly look at it again and let me know? I could probably easily make some minor alterations to adapt it.'

The importance of this breakthrough was only too apparent from Pamela's enthusiastic reply. 'I really cannot tell you how grateful, honoured and pleased I feel to know that something by you will appear in the front of my biography,' she wrote. 'Also,' she continued, 'I know that my father would feel just the same.'

But it was not long until Pamela discovered how far Bryant's administrative juggernaut had broken down since the misadventure of his advertisement in *The Lady*. Early autumn turned into deep winter before Bryant found time to execute the 'minor alterations' he had promised. Not even a steady stream of letters from his anxious correspondent jogged him into action.

'It might interest you to know,' one of these missives had politely observed, 'that my husband has kept your articles "Why we can still be rich and strong" and "Let Sir Alec take over as leader again" from the *Sunday Express*, as he says to him they are the only ones which make any sense in the British Press in 1968!'

At one stage, Bryant had to confess that one of his new secretaries had mislaid the typescript of her book and that he had inadvertently 'soiled' its cover. To his further embarrassment, he also had to admit to losing the copy of his original article, which Pamela had eagerly sent him at the outset of their correspondence. In the event, it was only at the last minute that the foreword appeared with the publisher in the run up to the book's publication in May 1969.

By this time, the connection between Pamela and Sir Arthur had blossomed into a friendship of sorts. Despite the former's debilitating self-effacement and repeated reluctance to disturb Bryant's 'important work', she had – following a correspondence with Miss Hoe about Sir Arthur's 'likes and dislikes' – dispatched an expensive bottle of Saint-Émilion as a New Year's gift. He, in turn, had offered to send her as many copies of his works as she would like – a proposition which elicited Pamela's most ecstatic response to date: 'I feel it would be altogether wrong for me to accept anything else from you, not, of course, that I shouldn't be most terribly proud to have *any one* of your distinguished books from *you personally* in the highest place of honour on my shelves – irrespective of any I may already have!'

While Bryant succeeded in forcing a volume of his *Story of England* upon her, he was unable to interest either her or her husband in his unwanted Jersey herd. 'It takes up so much of the time I ought to be giving to writing history,' he had complained, 'that I feel I may have to harden my heart and give it up … for the sake of the cows.'

The first clue of Bryant's colourful private life came in the form of a letter from his wife, Anne. This was a response to Pamela's invitation for the Bryants to attend a celebratory dinner at the Dorchester Hotel to mark her book's publication. Several aspects of the letter were unusual. Firstly, Lady Bryant explained that the invitation had arrived the day that her husband had departed, without her, for South Africa. As she had been staying with her sister in Weybridge, where she was still residing, she had known nothing of the event until her husband had written to her from Tenerife 'saying that he would be writing to you on his arrival in South Africa'. There was also a surprising reference to her husband's penchant for going away for long stretches of time 'on a combination of holiday and work'. Only tact prevented her from mentioning that he seldom went alone.

When Bryant, as promised, sent his response from South Africa, he further complicated matters by subtly altering his wife's version of events. 'I should have written before to thank you for your very kind invitation,' he scrawled from the home of his friend, the patriotic writer H. V. Morton, 'which was forwarded to me in South Africa.' Reiterating his wife's acceptance of the invitation, he explained that he would be returning to the country on the day of the party. It would, he reassured her, make his 'homecoming an additionally pleasant one' to be dining with her that evening.

In due course, the Bryants arrived at the Dorchester's private function suite for the long-awaited dinner. The table was set for ten, as Pamela had invited, besides her publisher and his literary team, some mutual friends of hers and the Bryants, Margaret and Derbe Berry, as well as her daughter, Miranda, who had just begun her undergraduate studies at Oxford and would be bringing her young boyfriend along too. Although Bryant would, before long, excoriate his host's alleged parsimony, the evening was underwritten by Pamela's husband, David, who generously provided his wife's guests with champagne cocktails and three bottles of Château Léoville-Poyferré '55 in addition to their gourmet dinners. It was practically the last time that the pair would go through the increasingly painful charade of still being happily married.

There was, however, little indication that Pamela would soon become involved romantically with Sir Arthur. Visibly exhausted by his long journey, he shuffled into the room looking more like an elderly caretaker than a latter-day Lothario. His well-preserved Edwardian dinner jacket hung loosely from his wide shoulders, and he shook all the proffered hands around the table with a certain limpness, even lethargy. He said little besides how sorry he was for being so bemused by his flight, and he and his wife were among the first to depart.

The following day Lady Bryant sent an especially kind letter of thanks. As well as expressing her gratitude for the hospitality, she indicated how much she had enjoyed reading Pamela's biography of her father. 'You must have turned yourself inside-out in the writing of it,' she perceptively commented. What had particularly resonated with her were the parallels she had drawn between A. G. Street and her own father, Bertram Brooke, 'who was [also] incapable of telling a lie or doing anything crooked'. Both women seemed to have found, in their respective parents, heroes in a world of moral pigmies.

So, in conventional circumstances, Pamela's connection with the

Bryants might have ended. But a week later came a second letter, this time from the famous historian himself.

'It is very much on my conscience that I haven't written sooner to thank you,' he wrote, 'for the inscribed copy of your beautiful and moving book ... and for so kindly asking us to the dinner which heralded its publication.' As well as referring once again to his 'awful arrears of work and correspondence', he returned to the theme of his state of mind that evening. 'Please forgive me,' he went on, '... for seeming so dull and dazed, as I must have done ... for though I greatly enjoyed it I was, I am afraid, terribly tired after all that flying.' He ended the main part of his letter by complimenting her on the 'little classic' that she had written. He was, he said, 'very proud to be associated with it' and would do all he could to ensure its success.

'I hope very much,' he concluded in the margin, 'that in losing one friend in your dear father, I have found another in his daughter.'

2

What Sir Arthur did not yet know was that Pamela was approaching a crisis. At the age of forty-eight, she had come to the terrible realisation that she should never have married the young army officer to whom she had become 'unofficially' engaged in the spring of 1941. Only the highly unusual circumstances of their courtship blinded her to the fact that they were completely ill-suited from the start.

The wedding had taken place in July 1945, within weeks of VE Day, and after a hiatus of four years during which the pair had not even seen one other. This had been due to David's posting to Egypt where, in December 1941, he was captured while fighting in the Desert War. He spent the rest of the conflict surviving in a series of overcrowded Italian and German POW camps.

Although distraught by these developments, Pamela had attempted to do all she could on the Home Front, serving both as a nurse in the Voluntary Aid Detachment and later as an officer in the women's branch of the Army, the Auxiliary Territorial Service. By the time that David returned from his long captivity, she had already, under the strain of these activities, suffered a severe nervous breakdown, and it was while still recovering from this that she agreed, as convention dictated, to go ahead with her marriage to the prematurely aged and balding stranger for whom she had been 'waiting'. Only later did she reflect that she had done so more out of pity than passion.

The peacetime years quickly revealed further disparities between husband and wife. Unlike Pamela, who loved to express herself through art, literature and poetry, David had never really questioned the stoical values and tastes that he had imbibed as a schoolboy at Radley. More troubling, David also found it hard, in the early years of their marriage, to find suitable employment. Having finally secured a position at a London stockbrokers' firm, he felt that the commute into the City was too reminiscent of his time as a POW, and it was not long before the couple returned to South Wiltshire, where David had undergone his officer training and Pamela had enjoyed a happy childhood.

With the utmost diffidence, David now asked his revered father-in-law, A. G. Street, if he would help him start again as a farmer. It was on this understanding that it was possible for the novice to obtain a large agricultural mortgage – as well as a loan from his parents – for the purchase of a six-hundred-acre farm at Steeple Langford, not far from A. G. Street's own farm in the Wylye Valley. Despite coming from a wealthy trans-Atlantic family, and inheriting a sizeable legacy of £10,000 from a grandparent, nearly all David's capital was absorbed in the running of the farm. Nevertheless, under his father-in-law's benign direction, it was not long before he had mastered the art of farming, and within a decade he was even able to purchase part of an adjoining farm, including its imposing Elizabethan manor house, Yarnbury Grange, which became the family home.

Life in the country was not, however, without difficulties for the McCormicks. For David, these mostly involved worrying pains in his chest, which were left untreated until he was eventually diagnosed with severe angina in the mid-1950s.

For Pamela, however, it was the birth, in 1949, of the couple's only child, Miranda, which inadvertently led to another major crisis. Having always known that she did not want children – preferring to 'create in other ways' – the burdens of motherhood quickly proved an intolerable strain. Her angst and unhappiness were exacerbated by the fact that Miranda grew to be a sickly child, suffering particularly from bronchial asthma during the harsh winters. Concerned relatives commented that Pamela was becoming 'obsessive' about the girl, and even her beloved father advised that 'a dose of healthy neglect' was in order.

Following consultations with various medical specialists, the couple decided to send Miranda away to boarding school: initially, to a prep school in the New Forest, and, latterly, to Pamela's old school in Salisbury, Godolphin. As the first of these experiments had not been successful – Miranda had to be withdrawn almost immediately due to an acute ear infection – they decided to start her off at Godolphin as a day pupil. When, however, Miranda became a boarder in her second year she was bullied unmercifully by her new companions, who viewed day pupils as somehow different. In January 1962 she ran away, making it as far as a great-aunt's cottage in Wilton.

This was the beginning of a downward spiral for Pamela. The shock, disappointment and anger initially provoked by Miranda's actions were soon eclipsed by feelings of guilt and failure. How, she wondered, had she not sensed her daughter's misery? While David increasingly took over in terms of family decisions – such as transferring Miranda to a school he had already put her down for near Ascot – Pamela endured a second, even more serious, nervous breakdown, which led to her being hospitalised, on and off, for some four years.

By the standards of the time, David was a patient and supportive husband throughout his wife's illness. He regularly took her to see leading Harley Street psychiatrists and was farsighted enough to veto one expert's recommendation of brain surgery as a quick panacea. But he still struggled to comprehend mental illness, especially as the stress he associated with Pamela's condition had worsened his own health problems: in 1971 it became necessary for him to travel to Chicago for a major operation on his heart. By the time that his wife had recovered in 1965, he had put some distance between the two of them, leaving her in the care of friends or professionals as much as possible.

Matters were further worsened by the death, in July 1966, of Pamela's beloved father, A. G. Street. Alongside the grief of this loss, Pamela was shaken to learn that her husband would not allow her widowed mother, Vera, to come and stay with them, even though she was herself unwell and would die of palsy only three years later.

It was against this grim backdrop of arguments and bereavement that the couple considered, for the first time, getting a divorce. But even in the 1960s, with its gospel of 'freedom' and 'emancipation', few marriages ended in this way, and such a step would have been a form of social suicide for the troubled couple.

Partly for this reason, David and Pamela initially tried to save their relationship through the assistance of marriage counsellors and even went through a brief reconciliation. Sadly, however, this did not last, and it was not long before Pamela's old grievances resurfaced, with predictable effects on David's own wellbeing. 'I feel I should prefer loneliness,' he wrote to one of their marital advisers, 'to this continual criticism and destructive animosity. It seems that Pam wants to keep my emotional state at fever pitch, even if the emotions registered are only negative ones such as irritation, anger and anxiety. I just want some peace.'

This peace was to be found by living increasingly separate lives. While Pamela occupied herself by writing a short biography of her father, David became accustomed to spending much of the week in Mayfair, where he owned a small flat. Early in their marriage he had bought the entire block as a one-off property venture, keeping only the top-floor caretaker's flat as a base, he hoped, for their daughter to complete a 'season' of dances hosted by the country's most influential families. Pamela had been rather against this venture, both on account of the extra borrowing it entailed and because she viewed the very concept of 'coming out' in society with suspicion, if not open disdain. When the time came for Miranda to undertake this bygone ritual in 1968, Pamela played the part expected of her as a debutante's mother with minimal involvement.

It was shortly after this milestone, with Miranda now an undergraduate at Oxford, that Pamela began to suspect that there was something more to her husband's frequent trips to London. What turned suspicion into certainty was the discovery in October 1970 – almost two years after contacting Sir Arthur about her book – of a highly incriminating cache of evidence. These were the stubs of a chequebook which revealed that David had been making regular payments to a mistress with whom he often stayed in the capital.

This, finally, was the end of the marriage: in a rare moment of fortitude, Pamela declared that she would be filing for divorce. If she did this with some degree of relief, the same was undoubtedly the case for David, who had long-since come to terms with the fact that their marriage was beyond repair, and had even started looking for a potential new home for Pamela in the Cathedral Close in Salisbury. This plan was only put on hold by the sudden urgency of the situation, which required Pamela to go and live in their London flat while the necessary arrangements could be made.

One thing that the couple were agreed upon was that her stay at 47 South Street would not be for long. On the fateful autumn day when David left her there, the emotionally fragile countrywoman took one look at the cramped flat – which she had always hated – and immediately pleaded to be taken back to Wiltshire, either to 'try again' or at least to find some less drastic means of going their separate ways. But her husband was adamant. 'You're a big girl now,' he said as he dropped the solitary suitcase that she had thought to pack.

Only when the slow process of obtaining a divorce was begun shortly afterwards did Pamela realise that she would be stuck in London for considerably longer than either of them had envisaged. Aside from this, she tormented herself with the idea that their mutual friends would be 'judging' her for the failure of her marriage. At times she wondered if she would ever return to her beloved West Country at all.

This sense of desperation was reflected in the political climate of the time. Earlier that year the Conservative leader, Edward Heath, had unexpectedly defeated the Labour prime minister, Harold Wilson, in a close-run general election. Lacking popular support both in his party and in the country at large, the somewhat unprepossessing Heath nevertheless attempted to push through a series of sweeping reforms, including decimalisation, a complete overhaul of local government and admittance of Britain to the continental trading zone, the European Economic Community. Connected with these policies was an intention to amend industrial relations, as well as to end state subsidies to failing industries. It was this concoction of initiatives that began the series of crises which engulfed Britain for the next fifteen years – a situation exacerbated by Heath's reluctance to carry through with his initial 'modernising' agenda. The result was that, even as early as 1970, the British public began to experience regular power outages, as the unions exerted their strength over the government. Pamela, along with the rest of the population, would soon become used to bathing in the dark and going to bed early for lack of warmth and electric lighting.

There were few friends to whom Pamela could turn at this difficult time. Other than a doctor and his wife who spent weekdays in London, she knew practically no one in the capital. And as she attempted, in a strategy to stave off depression, to see someone almost every day, it was not long until she thought of making contact once again with the Bryants. She had seen them at least twice since her dinner party at the Dorchester Hotel; once at a small drinks party at Yarnbury Grange, and on another occasion at the home of their mutual friends in the area, the Berrys. In addition to simply wanting some company, Pamela knew that Anne devoted much of her time to charitable work, and she was attracted by the idea of doing something similar as a means of giving her life a renewed sense of purpose and direction. With this objective in mind, Pamela overcame her habitual shyness and, one drizzly November afternoon, dialled the number for 18 Rutland Gate.

It was Lady Bryant who answered. Her tone was cheerful and encouraging. 'My dear Pam,' she would soon write, 'please call me

Anne.' The two women discussed the possibility of meeting for tea one day despite the ongoing industrial disruption which had plunged much of the country into despair and gloom:

> Arthur insisted I should get in a supply of horrible tin things [wrote Anne in her letter] in case there should be a general strike. It's too ridiculous to contemplate, but so have been the blackouts which have almost reduced me to the wreck I was during the war, & I don't feel safe unless my torch is within sight day and night. And we are so fortunate in comparison to the majority of the poor, long-suffering British people who are mucked about by the Government, damn!

Despite these inconveniences, it was not long before Pamela found herself perched on the green velvet chaise longue that dominated Anne's small drawing room. The younger woman did not need to go into too much detail for her companion to discern her situation. They had both, in their separate ways, battled with an appalling number of personal problems over the years: Anne herself suffered from depression and had for many years been overdependent on alcohol. Although now well into her sixties and without children, she had a strong maternal instinct and desperately wanted to assist her new friend.

'She was looking awful,' she later recalled of her guest, '[and] said that when she felt stronger ... she would like to work in some voluntary capacity.'

While Anne outlined some of the options available, her husband, who had not previously emerged from his study, entered the room for a 'very short time' to greet the visitor. He was intrigued by what he saw, later commenting that she had seemed to him a 'maiden in distress', ready for him to rescue.

It was at least partly on account of this sentiment that Sir Arthur, shortly afterwards, suggested that Anne invite the unhappy woman for dinner with them on Christmas Day. This was to be the couple's sole celebration that year, as the historian resented any break from his work, while his wife preferred to spend most of the festive period fulfilling her share of responsibilities at a local hospital. The only other guest, rather typically, was to be the former Lord Chief Justice, Rayner Goddard, who was an old acquaintance of Sir Arthur's.

Anne's invitation gave a clear picture of both the warmth and unconventionality of the Bryant household. Whatever her husband's motivations, the fact that she had specifically thought to include Pamela's daughter, Miranda, who would be staying with her mother over the Christmas period, suggests that there were, as yet, no grand designs afoot.

'Arthur & Rayner,' the letter ran, 'will wear dinner jackets & please, both of you, wear whatever is most comfortable. We only have one rule which is that we don't give or receive presents. It's your company we love.'

It was purely on account of serendipity that this convivial gathering was to be transformed into something rather more unholy. For when Miranda returned from Oxford a day or two before the party, she brought with her a hacking cough. Only a few hours before they were due to depart from South Street, she told her mother that, since it had still not cleared, she would prefer to stay behind. Pamela wondered for a moment whether it would be best to cancel after all, but her daughter was loath to spoil the evening. 'Go on, Mummy,' she implored, 'you've had a rotten time lately: I'll be quite happy looking at TV.'

For the first time since her youth, Pamela was to attend a party not as a wife and a mother but simply as a talented, single woman.

Nerves and anticipation propelled her onwards. Had she thought rationally about it, she might have doubted the wisdom of celebrating Christmas with two such formidable representatives of the British 'establishment' as Sir Arthur and Lord Goddard. Only when her taxi arrived at her destination did she begin to doubt her resolve. The house looked so grand and forbidding. More to the point, it looked strangely vacant. Other than a light coming from the first-floor windows, the entire property seemed as empty as the various embassies that were dotted around the square, apparently shut up for the holidays. Almost without realising, Pamela ascended the little flight of stairs to the entrance and rang the bell.

There was a slight delay before a blurred silhouette appeared at the windowpane. This belonged to neither of her hosts but to their housekeeper, Mrs Chalkley, whose style of dress quietly advertised that today was her 'day off'. If she was, on account of this, a trifle short with Pamela as she took her hat and coat, it was not the only cause of her vexation. By long-standing arrangement, she and her husband would be hosting the veteran Law Lord's own retainers in the basement, and she was not sure how long Herbert could be trusted stirring the pot.

Pamela was left, alone, in the small, candlelit dining room. As the minutes passed she felt a growing sense of embarrassment. Then there was a sudden patter of footsteps down the central stone staircase.

'Surely not the speedy, sure-footed sound of a septuagenarian?' she later reminisced. But it was.

'Pam,' he said, striding into the room, 'I'm so sorry. I should have been ready. Anne's cooking. Come up to the library ...'

He looked a lot younger than he had at their previous meetings: his face seemed fuller and his eyes sparkled in the candlelight. And there was an energy and an urgency about him that had completely passed her by until now. It almost frightened her.

Before she could mumble her own vague apologies, she was swept upstairs to the library, listening en route to a garbled discourse on the follies of the present government, whose ministers were unfavourably compared to the subject of his latest book, the first Duke of Wellington.

To these ruminations, Pamela could offer only the meekest assent. Although she had recently attempted to improve her academic credentials by taking an A level in History at the Salisbury College of Further Education, she knew nothing of Tory cabinets and Irish votes. Yet she instinctively felt, as a life-long Labour supporter, that much of what he said ran counter to her beliefs. Somehow it was just impossible to contradict him, even in the matter of what to drink. 'Yes,' she heard herself repeating as he handed her a glass of sherry.

The library was enormous. Encased by two massive windows and a series of groaning bookshelves, it seemed more like the reception room of a gentlemen's club than a private study. While her host arranged Christmas cards on the mantlepiece above the fireplace, she sat nervously in a leather armchair overlooked by a bust of an austere nineteenth-century writer or statesman – incongruously draped in ribbons. On either side of her were a pair of large mahogany writing desks, each scattered with an assortment of pink carbon papers, reference books and unanswered correspondence. Two bright chandeliers combined with the glow of the fire to create an overall impression of red and gold and splendour. After a few sips of her drink, Pamela realised that she was, in more than one sense of the word, intoxicated.

The sound of high-pitched laughter announced the arrival of Anne. She was, even more than Pamela recalled from their recent meeting, slim, elegant and, given her age, surprisingly vigorous and emphatic. She was amused by the sight of her husband still trying to arrange Christmas cards. 'I'm afraid,' he replied sheepishly, 'I'm always a little apt to leave putting them up until—'

The doorbell interrupted him. Lord Goddard, aged and infirm, had arrived with his small entourage. Pamela and her hosts came down to greet him in the hallway before moving straight through for dinner. The gentlemen sat at either end of the rectangular table, and, in the presence of his old friends, the former Chief Justice became almost expansive. He had first crossed paths with Bryant at the Inns of Court, when the younger man was reading for the Bar in the 1920s; later, shortly after the war, he and Winston Churchill had sat either side of the eminent historian at a special dinner at Gray's Inn. At the time of their first acquaintance, Goddard was already a successful King's Counsel, well known for his staunch conservativism – he had even run for parliament in a failed attempt to unseat a divorced MP. Subsequently he had gone on to acquire a reputation as the country's foremost 'hanging judge', presiding over the legal execution of countless miscreants, including a young man who had ambiguously told his armed friend to let a police officer 'have it'. This evening, however, his lordship, encouraged by Lady Bryant, recited in a splendid Stanley Holloway voice 'Albert and the Lion' – twice.

At the other end of the table, Sir Arthur was in prime position to monopolise Pamela. He spoke kindly of her father, and of her biography of him, which he was pleased to hear had already been through four impressions. She, likewise, complimented him on the latest instalment of his national history which he had been kind enough to send her and her husband some months previously. Then, picking up one of the silver salt cellars on the table, she asked how he had come to possess so many exquisite antiques. He smiled shyly and began to recount how his first wife, Sylvia Shakerley, had belonged to an old Cheshire family, and that these particular receptacles had probably adorned her forebears' dining table when his beloved Charles II had visited the county in the mid-1600s.

Pamela was on the verge of asking what had become of Sylvia when she looked up and found Sir Arthur watching her. Their eyes met; she turned away. Something raw and primitive had passed between them: it was neither welcome, nor entirely unwanted.

Lord Goddard was carried back into his car by his servants immediately after dinner, and the remainder of the party returned to the library for a nightcap. The topic of conversation unexpectedly turned to the operettas of Gilbert and Sullivan – one of Sir Arthur's favourite forms of light entertainment. Anne asked if Pamela also enjoyed their music. Eager to please, she replied in the affirmative. But then she inwardly hesitated, as the purport of what was being suggested dawned on her: her hostess wanted her to accompany her husband to a performance of *Trial by Jury* at the Savoy Theatre. In the country district in which she had been born and bred, wives did not suggest such things. She shot a confused look at Sir Arthur; he was beaming.

The arrival of Pamela's hired car, earlier than expected, prevented the matter going any further. It was, she thought, a lucky escape. Had the driver arrived just a few minutes later, she would have been forced to choose between compromising herself and disappointing her hosts.

Such accidents, however, could not guard her from the historian indefinitely.

3

Pamela made no mention of any of the curious conversations or happenings in her polite thank-you letter to Anne. A part of her saw no particular reason why she should ever see the Bryants again; she certainly was in no position to return their hospitality in the same style. Aside from the limited capacity of her flat, she was now fully occupied with her own affairs. Foremost among these was her attempt to obtain a divorce from David through the small firm of country solicitors which had handled her parents' estates. She was also busy correcting the proofs of her new book, *A Portrait of Wiltshire*, which seemed a fitting sequel to her biography of her father.

And yet Pamela continued to feel painfully downcast. When Miranda returned to Oxford at the beginning of the new year, her home started to feel like a prison.

'Sundays, five floors up in a silent Mayfair flat,' she would later write, 'however comfortable, were a special kind of agony.' Days might pass without seeing another human face, and there was something she found utterly 'distasteful and irritating' about the legal process in which she had become embroiled. Even her enthusiasm to correct her proofs could sometime flag. Depression, once again, reared its ugly head.

In such a condition, the ringing of the telephone one Sunday afternoon brought a rare moment of relief, even if it was simply the wrong number. Her expectations were exceeded when she heard, at the other end of the line, a gravelly voice enquire: 'Pam?' There was no need for him to say anything further by way of introduction, but he went on: 'This is Arthur …'

She stood up and clutched the phone a shade too tightly.

'I was wondering,' he continued a little uncertainly, 'if by any chance you weren't doing anything tonight. Anne suggested it. She is going to her sister's … Would you care to join me for dinner … as my guest … at my club?'

The request rather took her aback. Besides her husband, whom she had met at a local dance during the war, there was only one man who had ever asked her out on a serious 'date'. This was an American captain whom she had met two years after David had been captured in the Desert War. Given her conventional upbringing, Pamela had struggled to forget the appalling sense of guilt which she associated with this 'near affair', and she had vowed at the time never again to allow herself to fall so short of her strict moral standards. And yet she now heard herself accepting Sir Arthur's invitation. A part of her simply could not view the situation as in any way akin to her dalliance with that handsome American captain. Surely principled, married men and women did not go out on 'dates'? Hadn't Anne suggested it in any case?

But just as Pamela was trying to rationalise what she had done, the phone rang again. She knew exactly who it was this time.

'Pam?' returned the voice. 'I feel I didn't give you much choice … I mean, about where to go.'

She wanted to cut him off – to laugh, to say they could perfectly well see each other once Anne had returned from her sister's; but she simply clutched the phone tighter and tighter.

'Would you really like my rather vulgar club? Or there's a little restaurant in the Brompton Road.'

She mumbled something about not minding either way – she would later reminisce that 'a Lyon's Corner House would have been all right for me' – but he continued speaking to himself regardless. Although far too unworldly to realise this at the time, it obviously suited the historian to take her somewhere, unlike his various clubs, where he would not be recognised.

Pamela had more than enough time to select her outfit in the hours before Sir Arthur came to collect her. Since returning to London as a single woman, she had bought hardly anything new and was 'making do' with what she had packed in her little suitcase. Yet throughout her life she had prided herself on maintaining a 'capsule' wardrobe, in which all the garments were in tones of black, brown, beige or white, in order to mix and match easily. She favoured good quality fabrics in 'lady-like' styles, with high necklines, long sleeves and calf-length hems – a far cry from the miniskirts that Sir Arthur had recently praised in his newspaper column. Being tall and slender, she had always been complimented by her Wiltshire friends on her elegant appearance, and her new companion would shortly liken her to Lady Edwina Mountbatten, whose beauty and charm was widely revered. Pamela briefly considered buying something special for this highly unusual occasion but quickly decided against it; whatever the outcome, she must not look too 'keen'. One of her favourite Jaeger outfits would easily fit the bill.

The individual who arrived at her block of flats appeared to have a rather different approach to matters sartorial. Not a man for fashion or fine tailoring, he appeared to have acquired a few good suits in his thirties and simply had them altered as his waistline had expanded. More worrying was his demeanour. Pamela would later express surprise that although he was 'not exactly late', he was 'in great agitation'. He told her that he had walked across Hyde Park and now proposed that they try to find a taxi together. It was the sort of cost-cutting initiative that had long been a feature of Sir Arthur's romantic activities. 'I remember,' recollected Pamela, 'some discussion as to whether we should have to take a bus.' But, at length, they found a cab and were shortly seated opposite one another at the unassuming Polish restaurant, the Marynka.

The couple ordered starters and main courses, as well as a bottle of French wine. It had been a long time since Pamela had been out to a restaurant and she was beginning almost to enjoy herself. But, to her dismay, Sir Arthur barely ate anything.

'He *seemed* well enough,' she later wrote, '[and] was a most charming and attentive host, but, nevertheless, when the waiter came to clear the main course, his was almost untouched.'

She did not feel that she knew him well enough to remark on this curious behaviour. Only much later did he provide her with an explanation. 'Incredible as it still seems to me,' she wrote, 'he confessed that it was because he had fallen in love.'

Conversation, then, was not exactly free flowing. A man with 'absolutely no small talk', Sir Arthur was largely confined to stories about Salisbury and Wiltshire, the main connection between the pair. Herself lacking in confidence, Pamela listened attentively to his fond memories of the old markets he had attended as a boy, and how he had often sat reading poetry on the banks of the River Avon. He said that he wanted to help with her new book, though it was not exactly clear how this was to happen, the text having already been completed and set to type.

History was another topic that could fill any lulls in their conversation. Always in the midst of some exhaustive project, Sir Arthur explained that he was nearing the end of his research on Wellington and would shortly be retracing his footsteps on the long road to Waterloo. Despite his subject's Irish parentage, the biography provided Sir Arthur with the perfect opportunity to praise the qualities of a great Englishman – a description that he was only too glad to apply to Pamela's father, as others would likewise bestow upon himself. The finished biography was to outline these attributes in the historian's distinctive, seductive prose. 'An officer to command must be worthy of command,' he would write, 'be both a gentleman – honourable, faithful to his trust, truthful, self-controlled and considerate to others – and a soldier dedicated by study and experience to the mastery of his profession.

'Only so,' he continued, 'could he deserve and win the confidence which had to exist between men who faced death together and depended on one another utterly.'

While there was not much that Pamela could contribute to this sort of discussion, she was certainly starting to enjoy Sir Arthur's company.

As they travelled back to South Street, she debated with herself about whether or not to invite him in for coffee. 'It was still very early,' she later wrote, 'but I decided against it.

'For one thing,' she continued, 'I was getting a divorce; for another, I felt he himself would not have wished it and would, in fact, have been quite shocked at such a suggestion. In my naiveté, I imagined that people who had been made Companions of Honour actually were. How little I knew. What a lot I had to learn.'

Upon their arrival, Sir Arthur leapt, with surprising agility, from his seat and hurried round the back of the taxi to let her out. They stood rather awkwardly on the pavement for a moment. She offered him her hand. He bowed slightly, lifted it to his lips and kissed it.

———

'*Well!*' – this was all Pamela would write of her feelings on parting from Sir Arthur that dark January night. It seemed pretty clear what the historian's intentions and inclinations were towards her, however unlikely, given the gap in their ages: he, an over-ripe seventy-one; she, just shy of fifty. Yet, completely contrary to her better instincts, she found herself almost complicit in his schemes.

Sir Arthur had told her before returning to the taxi that he would ring her soon. But what did 'soon' mean? Pamela was by nature impatient and impulsive. However, as the days rolled slowly by following that extraordinary evening at the Marynka, she chided herself with the thought that this was a man whose idea of 'soon' was in terms of centuries, not seconds and minutes.

She was equally at a loss as to whether or not she should write to thank him. Could such a letter seem compromising? What if Anne opened it? Or one of his secretaries …? Maybe she had misread the entire situation.

Eventually, almost at breaking point, she settled on writing him a somewhat stilted thank-you note, before attempting to turn her mind to her more pressing matters.

She very nearly succeeded. By the end of the month, she had completed her proofs and had even arranged to stay for a weekend with an old school friend, Sybil Scott, back in Wiltshire. One Saturday afternoon she was just packing her bag in time to catch the one o'clock train to Salisbury when the telephone finally rang. She watched it nervously. *Could it be?* she wondered. Only a small part of her hoped that it wasn't.

She lifted the receiver without a word.

'Pam?' the voice returned. 'Arthur here ...'

She drew a deep breath.

'I would have rung before,' he said, half apologetically, 'but I've been driven off my feet by my book on Wellington. But I wondered ... next Friday ... Anne has to go to her sister's. Would you care to dine again? The Marynka seemed quite nice, didn't it? Eight o'clock?'

And so it was arranged. Unlike their last outing, there could be no doubt that this was more than simply an innocent dinner with one of her father's old friends. She decided not to mention it to her friend Sybil, let alone to her daughter, Miranda, who would be likely to report back to David. If there was one thing Pamela truly hated, it was any form of gossip or sordid speculation. Even secrecy was preferable to this.

When Friday came, she found herself sick with nerves. Her companion, however, was anything but.

'He was more,' she later wrote, 'how shall I put it? At ease? Sure of himself?' Whatever he was, he deigned on this occasion to eat his meal. He also made another alteration to his behaviour: he asked if he might come up to her flat afterwards.

He did so on the most ingenious of pretexts. Knowing how much

43

trouble she had endured writing her book on Wiltshire and how much she was now missing her home county, he said he wanted to read her a particular article from his recent book of collected journalism, *The Lion and the Unicorn*. 'A good line,' recalled Pamela of this casual suggestion. They made a detour on the way back to South Street for him to fetch a copy of the book from his library.

This was the first time Pamela would hear Sir Arthur read from one of his works. There was a seriousness about it, almost as though he were about to recite a sacred text. As he smoothed down the relevant page, he could not have been less interested in the cup of coffee she placed before him or the way in which she carefully prepared the lighting behind his armchair. When he was ready to begin, she took up a position at the far end of the small sofa immediately beside where he was seated.

The article was on his beloved Wiltshire and Dorset. 'Forced by my calling and obligations to spend much of my time in London,' he read in his slow, slightly lisping voice, 'I find myself, as I grow older, repeatedly daydreaming of those two dear counties, each so different yet so entangled with my life and memories.'

Pamela found herself moving up a little along the sofa.

'Journeying frequently from town to country,' continued Sir Arthur, 'from metropolitan scurry and uproar to woodland quiet and solitude, I realise I have many compensations.'

Captivated, Pamela edged further up. Before long, the pair were almost side by side.

'It never fails to make my heart leap,' he went on, 'to see, each time with the thrill of surprise at its perfection and beauty, the spire of Salisbury Cathedral rising from the cup of the downs as the winding

London road descends from the Plain into the valley of the Avon; to glimpse, from a distant hillside, the woods of my deep western coombe and the silhouette of barns filled with hay borne home on summer evenings, to hear the rooks cawing in the beeches as I stop to open the gate before entering the descending tunnel of trees at whose far end lies home.'

Sir Arthur stopped abruptly. For a moment Pamela thought he was about to say he had to go. Then he held out his hand. She reached for it. One small tug was all it took. Suddenly Pamela found herself in the arms of the great historian, exchanging kisses more passionate than any she had previously experienced; or, she imagined, had he.

Guilt hit her like a cannonball. 'What about Anne?' she said quietly.

'You don't need to worry about Anne,' he said.

She made no response. He wondered if she had heard.

'No,' he repeated, 'you don't need to worry about Anne.'

4

―――――

Sir Arthur did not stay long that evening. It was as though a signal had sounded in his conscience just before sexual infidelity could take place. He left the flat without having ever removed his tie or shoes.

Pamela collapsed back on the sofa in total confusion. Ashamed, frightened – but also unexpectedly aroused – she wondered what had made her guest leave so precipitously. Was it that she had seemed too willing? Or was it, she found herself asking, that he was too enfeebled to have sex? Little did she know that there was a more worldly consideration: Sir Arthur had already decided that she was not to be sexually compromised until her decree nisi, formalising her divorce, had been issued by the courts. From what he had gathered so far, it would not be long to wait.

Pamela was still trying to make sense of the evening's momentous events when the telephone rang. 'Pam?' returned the familiar voice, with its curious mixture of surprise and formality. 'This is Arthur.'

She wondered who else he thought might be calling her at such a time. He said that he wanted to tell her something urgently.

'I have another telephone number,' he whispered conspiratorially. 'You can ring me on it anytime – any time of the day or night.'

Pamela once again found herself unable to formulate a coherent response. When she could finally articulate her thoughts, she asked if there was a possibility of someone else answering.

'No,' he shot back, 'it's a private line. I carry the instrument around with me, plug it in wherever I happen to be.'

The gears inside Pamela's head shifted noiselessly. *So strange*, she thought, *so exciting. What an odd man!*

Over the coming weeks, Sir Arthur made a point of walking across the park to visit her for tea. A great believer in exercise, he told her that the distance between Rutland Gate and South Street was the perfect antidote to a morning battling with his biography of Wellington.

While his attention – and clear affection – was certainly appreciated, Pamela could not help feeling slightly irked by his presumption. Whenever he opened his diary to enquire when he could next visit, he smiled as if to say he knew how much he already meant to her. It was as though his presence was a great favour that he might have expected her to pay him for.

But just as Pamela's doubts began to return, Sir Arthur had a way of winning back her affections. He did this not only by constantly praising the neatness of her small flat and the quality of her appearance, but also by hinting that he could 'open doors' for her. Perhaps, ultimately, he might even help her with some of her own literary projects and aspirations.

The first step in this journey began when Sir Arthur raised the matter of how Pamela was going to secure an income while awaiting a settlement from her ex-husband. He seemed genuinely concerned about this, without any personal interest, and listened attentively to her ideas about applying for a position at an upmarket florist's, perhaps Constance Spry just around the corner, or some other local business. At no point did either of them seriously consider that she follow a literary path, despite her clear talents and achievements in this line; nor did it seem obvious that he was in need of any extra assistance with regard to his own projects and administration. But as Sir Arthur drained his china cup one crisp spring afternoon, he simply came out with it: he wanted her to come and work for him. 'Just for an hour or so,' as he put it, 'to take down some letters.'

The notion of working for any professional writer – let alone one as famous and distinguished as Sir Arthur – thrilled and terrified Pamela. She told him so quite frankly, but he merely batted away her concerns and told her to come round to Rutland Gate for a trial one day the following week.

Careful preparations were made in advance of her visit. Miss Hoe, a dangerous potential rival, was told to depart early that day; Mrs Trevett, too, was kept out of the picture. Sir Arthur knew perfectly well that the secret to a successful intrigue was to ensure that each admirer was in the dark about all the others. 'Arthur,' his wife would soon confide in Pamela, 'never tells anyone anything.'

Pamela paced up and down the Kensington Road in the minutes leading up to her appointment. No matter how much she saw of Sir Arthur, she lived in constant fear of causing him any kind of inconvenience or distress. Despite the pouring rain, which she hoped had not breached her umbrella and silk headscarf, it was vital that she should arrive at exactly the appointed hour.

At length, she turned into the square, walked past a procession of elderly nuns and rang the doorbell. Once again it was Mrs Chalkley who answered. She made no acknowledgement of their prior acquaintance but simply gestured to the staircase. Pamela had a presentiment that all was not well with the master today.

She could hear him talking in animated tones as she entered the library. '*No!*' he yelled into the mouthpiece of his telephone. 'I want to speak to the *chief* supervisor.'

He saw her and, with an incongruously casual sweep of his hand, beckoned her in.

'*Not available!*' he screamed. 'What, is she drinking herself to a standstill on coffee in the canteen!'

He threw down the receiver and flung himself into a nearby armchair.

'Is everything all right, Arthur?' Pamela said at last. 'If it's not convenient, I can—'

'No, no,' he cut in, 'of course it's convenient. Just a recurrent problem I've been having with the wretched operators at the London telephone exchange – I've been inundated with calls all morning by people wanting—'

The telephone rang again. With a weary sigh, Sir Arthur grabbed the receiver. Pamela heard a woman squawking about tickets for a concert at the Albert Hall.

Sir Arthur let out a cry of frustration. '*Madam,*' he continued with cold politesse, 'this is neither the box office nor the conductor's dressing room – this is a private residence, and its resident is being prevented from conducting his life and affairs because' – his voice suddenly became tense and shrill again – '*he is being pestered by a gaggle of pleasure-seekers who want to spend an "Evening with André Previn" – whoever that is!*'

He hung up with a mechanical jerk of his wrist, before immediately dialling another number, one he clearly knew by heart. For some minutes he was engaged in a frantic diatribe, sometimes invoking the authority of the chief supervisor or engineer – even, at one stage, the postmaster general himself.

Beside herself with embarrassment, it was with relief that Pamela watched Sir Arthur slam down the receiver for the last time. She was even more happy to see, in the ensuing silence, the faintest hint of a smile play upon his lips.

'I suppose the powers that be,' he said dryly, 'are all saying, "There's that man again!"'

He stood up and, taking a large set of keys from his desk drawer, said that he wanted to give her a brief tour of the house before they set to work. Although she agreed to this, Pamela could not help wondering at the keys. They were needed, she soon discovered, for the unlocking and relocking of every door in the property – a ritual he performed with no further explanation than a murmured comment about burglaries and the need for 'internal vigilance'. Neither this nor his inexplicable decision to pass over the second floor of the house entirely filled Pamela with confidence. But she did not dare express the one thought that was racing through her mind – *What on earth have you got all those doors locked up for? Are you Bluebeard?*

Unbeknown to her, she had passed the first test already. Before they had even returned to the library to commence their labours, Sir Arthur's belief that she was ideally suited for his complex requirements had been confirmed absolutely.

This was just as well. With little secretarial experience besides helping her father with his correspondence and farming operations during the war, Pamela did not know shorthand and had only a vague idea about many aspects of business administration. When Sir Arthur, after handing her a notepad and a pencil, began to dictate a vehement letter to the editor of *The Times* opposing a local planning application, she promptly snapped the lead and watched in horror as the papers slid noisily onto the floor. Only Sir Arthur's indulgent gaze assured her that all was going perfectly well.

At the end of the ensuing ordeal he insisted on marching her – with all her scribblings indecorously shoved in her bag – to the underpass on the east side of Hyde Park, exactly halfway back to her front door.

It was the beginning of a routine that would soon come to dominate Pamela's entire existence. Like the opening strains of a Wagner opera, there was no clue from the pleasant first stages of the chaos, confusion and sheer intensity that was to come. She had only a warm sense that she was truly *needed*. Initially this was merely to go to Rutland Gate for a couple of hours in the morning, take down some letters and then return home – always accompanied halfway by Sir Arthur – in order to type them up. Then the workload was suddenly increased. The first reason for this was that Miss Hoe, whom Pamela had only met a few times, joined the throngs of women to abandon their posts with Sir Arthur. On her last day in the job, the three of them went up to the little secretary's room at the top of Rutland Gate to acquaint its new incumbent with its antiquated stationery and illogical filing system. Some sisterly sixth sense told Pamela that the girl had not left wilfully; hot tears stood behind her big green eyes.

Then, within a few weeks of commencing work for Sir Arthur, Anne departed. Although ostensibly in the interests of her health – she had a persistent bronchial infection – and also because of her close attachment with her sister, with whom she was going to live in Weybridge, it was clear that her decision was motivated by other considerations too. She had not been married to Sir Arthur Bryant for nearly thirty years without knowing when he was 'smitten'. And though she may not have known the precise details about what had transpired between her husband and his new secretary in the latter's Mayfair flat, it was clearly more than filing and administration. Indeed, the couple had finally consummated their relationship in the small master bedroom on 25 March – the very day that Pamela had received her decree nisi from the courts. Her diary entry for that date, marked with a revealing little asterisk, read: 'I am definitely & delightfully divorced!' From then on she continued to experience, contrary to her earlier expectations, the most wonderful, passionate sex that she had ever dreamt possible.

Anne knew that it was beyond her powers to prevent what was happening. But she did make a final, valiant attempt to discover just how far things had gone. She told her husband that she had been disappointed that he had taken Pamela on as his secretary without first asking her permission. It was particularly painful, she told him, on account of the fact that she herself had brought the distraught woman into their home. All she now wanted to know was: Did he love her? 'He said "no",' she later wrote, 'but that he cared for her emotionally and that her help to him was invaluable and that her brain worked as fast as his did.' Despite protesting, continued Anne, that 'he still loved me and his involvement with her made no difference to his feelings for me', she still felt forced out of her own home.

It was typical that, before bowing to the inevitable, Anne did all she could to make the change of régime as seamless as possible. On one of the rare occasions that she emerged from her little set of rooms on the second floor, she told Pamela about many of her husband's personal requirements. She indicated such details as the make of his favourite kind of toothpaste (Pearl Drops) and how he liked his steak (medium-rare); for it was clear that the younger woman would now be shopping and cooking for him in addition to her usual secretarial functions. Despite the old lady's evident sadness, her successor could tell that she was also partly relieved. It was as though she was handing over a responsibility which had become too much for her.

Throughout the ensuing summer and autumn, Pamela tended to Sir Arthur's every need. Her day would begin with a visit to one of his favourite shops to purchase his evening meal. Then she would report to Rutland Gate, where she would usually find him on the back terrace, surrounded by his beloved pigeons, furiously scribbling the latest chapter of *The Great Duke*, as his biography of Wellington was now entitled. Hours would subsequently be passed typing and retyping the endless versions of the text; occasionally a phone call from the offices of the *Sunday Express* or the *Illustrated London News* would precipitate a crisis, as Sir Arthur sent her all over the house looking for his notes on 'communism', 'crime' – or whatever else his editor had asked him to write about.

Around five o'clock, he would march her to the underpass and then return to his labours for a final couple of hours. At about seven he would appear at her door, often clasping flowers, before sitting down for dinner. He did not, at first, stay the night – nor did he offer her any payment beyond the cost of her direct expenses. He said that a salary might lessen the amount she received in settlement from her ex-husband.

Pamela was initially willing to tolerate this arrangement; she was simply too happy to question it. And Sir Arthur was a past master of making a woman feel utterly adored, as proven by his latest candidate's entry in her pocket-diary one hot summer's day: 'I have had a strange life – 26 years of marriage & yet at 5am this morning I was awakened by someone just to tell me *"I love you"* on the telephone. It will remain for ever.'

Before long these impromptu performances would be supplemented by vast, gushing letters, often written just before he caught the train to his Buckinghamshire home, the South Pavilion, near Wotton Underwood, where he inexplicably liked to spend twenty-four hours each week.

'I owe so much to you in everything I now do,' he wrote in one of these dispatches, 'and no blind man is more indebted to his dog than I to you on whom I so much depend.'

On another occasion he preferred to reach for a military analogy. 'I feel rather as General Eisenhower did,' he declared, 'when he took the parade of the Guards Division in Germany in 1945 – and said, with tears in his eyes, "Who am I to command such men." How less worthy am I to command such an incomparable secretary.' He said that her presence in his life had restored his faith in human nature – 'even in my own' – and that he could not have been prouder had Jane Austen been on his staff.

Nor were these entreaties destined for stony ground.

'I have so much to thank you for also,' replied Pamela during a brief parting towards the end of the year. 'I *truly* believe I have experienced a miracle – I know that whatever else happens in my life I have known, during this time, such happiness that I never thought possible and am so very grateful. Knowing you and working for you have given me something that I think I have always unconsciously been looking for and I realise that, although I am still the same person in many ways, there is a difference and that more than anyone else in the world you have helped me towards finding myself.'

When the book was finally published at Christmas, it was as though their physical and psychological union was complete. 'Congratulations and heartfelt gratitude,' he telegraphed her in Salisbury, where she was once again staying with her old school friend, Sybil, 'on publication day of a book for which your tireless and devoted work did so much.'

———

As much as Pamela was enjoying her newfound happiness, a few doubts lingered about Sir Arthur. At first these had been relatively small, no larger than a cloud the size of a man's hand. But as the months passed, it became increasingly difficult to accept that he was being entirely honest in his conduct and behaviour. It hardly mattered to her that several reviewers of *The Great Duke* chuckled that innumerable passages had been recycled from his earlier books, nor that some of these critics feigned surprise that such a patriotic writer had formerly been a zealous advocate of Neville Chamberlain and his policy of appeasement. Her suspicions were rather more personal.

The most pressing of these concerned Sir Arthur's weekly trip to his other home, the South Pavilion. An imposing outhouse on the Wotton estate, it took its architectural cues from the nearby residence of every British prime minister since 1921, Chequers – it is no coincidence that a later holder of that office, Tony Blair, would buy the property on his resignation from parliament in 2007. Sir Arthur had told her little about what he did when he was there, only that she needed to provide him with a packet of ham each time he visited – 'for my breakfast', as he explained. Although Pamela had no desire to jeopardise her current happiness, she could not help but find this request somewhat strange. If he was so unable to cater for himself, what did he eat the rest of the time he was there? In moments of debilitating insecurity, she found herself wondering if there was someone else, waiting each week for his unfailing visit.

This supposition was confirmed in a most unexpected way. One day that summer, Sir Arthur returned from the South Pavilion with a small packet of heirloom runner beans. When Pamela took them home to prepare their dinner, she was surprised to find a note folded up inside the bundle. Unravelling it, she could see straightaway that the handwriting was not Sir Arthur's. In contrast to his squiggly, disjointed style, these characters were smooth and rounded; and while the historian invariably wrote in pencil, the message was penned in bold green ink. The recipient was presumably intended to be Mrs Chalkley, as it explained in some detail how best to prepare the legumes.

Pamela endeavoured not to create a scene. But when Sir Arthur later arrived with a bunch of flowers to partake in their meal, he made the fatal error of complimenting the beans. Seizing her opportunity, Pamela nonchalantly replied that she had merely followed the instructions. On seeing her guest's puzzled expression, she showed him the scrap of paper. Instantly, she could see his discomfort. It was almost as if she – Pamela – had inconsiderately decided to upset their very happy arrangement.

After a long silence, he finally explained that the note had been written by Alwynne Bardsley, the wife of an old friend, Geoffrey, who had formerly looked after his pedigree Jersey herd at Crafton Farmhouse, some twenty miles away from the South Pavilion. Alwynne, he explained in a series of halting sentences, kept an eye on the vacant property, as well as maintaining the garden, and came over to see to his needs on the day of his weekly visit.

But who exactly was this other woman? And why was she so concerned to look after a man who was, apparently, little more than an acquaintance of her husband? At length, a version of the story came out. In her youth – nearly fifty years ago – Alwynne had attended the historian's lectures at the Conservative training college at Ashridge, where she had soon fallen under his spell. In the ensuing years, during which she had married and brought up two sons, the pair kept in distant touch until, about a decade previously, Sir Arthur suggested a scheme which seemed to satisfy all of them. Unable any longer to afford his home in the West Country, Smedmore House, as well as the pedigree herd which he kept on the estate, Sir Arthur had asked the Bardsleys to move from Cheshire to South Buckinghamshire, where they could live at a nominal rent in a Tudor farmhouse owned by his friends at the Merchant Adventurers. Now that Geoffrey had retired from business, he hoped the couple would help look after the displaced animals and also take a turn, when required, with the maintenance of his nearby mansion. Although the enterprise had proved costly – Alwynne's younger son, Daniel, recalls a fellow vet telling him that it seemed pointless to write books only to throw the proceeds away on such a farm – the arrangement had persisted even after the historian's recent sale of the herd and machinery.

What little of this history Sir Arthur revealed to Pamela only presented more questions, as her imagination proceeded to run wild. Where, she demanded to know, did Alwynne sleep when she came to the South Pavilion?

It emerged that she had her own designated bedroom at the property.

'So you and she sleep alone under the same roof when you're both there?' she could not help blurting out.

Sir Arthur admitted that this was the case but quickly added that his relationship with his former student had always been platonic. In magnanimous tones, he went on to explain that he allowed her to look after him for one day a week as acknowledgement for her unfailing devotion throughout the decades.

'I promise you,' he said with just a hint of accusation, 'it's simply an old friendship. I have … obligations. You must know you're everything to me now. You mustn't grudge poor Alwynne what little occasional happiness I can give her.'

A strange feeling of being at once jealous, guilty and selfish swept over Pamela. All she could do was apologise. She so badly wanted everything just to remain the same, no matter how untenable Sir Arthur's story appeared to be.

This was a pattern that would recur time and again throughout the years to come. Whenever Pamela's 'bugaboos' – as Sir Arthur dismissively termed her nagging fears – grew louder, he had a way of winning back her affections. As she would later recall: 'Although he could be bewildering, unreasonable, irrational, inconsiderate and sometimes extremely bad-tempered, underlying these temporary lapses there was an unfailing quality of … lovableness.'

This did not, however, make problems entirely vanish. One of the most glaring of these remained the position of Anne. She had, Pamela gradually came to realise, not left Sir Arthur as willingly or as happily as the younger woman had been led to suppose. Occasionally Sir Arthur had hinted that she had suffered from psychiatric problems in the past and was rather too partial to alcohol. Her move to Weybridge, where her sister and brother-in-law could look after her, was not necessarily going to be as permanent as originally advertised.

A sure sign of this was the unending series of letters that passed between the estranged pair.

'Like you,' wrote Anne in one of these jeremiads, 'I too feel it is a sort of worse than death for both of us, this parting.'

Even when Sir Arthur took Pamela to watch his old school, Harrow, playing cricket against Eton at Lord's that summer, he was furtively keeping up their correspondence in the safety of the all-male Long Room.

'I was so utterly touched by your thinking of sending the cornflowers,' he wrote with reference to the carnation he was wearing. 'It was characteristic and dear of you and almost made me cry.'

After detailing the trials and tribulations of the Harrow batsmen, he concluded: 'I did want you to know how much your thought and kindness meant to me. I should have forgotten them, too, myself.'

There was certainly no doubting Sir Arthur's affection for Anne – 'Darling,' he wrote in another letter from this period, 'you are *everything* to me … I love you unutterably – far above everyone I have ever loved or could.'

The difficulty was that they had proved strangely incompatible. Whereas Anne enjoyed companionship and family life, Sir Arthur had little time for anything besides the writing of history – 'the only justification of my existence', as he often told her. Having suffered from mumps in his youth, he was unable to have children, and the inevitable void had been filled by a series of increasingly spoilt dogs, one of which had even, several years previously, been subjected to biographical treatment by its famous owner: *Jimmy: the dog in my life*. The loss of his latest terrier, Hamish, who went with Anne to Weybridge, was almost the worst aspect of the separation from his point of view. In moments of desperation he would gaze out of his study window in search of a new companion. 'I ... saw the boy with the little white Westie,' he wrote to Anne that November. 'I think I shall try to find out his name to see if he'd like me to take the little dog [for] walks sometimes during the day!'

Matters were complicated, as they inevitably were for Sir Arthur, by money. His own income from writing had always been sporadic and he had inherited precious little capital from his father, Sir Francis Bryant, who had spent a lifetime working as a clerk in the Royal Household. Only a bestseller every couple of years could sustain his current lifestyle: a feat that was increasingly difficult for a man in his seventies beset by competition from a new breed of angry young historian. It had been this uncertainty which had initially made his marriage to Anne so useful. The descendant of the nineteenth-century explorer Sir James Brooke, her forebears had run the island kingdom of Sarawak, situated at the foot of the Malay peninsula, as a private enterprise right up until the end of the Second World War. However, since the death of his father-in-law two years previously, Sir Arthur was now liable to pay surtax on all of Anne's investments, including a fifty per cent share in Rutland Gate.

Sir Arthur was quick to point out the financial inconvenience this caused him. 'The classic example,' he wrote to her with some exaggeration, 'was William Charles Crocker who married a wealthy American widow as his second wife – who never told him how rich she was! – and then discovered that the effect on his own professional income was that he was unable to afford to live any longer in England!' It was for this reason, at least in part, that Sir Arthur now asked Anne for a legal separation.

The difficulty with this plan was that Sir Arthur would have to stump up the funds necessary to buy Anne out. Besides this being her legal right, Anne explained that she could hardly continue living with her sister and brother-in-law without making a significant contribution to their household expenses – to say nothing of recouping what she had recently spent improving Rutland Gate. Reminding her husband that, while he had usually been 'so generous with money', when it came to paying for such unglamorous necessities as a new gas boiler, it had invariably been her who footed the bill. She told him that she was prepared to forego the repayment of these expenses, as well as her share of the house, so long as they remained married and that he agreed to make her a small living allowance.

But Sir Arthur squirmed at this proposition. Incapacitated by a back injury sustained while reorganising his entire library, he scrawled an interminably long draft rebuttal to her proposal.

'It wouldn't be arithmetically possible,' he pleaded in one section that made it into the final letter, 'out of my taxed professional earnings for me to ... defray the running costs of the house and pay the surtax due on your private income ... simultaneously, paying also you interest on that additional £25,000 you invested in the house.'

What he proposed instead was that they proceed with their legal separation and that she accept a modest five per cent annuity on her investment in the property in lieu of a financial settlement. He was, he rather tactlessly added, now being very competently looked after by Pamela, whose skills and abilities both as housekeeper and author were fully enumerated. She was, he prophesied, going to become a great writer – 'A far better thing than being an old man's bottle-washer', he disingenuously added.

Never able to resist an attack on the modern world, Sir Arthur warmed to his theme.

'All round me,' he continued, 'everyone seems set on destroying something – from the shallow Common Marketeers who are blindly trying to destroy a thousand years of British history, to the money-grabbing tycoons who, as I write … are smashing down the beautiful Victorian house overlooking the gardens at the back – and I find it consoling to think of someone wanting and starting to create something worthwhile instead.'

After a further week of backsliding about her request for a settlement, he suggested that if she really insisted on her legal rights, she was welcome to return to Rutland Gate to live with him and Pamela.

Only Anne's superior knowledge of human nature prevented this scheme getting any further.

'The house is obviously running very well under Pam's capable management,' she responded, 'and it could only lead to trouble for all of us if I returned. No man, darling, even you, can be emotionally involved with two women under the same roof and one of these a wife without tension building up. And all three of us are particularly sensitive to this.'

Anne had been here before. Only a few years previously, her husband had asked her permission to bring yet another old flame, Barbara Longmate, into their lives. Back then, both were agreed that this affectionate divorcee would be the ideal helpmeet to Sir Arthur in his old age.

'You and Barbara,' wrote Anne at the time, 'love each other as a man & woman should & I feel in my heart that you should be together & that it is wrong and silly & wasteful for you to be apart in loneliness & unhappiness.' She said that she wanted him not to worry about her own feelings in the matter.

'I *knew*,' she wrote in a moment of revelation, 'with the whole of my being that *all* my doubts had disappeared, that there would be no need to exorcise anything, and that I should be happy to know that you were happy in Barbara's company in Norfolk instead of among the strange and motley collection [of women] you have gathered round you [at present].'

While the plan had evidently not worked out, Sir Arthur still made a point of going to stay with Barbara every few months; indeed, he had been on his way to see her when he had written to Pamela comparing himself to General Eisenhower at the Guards Parade.

Despite her suspicions, as well as Sir Arthur's curious habit of phoning her up when he was actually staying with another woman – either from a cliff-top callbox or with one hand partially covering the receiver – the full extent of the historian's control and deception had not yet dawned on Pamela. Yet the cord between them had already started to fray by the late summer of 1971, when he began turning his attentions to managing her domestic affairs.

The first instance of this concerned Pamela's daughter, Miranda.

After completing her studies at Oxford that year, she planned to come and work in London. She had taken it for granted that she would be able to stay at South Street until she could find more suitable accommodation with friends of her own age. She assumed that her mother, who had been so grateful for her company only the previous Christmas, would once again be delighted at the prospect. And ever since – albeit rather in spite of her mother's reservations – completing the 'season' in 1968, the young woman had regarded the flat as her London home. She was, accordingly, mystified when her mother turned down her perfectly reasonable request. The explanatory letter she subsequently received was even more hurtful. Unlike her mother's hitherto affectionate style, this was formal and lawyerly, as though it had been composed by a totally different person – which, indeed, it had been.

Pamela would later recall what took place. Upon telling Sir Arthur of her daughter's request to stay in the flat, even for a short period, he had become 'demented' with rage. He then demanded, for the first time, that he compose a letter on her behalf.

'I have done my best to see this thing from your point of view,' the text ran, 'even so, I was surprised that, considering you have been very much living your own kind of life … you should actually want to live with me again in so small a space with all the complications which would invariably arise.'

These 'complications' were then carefully reviewed: 'my wanting to chain and lock up … when you were out on the tiles'; 'you wanting to watch television … and my wanting to write' and 'both our smalls and other washing overflowing in the not-too-commodious bathroom.'

'Pamela' wondered whether her daughter would have made the same request had it been her father living alone in the flat.

'I can't help feeling it would be very difficult for both of you,' the letter ran on, 'what with the disparity in your ages and the different ways in which you would both want to conduct your lives.'

There was even a passing shot at the fact that David 'was trying to hound [her] out' of the property. It was no surprise the relationship between mother and daughter was never quite the same.

And nor was it with Sir Arthur. Emboldened by his unrestricted access to the flat, he now strove to ensure that its ownership would pass from David to his ex-wife as part of their divorce settlement. Up until this point, Pamela had relied entirely on the small legal practice that had advised her parents, and which had, in line with her wishes, made few financial demands upon David. It fell to Sir Arthur to alert her to the fact that her husband was a comparatively wealthy man and that, without a substantial settlement, she would have few resources – and certainly not the property in which the most part of their liaison had been conducted. He insisted that she instruct his own, far more litigious, firm of solicitors to take up her cause.

This threw up an unexpected issue that was to do tremendous damage to Pamela's relationship with Sir Arthur. The problem concerned the thorny 'grounds' for her original petition for divorce. These were based on David's proven infidelity with the woman to whom he had been found to be paying an allowance. Pamela had initially wanted to slur over this issue to avoid causing unnecessary pain and scandal, but her new lawyers, as well as Sir Arthur, were eager to flesh out every particular. Both knew that the size of any settlement was likely to depend on the enormity of David's transgressions.

Throughout the autumn and winter of 1971, a series of claims and counterclaims were accordingly exchanged between each party's representatives – by the end of negotiations, in March 1973, the legal fees alone were to reach the dizzying figure of £10,000.

'Your solicitors keep asking for more and more obscure papers,' complained David at the height of the dispute. 'It has taken a fortnight to get details of the little account I used to have at Menton [in the South of France, where his parents had retired for tax reasons in the 1950s], which can mean nothing. Now they want (God knows why) a copy of the next American Trusts accounts, which won't appear till after the meeting in May.'

A protective order was placed on the South Street flat and progressively inflated sums of money were demanded as part of the final settlement.

'If it is any consolation,' concluded David in the same letter, 'I feel lonely as a single man as I expected to be – but it is better than all the nagging and rows, which would surely have shortened my life span. I gather you are better off as a career woman. I thought you would be and am glad for your sake.'

David could hardly have imagined that Sir Arthur was the driving force in these wrangles, but the historian was already in complete control of his latest muse.

'You have all the dear tender human virtues … and capacities,' he told her in one letter, 'except in defending yourself against the cruel wrongs done you when, unlike everyone else, you are so blind, dear cheek-turner, so that, except in this one thing one never has to explain anything to you for you instinctively understand.'

Ignoring the fact that he had just persuaded his own wife to forego a financial settlement, he bombarded her with letters and quasi-legal statements outlining her rights. One of these, scribbled on pink carbon paper one hot summer night in 1972, summed up his opinion as succinctly as he could:

> A woman of fifty-one after twenty-five years of marriage to a man with a large house, an agricultural and shooting estate of 1,000 acres worth at least £400,000, a sixty-one-year lease on a Mayfair flat worth £40,000, and a tax-free allowance of £4,000 p.a. from his octogenarian father to whose Chicago-based properties he was joint heir under entailed trusts, found that her husband was making regular payments to a woman in London ...
>
> ... Through his solicitors the husband ... intimated that if the wife sought a legal remedy for his failure to provide her with a share of their former marital home, he would rely on Tumath v. Tumath with the implication that she had been a bad wife and was solely responsible for the breakdown of their marriage.
>
> ... She now in self-defence placed her affairs in the hands of more experienced solicitors with a large divorce practice, paying her former ones for their services, including the costs of the divorce which they had not obtained from her husband who was liable for them.

Presenting her with this enormous document when she arrived for work the following morning, Sir Arthur implored Pamela to stiffen her resolve against 'that self-satisfied, heartless egoist' of an ex-husband. He said that he could barely comprehend his 'callous unkindness and obsessional meanness' towards her.

But as these painful negotiations dragged on, Pamela felt increasingly uneasy. For one thing, the man who described himself as her 'utterly disinterested and devoted' champion began dropping general hints that she might like to invest part of any future settlement in Rutland Gate. There was also the small matter that she was suing David for an offence of which she was now equally guilty. One afternoon, while tending to Sir Arthur in his sickbed, she raised this contradiction, telling him that she was going to inform her solicitors, without mentioning any names, of her new situation. The patient winced; whether from the implications of her disclosure or the pain in his back, he was careful to disguise. He said that, seeing her mind was made up, she was free to do as she wished but added, as casually as he could, that such an admission would, besides being embarrassing for her, be irrelevant to proceedings. The new divorce laws, he explained authoritatively, did not take into account a woman's 'future prospects'.

How wrong he was. The legislation to which he had referred only applied to divorces filed after 1 January 1971 – exactly two weeks after Pamela had submitted her petition. Sir Arthur, it was now clear, was going to make all the difference to the outcome of her settlement: Pamela's solicitors immediately demanded a written statement outlining when and whom she was marrying, as well as her future husband's means.

Sir Arthur's response was more explosive than ever – Pamela had never seen his face quite so contorted with rage. Throwing aside his notes for his latest book – a regimental history of the Rifle Brigade – he began denouncing her for creating a hugely dangerous and embarrassing situation. Foremost in his mind, at the present moment, were his other muses. '*Think how it would hurt Anne and Alwynne!*' he declared with indignation. Calling upon his secretary to take down a letter at once – ostensibly from her – to her new solicitors, he began to dictate a face-saving letter.

'As I have now had time to consider the matter,' it began, 'I am writing to inform you that I have no reasonable prospects – whatever I may wish – of remarrying in the foreseeable future.' The letter then proceeded to itemise the impediments:

> (a) The only person I care for is married and has been so even longer than I, and, though he and his wife, who is a sufferer from chronic asthma, live apart under a Deed of Separation and Settlement, they are still very fond of each other, and it could hurt her deeply and he would consider it wrong – as would I – for him to put her through the pain of asking her to divorce him.
>
> (b) Because he is many years older than either of us and has only a very short expectation of life, time is very much against us ever being in a position to marry.

When Sir Arthur's dictation was done, he told Pamela to repeat the letter to him. He nodded with approval before demanding that she allow him to keep the only copy on the pretext that it concerned him so intimately. It was in this way that Sir Arthur first made it clear that he had no intention of marrying her whatsoever.

This fact was only too clear to Pamela as she, as instructed, proceeded to deliver the letter by hand to the solicitor's office. Sitting in the back of a taxi – one of her few extravagances, as she did not own a car – her eyes welled with tears. All the hopes and dreams she had been nursing during the early months of their relationship seemed to be fading to nothing.

Such a state of affairs was confirmed when, shortly afterwards, Anne made one of her rare visits to Rutland Gate to pick up some of her belongings. Although she had seemed friendly enough towards Sir Arthur to begin with, she suddenly turned on him in a different manner, asking with bitterness: 'Do you want a divorce?' Taken off guard, he murmured something about having already given her enough pain and not wanting to cause further distress. But the matter was left to be resolved when she returned to the house the following week to remove her final items.

Pamela, who had wisely absented herself during Anne's visit, was now required to decide what he should do.

'Next Sunday,' asked Sir Arthur, helplessly, 'when she comes again, what shall I say?'

Torn between her wish to keep her word to her solicitors and her desire to become the historian's wife, she hardly knew what to suggest. But her fear of committing perjury, in the unlikely event that her divorce case ever went to High Court, proved the deciding factor.

'You'll have to say "no",' came her whispered answer.

'If I do,' responded Sir Arthur gravely, 'she'll never forgive me if I asked later on. I shall have to stick to it.'

There was a long pause, as the full implications of this sank in.

She was trapped.

5

Little evidence of these machinations could be detected in Sir Arthur's public life, which continued its usual charmed course throughout the entirety of 1971–2. Even during the month that he was largely, on account of his backache, laid up in bed, his extramural activities had included: delivering the eulogy at A. P. Herbert's memorial service at St Martin's-in-the-Fields, attending the Lord Mayor's Banquet, lecturing on Samuel Pepys at the Royal Society of Literature, promoting *The Great Duke* in Newcastle and Cheltenham, and dining with the Queen at a veterans' luncheon at the Royal Hospital Chelsea. In addition, he was, as President of the Common Market Safeguards Committee, busy lobbying the government, both directly and through the columns of the press, in opposition to Britain's proposed entry into the nascent European Union.

'I had a talk to the PM at the Stock Exchange Dinner,' he wrote to Anne at the height of the agitation, 'and told him that, right or wrong, it would be a national disaster to go into the Market without his having first persuaded the British people that it was the right course.'

Sir Arthur thought himself well placed to 'guide and help' Heath, since he was, as he put it, 'older and have studied more … [and] understand better than he.' Nor did he think his advice was likely to be ignored.

'He always seems to go out of his way to be nice to me,' he went on, 'for I think he realises that, diametrically opposed as our views are, I am as sincere about it and feel as strongly about it as he does.'

Only occasionally did Sir Arthur's two worlds collide. One such instance had been the Lord Mayor's banquet that November. The incumbent for 1971, Sir Edward Howard, had asked him, as a personal favour, to compose the speech by which he was to introduce Heath – a service that was to be rewarded by an especially prominent place for Sir Arthur and his wife at the High Table. But as the event drew nearer, it became clear that Lady Bryant would not be willing to accompany her wayward husband any longer.

'I'm dreadfully distressed that I am disappointing you by not going with you,' she wrote following a similar invitation to Windsor Castle, 'but I'm just not tough enough at present to be with you at so illustrious an occasion as a separated wife.'

When the Lord Mayor's secretary, a retired admiral, remonstrated with the beleaguered author – *'Haven't you got a daughter who could fill the vacant place?'* – Sir Arthur was forced to divulge a shade more about his private life than he would have wished. Despite a lifetime's experience in making obsequious apologies and excuses, he was beginning to look dangerously exposed. Not even his attempt to make light of the situation by suggesting, to Anne, that he take their terrier in her place – *'He would have looked so sweet sitting up at the table among all those aldermen!'* – could disguise his growing sense of unease.

What Sir Arthur required, more than anything, was a loyal companion who would follow him from one end of the earth to the other without ever asking for anything in return.

'I am not very interested in other people's lives,' he had confessed in one of his more introspective letters to Anne. Only dogs, he often suggested, came close to providing him with the kind of contentment and fulfilment that others seemed to find in more orthodox relationships. As he had written in his curious 'biography' of Jimmy: 'He gave a love as single-hearted and unquestioning as I have ever witnessed in any creature, human or animal.'

On occasion he would regret that his faith in bipeds ended with the arrival of his childhood nanny, Sarah Oakford, who had sternly governed the nursery of the mews house beside Buckingham Palace where he and his late brother, Philip, had grown up. No one after that date, not even his devoted mother, Margaret, had come close to satisfying his emotional needs – or so he sometimes liked to suggest to his legion of female confidantes.

Sir Arthur did, however, encounter one woman during these tangled months who almost lived up to his ideal. Her name was Ruth, and he met her through the pages of that other source of moral guidance to which he so often turned: the Bible.

'I can't tell you what comfort I found reading those four beautiful chapters,' he had written to Pamela while awaiting a train to see Alwynne during the summer of 1971, 'and written in that wonderful language with which our country ancestors, yours and mine – for the soil of the Christian England of the past is in our blood – expressed their feeling for God.'

He was profoundly moved by the story of this widowed handmaid whose many hardships were ended by her loyal and selfless love for an elderly relative, Boaz, to whom she was later married according to the custom of the Ancient Hebrews. Divinely inspired, Sir Arthur proceeded to compose a solemn promise to Pamela on a piece of paper which he accidently tore into shreds while extracting from his bag.

'Whither thou goest I shall go,' he wrote, 'and shall love and honour you all the days of my life as the dearest, kindest, helpfulest, the most understanding and by far the most companionable and quick and intelligent creature I have ever known. And if there is to be any happiness in this world for me I know it depends on you.'

Suggesting that she use her 'clever artist's fingers' to reassemble the fragments of paper, he implored her to go out at once and get a Bible – to his horror she did not have one at South Street – so that she, too, could enjoy the edifying tale. From now on, he continued, he wanted her to address him, at least in letters, as Boaz: '[the] restorer of thy life and a nourisher of thine old age'.

Yet, unlike his predecessor, Sir Arthur found it hard to cleave to a singular woman for any length of time. He seemed to have no difficulty in writing two, almost identical, love letters to Pamela and Anne throughout this entire period.

'Dearest love … my heart yearns for you,' he wrote to Anne, shortly after he had declared to Pamela that he loved her 'deeply and tenderly', and that whenever he climbed alone into his 'attic four-poster' he thought of all she had done for him 'with a gratitude and tenderness no words can express'.

When he was occasionally caught out, such as when Pamela discovered that he was paying a secret visit to Alwynne in Nuneaton, or when he tried to persuade Anne to spend Christmas with him at Rutland Gate while Pamela was staying with her friend Sybil Scott in Salisbury, he was adept at turning defence into attack.

'Oh darling,' he wrote to Pamela over his compromising Christmas plans, '... I hadn't the imagination to realise that your lack of confidence in yourself and your fate could cause you to suppose anything so diametrically opposite to the reality, which is that I am like a ship without its rudder without you – hopelessly lost.'

But he could scarcely reconcile this position with his decision, in the very month that he told Anne he did not want a divorce, to hang his wife's portrait in his room. It was, he told her in another letter, 'the most wonderful likeness of you as I first knew you, the most transcendently lovely girl with those strange eyes'.

While Anne was, far more than Pamela, willing to accept Sir Arthur's vagaries, she was not without a certain jealousy for her latest batch of competitors.

'It must be merciful for my sex,' she wrote after one of his many visits to Weybridge, 'that there is only one Arthur ... All that is dynamic & exciting left with you at 10:24 this morning. And I'm certain that all your lady friends feel the same way as I do as you flit from one to another of us. Each of us hating the guts of the others as you pass on your way.'

The position with Alwynne was altogether more tricky. For years she had been Sir Arthur's most devoted admirer of all, virtually living for his weekly visit to his Buckinghamshire home. Even during the early 1970s, when her elderly husband was suffering from terminal cancer, she continued to prepare the big house for the historian's weekly stay as a matter of priority.

In return for her seemingly limitless affection, Sir Arthur had offered her little besides allowing her, when circumstances required, to drive him to and from important engagements.

'After lunch,' wrote a slightly confused military friend, Lieu-tenant-General Sir Richard Fyffe, 'we can deliver you where you wish. Or Mrs Bardsley could come over if she'd like that?'

The difficulty arose when Anne made it clear that she wanted to return to London; a move that would require her to recoup her invest-ment in Rutland Gate to buy the new property. Only by selling the house, as well as the South Pavilion, would Sir Arthur be able to make this possible, while also ensuring that he had enough capital left over to purchase a suitable home for himself and, as he had often hinted, Pamela. One bleak winter's day towards the end of 1972 he headed down to Wotton Underwood to drop this bombshell on Alwynne, to whom he had long promised use of the mansion for the remainder of her lifetime.

'I could not feel compassionate [towards her],' wrote Pamela with just a touch of *Schadenfreude.*

As Sir Arthur was only too aware, there was a danger that these complex manoeuvres could have alienated him from each of the lonely ladies in his life: Pamela, who felt he had deliberately made their marriage an impossibility; Anne, who did not want to let go; and Alwynne, who simply wanted to be included. At one level Sir Arthur genuinely hoped that they could all be friends.

Following his heart-breaking disclosure to Alwynne about the fate of the South Pavilion, he had arranged to take his 'new secretary' – as he guardedly referred to Pamela – down to Buckinghamshire to intro-duce the pair. The latter recalled Sir Arthur's latest cast-off as a 'small, sad doll' of about sixty-five with dyed blonde hair and cream-co-loured clothes. The get-together, predictably, was not a success: at one point during dinner Alwynne burst into uncontrollable sobs.

'I always seem to make women unhappy,' lamented the organiser of this spectacle shortly after returning with Pamela to London the following day.

Sir Arthur's next plan was to take each of his lady friends on a holiday. 'I suppose that even if ... you had a separate home of your own,' he had recently written to Anne, 'they [the tax authorities] couldn't stop me coming to stay ... or perhaps even our having our holidays together!'

However, alleging that going with him at the present time would cause her too much pain, he proposed that she travel instead with her sister, Betty, whose husband, Terence, had recently died; a tragedy compounded by the death of their beloved terrier within a matter of weeks. Agreeable as this prospect was for Anne, it was harder for Sir Arthur to satisfy the needs of both Alwynne and Pamela, who were unlikely to tolerate being shipped off to warmer climes: the former admirer had, three years previously, accompanied him to South Africa, albeit as his 'personal assistant' so that her expenses could be recouped from the taxman. On this occasion, Sir Arthur decided, it was Pamela's turn.

'How I wish I could take you away into the sunshine,' he wrote during the early phase of their romance, 'and let you rest.' The pair would pass two weeks that March on the Algarve. Alwynne, meanwhile, was asked to stay behind to show prospective buyers around the South Pavilion.

Everything, it seemed, was perfectly in hand for Britain's foremost popular historian.

———

The holiday, however, did not get off to a good start. Never an easy traveller, Sir Arthur had not begun to think about packing until the last possible minute on account of his total absorption in his work. Having published his regimental history, *Jackets of Green*, the previous Christmas, he was now labouring at *A Thousand Years of British Monarchy*, a collection of royal biographies from Edgar to Elizabeth II for an American firm specialising in gold medallions. Sir Arthur's offering was intended to entice subscribers to a new series of collectable medals, and was, even by his standards, extremely well paid. The only difficulty was that, owing to his doubts about the bona fides of the Franklin Mint, he had not commenced any writing or research until the long-delayed contract was signed and delivered. That left him just under five weeks to complete the book – less than one day for each monarch in the island's history.

It had been Pamela's perseverance with the kindly directors of the Franklin Mint that had secured the commission; left to his own devices, she believed, Sir Arthur would have 'slammed the receiver straight down again'. Yet his gratitude for these services did not extend to emerging from Rutland Gate at the agreed hour for their departure. He had engaged his usual driver, Mr Colin, to take them to the airport partly on account of his great skill in meeting his rushed deadlines, but also because his car did not happen to have a meter. Only after she had waited for some twenty-five minutes outside the house did its occupant finally appear. Looking at him from the back seat, Pamela was surprised to see him laden with a vast steel container – his portable library – as well as a small holdall crammed with, she would later discover, miscellaneous items of clothing, a portable typewriter (for her) and an indescribable accumulation of unanswered letters. After throwing all this into the boot, he casually climbed into the front passenger seat and said: 'Heathrow, full steam ahead!'

Mr Colin need hardly have bothered. For no sooner had he deposited his passengers at the terminal, where Sir Arthur caused a huge row with the check-in clerks about the steel container – somehow allowed aboard as hand luggage – than it was announced that their flight was unaccountably delayed. Packed into the sterile boarding lounge, they were forced to occupy themselves as best they could.

While Pamela alternately read a novel and tried to calm an excitable lady who was convinced that their plane was doomed to crash, Sir Arthur wrote a long letter to Anne. Without dwelling too much on his present consort, he outlined his plans for his time away.

'I hope to be able to swim every day,' he wrote. 'There's a heated swimming pool as well as a private beach just below the hotel.'

Although he was going to need to work extremely hard to complete his book in time – 'I don't believe anyone but I could possibly do it,' he boasted – he looked forward to writing to her again from Portugal, 'in more peaceful conditions than those of the last few months'. After signing off, he handed the sealed envelope to Pamela and asked her to return to the terminal in search of a postbox.

This was an ominous beginning. But it was soon to get worse.

'I was kidding myself with thinking how comforting it would be to get into that plane (a Portuguese one),' wrote Sir Arthur in his next letter to Anne. For when they were finally herded onto the aircraft, it was only to sit on the runway for a further two hours before being returned to the boarding lounge; this time because of a bomb scare in the control tower.

When they were finally allowed to commence their journey, they were informed that the plane was to be diverted to Lisbon before arriving at its scheduled destination of Faro. As a result of these complications, it was not until 3am – 'more dead than alive' – that the weary travellers passed through customs at the other end.

'By some miracle,' continued Sir Arthur in the same letter to Anne, 'they don't seem to worry much about time in Portugal, the taxi which had been ordered to meet the plane at 5:30pm was still there, nearly twelve hours later.'

It was then but a short journey to their hotel, although Sir Arthur complained that their driver's penchant for pop music made this 'almost the worst ordeal of all!'

Nor were Sir Arthur's travails to end there. For when they arrived at the holiday resort and were shown to their personal chalet by a porter who spoke no English, it became clear that there was a new problem, or series of problems. As well as having no keys to their accommodation, their guide had to convey to them, by a series of signs and gestures, that it was currently without electricity. Not for another thirty minutes were the pair finally admitted to their quarters. Exhausted as much by Sir Arthur's 'angry expostulations' with the hapless janitor as by this man's laborious search for keys, candles and matches, Pamela immediately found her way into the spare room and passed out fully clothed on the bed.

The new day only worsened matters. Most obviously the weather was disappointing: unseasonal gales had battered the coastline for several weeks, and these had not yet entirely abated. When Pamela emerged from her room shortly after 9am, she found Sir Arthur, wrapped in a dressing gown, trying to finish off one of his

Anglo-Saxon kings on a low coffee table on the veranda. The sight was almost pitiable. To guard against the wind, he had placed rows of large stones along the edges of his fluttering carbon papers and open reference books. It had long been a part of his working habits to complete the bulk of the day's work before breakfast, and in spite of his pledge to enjoy their time away, it was clear that he intended to continue with his usual routine.

Barely acknowledging her presence, he muttered something about the swimming pool. Pamela glanced at it. An assortment of planks and a forbidding sign written in the native language suggested the worst. She returned her gaze to Sir Arthur. He did not look up but remained fixed on his task. She saw that he gripped his pencil harder than usual and was writing in a sharp, jerky manner. It would only be a few moments until his next eruption.

She managed to make it back inside before this took place. It was precipitated by one of his completed foolscaps discharging itself from its moorings and flying off in the direction of Faro. She watched him as he raged at the bleak horizon like King Lear.

In a few moments he was back inside, searching for the only pair of outdoor shoes he had brought with him. Pamela, meanwhile, slipped on her sandals and wearily went in pursuit of the runaway text. When she finally returned with the offending page – providentially caught up in some low-lying shrubbery – her companion was already remonstrating with the hotel's manager, who had chanced to bid them welcome at a particularly inopportune moment.

Despite this gentleman's charming apologies and assurances, Sir Arthur remained implacable. For some twenty-four hours he wrote a series of furious letters to the travel agency in London, threatening legal action and exposure to the Portuguese ambassador, with whom he was to be lunching on his return, unless full recompense for their gross incompetence was made with all haste.

It seemed that each time Pamela returned from dispatching one of these philippics at the nearest village – Sir Arthur did not trust the concierge – another grievance had already come to light. Among the most irksome of these was the racket that soon commenced from a nearby building site.

'All day long,' wrote Sir Arthur in his post-holiday letter to Anne, 'the noise of bulldozers and earth excavations continued.' How different, he told her, from his previous visit to the Algarve in 1935, when he had spent five carefree weeks swimming in the warm ocean and scribbling the second volume of his biography of Samuel Pepys. He did not add that he had, at that time, just sent his alcoholic first wife on a cruise to the South Atlantic to 'find a lover, or someone to love'. Nor did he make any mention of the fact that Sylvia had died from ailments associated with her addiction within a few years of their subsequent divorce.

The situation for Pamela was not quite so miserable, though she had no knowledge of her predecessor's fate either to console or to terrify her. As ever, Sir Arthur kept her completely in the dark. When, at length, he returned to his Anglo-Saxon kings, she took herself off for long walks along the cliffs and began planning a new book of her own. For a few days the pair were almost happy.

Then the letters arrived. Written in green ink, and in the same looping minuscule as the note stowed away in the runner beans, there could be no doubt as to their authorship. But Sir Arthur refused to discuss them. Even when a telegram arrived from the same source, he merely folded the incriminating evidence away and made excuses.

This was too much for Pamela. She told him that she could not remain with him if this caused so much pain and distress to any other woman – or women – in his life. Still, however, Sir Arthur argued his case.

'Weren't you the one,' he said, as if to settle the matter, 'with whom I wished to go away?'

Dispirited and defeated, Pamela retreated into their little pavilion and began typing up his six-hundred-word life of Ethelred the Unready.

This pattern continued until the time came for them to embark on their return journey, which happily passed without event. Sir Arthur immediately wrote to Anne to say that he felt as though he had not really had a holiday; though to Pamela it was a different story: the fortnight away with her, he said, was 'one of the happiest [times] he had ever known'.

In any case, Sir Arthur did not hang around long after their return to Rutland Gate. Unbeknown to Pamela, he had arranged to spend the ensuing weekend with the Earl of Leicester at Holkham Hall in Norfolk.

'It was only a very small party,' he wrote contently to Anne on his way back, 'consisting of Lady Macleod (Ian Macleod's widow), a cousin of Tommy Leicester's and myself.'

While lamenting that another of the earl's frequent guests, the Lord Chancellor, Quintin Hogg, had been unable to attend on this occasion, Sir Arthur was glad that, with the exception of mealtimes, he had been 'free to work in complete peace in that lovely, peaceful place ... amid all the glories of Coke of Norfolk's great palace and park.'

Whether or not he combined this sojourn with another visit to Barbara Longmate he did not say.

Left to her own devices in London, Pamela turned her mind to the book she had been planning. A rather good subject, she thought; perhaps too good? Maybe the truth would never be believed.

6

The idea of writing a short biography – or 'portrait', as she preferred to call it – of Sir Arthur had first occurred to Pamela soon after she commenced working for him. But it was not until she had completed a few chapters that she overcame her innate reserve and let him know of her plan. She feared that the drawbridge into his soul would quickly be lifted if he suspected that she was observing him with, as it were, a professional interest.

She chose her moment carefully. It was one bright spring morning, shortly after their return from Portugal, when Sir Arthur was in unusually high spirits. From time to time he was not above laughing at himself, and today he appeared to be mimicking Colonel Blimp as he scoured the *Daily Telegraph* for useful articles – '*What is needed in this country,*' he once blustered, characteristically, '*is for everyone to work harder, look forward and stop belly-aching.*' For a moment he made no response to her suggestion. The blue pencil that was as often between his teeth as in his hand rattled noisily to the floor.

Slowly, he put down the newspaper and became terribly serious. He told her that while he was flattered that she should wish to write about him, he feared that his life was far too boring to be of interest to the public. 'And besides,' he intoned, 'the lives of living subjects are seldom satisfactory.'

Pamela begged to differ. Had he not himself written biographies of living people? Had he not once written that the highest goal of his vocation was to 'make people feel that the past actually happened and that the names in their history books were those of real human beings'? And had he not always advised her to write about what she really knew, as, indeed, had her father, A. G. Street?

There was a pause while Sir Arthur contemplated his options. Maybe she had a point. Also, he was quick to realise, Pamela's idea could be turned to his advantage. Nothing would tether her to him more than an exhaustive project of this kind. And if what she had so far written turned out to be any good, it could even help stimulate some sort of revival in his flagging literary fortunes: the previous autumn, shortly after Heath had committed Britain to joining the EEC without a referendum, the *Sunday Express* had cancelled his retainer in the hope of moving with the times. Much of the book might, in any case, be written by himself, as a sort of autobiography by proxy. Both to humour Pamela and give himself more time, he asked to see the first chapters. Trembling within, Pamela handed over her precious typescript before retreating upstairs to cut out the articles that Sir Arthur had earmarked for his collection.

On her way back downstairs, her task completed, she heard the rare sound of Sir Arthur chuckling. Tiptoeing to the doorway, she realised he was no longer at his desk but relaxing in an armchair with a smile on his face, still engrossed in what she had written. As quiet as a mouse, she retraced her footsteps and set about the perennial task of filing.

When she returned a little later, however, she found Sir Arthur back at his desk, seemingly unmoved by her opening chapters. Gravely, he told her that he would consent to the book only if she adhered closely to his instructions. These had been carefully outlined in an essay on biography that he had written at the outset of his career. He placed this text solemnly at her disposal.

'We do not need the details of Shakespeare's private life,' the treatise declared, 'to understand what manner of man he was.' Rather, it was the first duty of the biographer to appraise 'the work of his hero'. 'A Rhodes or a Loyola,' the text ran on, 'is our friend or enemy, as we approve or detest the giant structure he raised: we apprehend him, though we know nothing of his loves, his private hopes and fears, his struggles with himself.'

Sir Arthur's views in these matters had, if anything, only hardened during the social and political revolution of the ensuing decades. As he was shortly to put it in a new edition of his 1932 biography of Lord Macaulay, he detested 'would-be biographers' who searched 'the memorials of the illustrious dead for evidence of sexual perversities and scandals, rather as little dogs seek out truffles'. His own 'truffles', then, were not to be unearthed.

'Even for a quick worker like you,' he told Pamela, 'the preliminary work of assembling and arranging such a vast mass of material would take a long time; from my own experience of preparing and writing biography I should say three years.' Passively, she listened as he reeled off everything that she would have to include: 'My experiences as a teacher of boys in the London County Council school and the Harrow Mission; the intensive work of transforming in two years a provincial art school with 80 students into a technical college with

2,000; my studies for the Bar and my production of pastoral plays and pageants between 1924 and 1931; my work as an adult education lecturer in Buckinghamshire and Oxfordshire at Ashridge and for H. M. Forces and the Ministry of Information; political ambitions, offers and experiences; my attempt after the war to prevent the high-handed annexation of Sarawak.'

Bombarded by this litany of information, Pamela's eyes started to glaze over. But Sir Arthur went on regardless: '... my three years' unsuccessful battle for the independence of Ashridge ...,' he continued, staring at an imaginary horizon, '... my frequent broadcast talks and my public lectures, speeches and addresses ... my restoration first of Rapsgate and then of Smedmore and the South Pavilion ... my farming and forestry ventures ... my membership for a number of years of the BBC Advisory Council and of the Committee for Education in H. M. Forces, and of one of the Committees of the National Trust ... my work on the official shorter *Naval History of the War* ... my lectures during and after the war at the staff colleges of all three services and of the Imperial Defence College ... my chairmanship of the Ashridge Educational Council and of the Authors' Society and for the past twenty-seven years of the St John and Red Cross Hospital Library ... my successful battle over the North Buckinghamshire high tension pylon line ... my ten years' unsuccessful opposition to the Common Market and presidency of the Common Market Safeguards Committee ... and my founding and Presidency of the Friends of the Vale of Aylesbury.'

He drew his breath, then looked at Pamela for the first time since commencing his discourse. She looked totally bewildered. Regaining her composure, she tried to explain that such a book was not at all what she had in mind. For, despite her recent History A level, she did not regard herself as a professional historian or biographer. She simply wanted to write a short 'portrait' of him, like the surprisingly successful memoir she had written about her father – the 'little classic' that had brought them together. Her mentor merely leant towards her, gripped her by the hand and flashed one of those penetrating smiles that he reserved for just such occasions. He told her that he was going to set it all down in a memorandum for her anyway.

When Pamela later tried to make sense of this constitutional document, she realised that the historian revealed more about himself by what he left unmentioned. Of his two wives, as well as countless other companions over the years, there was not even the briefest acknowledgement. Nor did Sir Arthur want anything said about his covert wartime activities. Naturally, he had no problem having the public side of this work fully detailed, including his personal friendships with the likes of Lord Alanbrooke and General Montgomery. He was equally content for her to quote extensively from the rave reviews of his patriotic histories – *The Years of Endurance*, *The Years of Victory* and the rest – which had, in 1954, helped secure his knighthood. What she was not to explore too closely was his unofficial attempts to broker a peace agreement between the British government and the Hitler regime during the summer of 1939. Due to the assistance of his friends in government and the civil service, much of this awkward history had been shielded from prying eyes – though not without a few questions being raised about his version of events: one official tartly observed that the historian's travel expenses to Salzburg had not been paid for from the 'intelligence fund', as he had often claimed. At the behest of the prime minister of the day, Harold Wilson – another of Sir Arthur's many 'fans' – the public records of this episode were sealed until the end of the century. The historian could not have been more relieved.

'Thank you so much for all your kindness and trouble,' he wrote back to the cabinet secretary at the time. 'I am most grateful. What anyone will make of my well-meant but futile efforts to avert the unavertable in 1990 I have no idea! – but I shall not be here.'

And the biography was by no means the only way Sir Arthur planned to keep Pamela at his side. He also kept up his steady stream of love letters.

'I now see you as the reality you *are*,' he told her shortly after their return from the Algarve, 'and *how dear* – and not just as a dream; I know my life can never be what it should and could be, and what I want to make it, *without you*.'

He realised that she was still upset about his increasingly obvious reluctance to marry her, especially now that her divorce from David had been agreed. He wanted her to remember that, while he enjoyed the company of scarcely anyone, he made a particular exception for her.

'I *have* loved and admired a few human beings very much,' he wrote in another letter, 'so it is quite a compliment really that I do respect and admire and like being with you more than any other human being I've ever known.' It was, he constantly intoned, her destiny – her *fate* – to be with him.

But like that other great pragmatist, Vladimir Lenin, Sir Arthur was not loath to give historical inevitability a little shove on occasion. Forced, as he was, to reshuffle his property portfolio to facilitate Anne's return to London, he now proposed to resettle in the town of Pamela's childhood: Salisbury. Nothing could have been more calculated to appeal to his secretary's innermost passions and emotions. Even from the time of their first dinner at the little Polish restaurant on the Brompton Road, Pamela had told the historian of her happy upbringing in the district where her father, after struggling through the agricultural depression of the 1920s, had risen to national fame as a writer and journalist. The thought of returning here to pass out a comfortable and carefree retirement was as great an enticement as could be imagined. It was no coincidence that Pamela's ex-husband had made precisely the same offer while attempting to coax her out of his precious Mayfair flat.

The house that Sir Arthur had in mind was only a few doors down from the property that David had previously suggested. It was an imposing eighteenth-century mansion called Myles Place, prominently situated in the Cathedral Close. After making an exploratory visit to the property in the early summer of 1973, Sir Arthur arranged to give Pamela a personal tour of the premises shortly thereafter. Proudly he explained that the house was large enough for her to be installed in a separate flat on the top floor. For this privilege, he told her, she might like to invest all the money – some £20,000 – that she had, a few years previously, inherited from her mother.

'It would make all the difference to me,' he wrote, 'and free me from the necessity of an immediate, as opposed to gradual, removal from Rutland Gate.'

Although Pamela eventually avoided making such a rash commitment, her elderly friend kept up the pressure by offering, just as he had to Alwynne in connection with the South Pavilion, to insert a clause in his will to the effect that she could go on living in the house until the lease expired in 2004.

Not for the first or last time, Pamela felt like an insect trapped in a spider's web. In the face of her half-hearted resistance, Sir Arthur wrote her copious letters, employing every trick in his toolbox to win her support and approval.

'There is nowhere I should so love to make my home,' he pleaded, 'provided it could be with you.'

When this enticement failed, the historian tried a little flattery instead, saying that the move was inspired by her 'wonderful description' of the Close in her *Portrait of Wiltshire* – a book that he had once dismissed to Anne as a mere 'guidebook'. In yet another letter, Sir Arthur opted for more direct means, writing that he was going to shower her with 'little treats ... theatres, jaunts to interesting places' – he hoped that in the course of these entertainments their difficulties would 'iron themselves out a little'.

Even on the very day that he was due to exchange contracts with the current owner of Myles Place, he told Pamela that he was only relocating to the West Country for her sake, and that he would gladly withdraw from the purchase if she only said the word. Yet, as ever, there was a strong personal agenda too. As he wrote to Anne at the same time, he envisaged the property one day becoming a kind of permanent monument to his life and work.

Pamela's principal objection to the scheme was that they could hardly go and live in an area where she was so well known – particularly in the Cathedral Close, of all places – without being man and wife. This had, ever since the distressing scene over the lawyer's letter, always been a source of disagreement between the pair. Each had such profoundly differing versions of what had taken place: Sir Arthur always swore blind that it had been at *her* insistence that they had not gone through with their planned marriage. In any case, as the historian hinted, the situation might change: 'let's wait and see' was a phrase often on his lips. But to Pamela's ears, these equivocations and half-promises merely added up to the words she had learnt, as a schoolgirl, of the Temptation of Christ. 'All these things I will give You,' the Devil crows, 'if You will fall down and worship me.'

Hardly less troubling for Pamela was how exactly Alwynne fitted into Sir Arthur's new arrangements. It seemed extraordinary to her that this faithful 'old flame', as the historian continually referred to her, had agreed to assist quite vigorously in the sale of the South Pavilion – she even suspected, rather unfairly, that the older woman had allowed the eventual buyer, Sir John Gielgud, to suppose her to be Lady Bryant. But it was only a matter of time until Pamela discerned that Alwynne was to be compensated for these endeavours, as well as for the loss of the South Pavilion. This was to take the form of permanent access to one of the spare rooms at the new house; a lodging that was to be a near replica of her quarters at the former property: an over-furnished boudoir dominated by an enormous four-poster bed. For convenience, this room was to be situated just next door to the master bedroom, which was itself directly adjacent to a narrow staircase leading up to the small flat on the top floor in which Pamela was to be installed.

The same attention to detail was clear from Sir Arthur's oversight of the transference of all his goods and chattels from his other two residences. Oblivious to his great age as well as to the usual practices of removal firms, he arranged for Alwynne to ferry him between Rutland Gate, the South Pavilion and the Cathedral Close so that he could personally attend to the packing and unpacking of every last clock and hourglass. By the time that the operation was complete in the late autumn, Pamela's doubts and reservations had become more acute than ever. Besides the casual way in which Sir Arthur had conscripted another woman in his fold – especially one so clearly besotted with him – she was beginning to observe with a disquieting new objectivity the historian's inner dictator. On the day that the ill-suited couple at last moved into the property, Pamela watched in semi-horror as he stood on the threshold of the house, surrounded by a group of 'slightly bewildered females', double-checking that all his instructions had been obeyed. It was as though his childhood dream of emulating Napoleon had finally come about.

Pamela was just dwelling on this thought when her eye was drawn towards a clerical figure walking up the driveway with a bunch of chrysanthemums. This was Canon Ian Dunlop, the Chancellor of Salisbury Cathedral, who happened to be related, by marriage, to Sir Arthur's first wife, Sylvia. He had come to extend a special welcome to the Close's newest resident on behalf of the entire chapter.

For once, Sir Arthur's impeccable public relations failed him. Barely had the kindly visitor handed over the flowers, with a few generous words, than Sir Arthur thrust them at Pamela – much, she thought, 'as a bride might have divested herself of her bouquet'. Immediately after the canon's hasty retreat, a cheerful old lady appeared brandishing a box of poppies.

'Would you …' she began, charmingly and expectantly.

'No,' replied Sir Arthur, waving her away, 'not *now!*'

A tallboy presented itself at the bottom of the steps and the lady, wraith-like, followed the canon into the West Walk.

From these unpromising beginnings, the move to Salisbury quickly proved to be a total disaster for Pamela and Sir Arthur. For one thing, the latter was completely unequipped to attend to the various tasks which came with the ownership of such a property. While he may have, in his youth, been able to undertake substantial renovations of old houses, in the intervening years the cost of labour had increased to an even greater extent than his own staying power had diminished. He seemed to think that a busy handyman and builder, Mr Robson, whose name he had chanced upon in the local directory, was prepared to serve as his personal factotum, day and night, twenty-four-seven. For some weeks he took to phoning him up early in the morning with long lists of queries and demands. 'The library ceiling ... the drawing-room paint ... the gallery, is it sagging? And what about the heating? I foretold trouble with these oil sheikhs years ago ...,' he would rail on and on.

A large part of the problem was the difficulty Sir Arthur had engaging a live-in housekeeper. Having relied on the services of the Chalkleys for nearly thirty years, it came as a shock to find that there was no one on hand, when required, to undertake all manner of domestic tasks, from doing his laundry to repairing old joinery. For a short period a young couple agreed to occupy the basement, but this arrangement broke down when the extent of Sir Arthur's demands became abundantly clear.

'She is not only the best tidier and polisher we have had,' he wrote contentedly a few days after their arrival, 'but she has got a wonderful bearded ... husband who ... has already made metal bars to all the window shutters. It would have taken Mr Robson another year!'

After several weeks of slaving for the historian in this manner, the pair decided that there were easier ways of obtaining the use of a damp cellar and quietly moved on.

Another problem was rodents.

'The mice have almost taken over the house,' declared Sir Arthur on the telephone to Pamela during these hectic months. He wanted her to find him a cat to resolve this issue quickly and inexpensively. With the help of her local friend, Sybil Scott, it was but a short time until she had found a suitable animal. Octopus, as the creature was known, was a large mass of marmalade fur, remarkable, like its new owner, for combining longevity with an undiminished appetite for prowling and pouncing. Perhaps the likeness was too exact, as the pair did not hit it off. After spending a week confined in the basement with another temporary housekeeper while Sir Arthur and Pamela were staying at South Street, the animal appeared to have acquired a strong dislike for the master of Myles Place. When the pair were introduced in the library late one Friday evening, Octopus darted beneath the tables and chairs, refusing to let the historian so much as touch a whisker. Despite his proud love of animals, Sir Arthur had to admit that this venture had been a failure. After the departure, shortly thereafter, of the latest housekeeper following a row over her unauthorised use of a favourite corner of the garden, he proposed that Pamela should either find the cat a new home – or arrange to have it put down.

This was almost the greatest shock of all. While Pamela had long since deduced that there was a 'startling difference between what he wrote and how he lived', it was not until the Octopus affair that she fully appreciated the extent of Sir Arthur's duplicity. She had finally realised that he did not simply deceive others; he deceived himself as well. In the guise of national historian and public moralist, he wrote endlessly about his love of animals and the natural world. The private man was equally forthright: he chided Pamela for killing any of God's creatures, even wasps. Yet, when he took a personal dislike to an elderly cat whose only fault, besides not liking him, was a preference for young birds over mice, it seemed perfectly reasonable in his own mind that a lethal injection was the best and fairest solution. There was, perhaps, a small clue in one of his earliest books, in which he had observed that holding two contradictory views at the same time was part of the English national character.

Thanks to the intervention of another friend, Pamela was able to save Octopus and the crisis was soon forgotten. But her relationship with Sir Arthur was now becoming intolerable. As well as continuing to work for him round the clock – typing, fact-checking, taking dictation – she was also expected to cook his meals and play the role of charming hostess, as required. Since much of her companion's professional life remained in London, these services were often transferred to South Street – a property that Sir Arthur said he preferred to Rutland Gate on account of its relative tidiness and compact nature. Even after moving into the Close, he continued to spend long stretches of time working here, much to its owner's increasing irritation. Aside from the continued burden of his usual administrative requirements, Pamela complained of her guest's curious habit of wandering around the flat noisily during the night; a practice for which she gave him the nickname 'Large Heavy Mouse'. Added to these gripes was the problem of his propensity to cause himself accidental injury. In the course of one week alone he managed to break a toe by dropping a metal stamping machine on his foot, as well as slicing open his thumb in an unsuccessful battle with a jammed window.

While Pamela continued to nurse and help Sir Arthur in all manner of ways, he had still not put Rutland Gate on the market. The reason that he gave for this anomaly was that he did not want to evict his elderly retainers, the Chalkleys, from their subterranean accommodation. Pamela might have accepted this chivalrous explanation had it not been used in other, less believable, circumstances. For Sir Arthur used precisely the same logic to account for the constant appearance of Alwynne at the Close, even though she had retained possession of Crafton Farmhouse after the recent death of her husband. It was only thanks to Anne agreeing to delay her move to London that allowed Sir Arthur to hang on to Rutland Gate for many months longer. When not incapacitated by work or injury, he would occasionally creep back to his old quarters either to attend official dinners or to partake in more intimate gatherings. Among the most notable of these amusements was a dinner party, hosted by Alwynne, for Sir John Gielgud, and a trip to the annual RAF Benevolent Fund concert with Anne.

In later years, Pamela would wonder why she tolerated this situation. 'Learn to walk away,' her father had once told her. 'Always make clean breaks.' But Sir Arthur had a way of keeping her right where he wanted her.

When she told him that the only way she could afford to invest in Myles Place was to sell her flat back to her ex-husband, he became almost apoplectic with rage.

'If you go on deploring and trying to put into reverse the necessary … financial adjustments between you and David,' he wrote, '… life becomes a complete nightmare for anyone closely associated with you, let alone who loves you.'

Describing her as a 'compulsive mental masochist', he said that the 'perpetual self-torment' to which she subjected herself was 'pure Hell' and made his mood and conduct just as bad as her own. During the course of one of their numerous rows over their properties, he burst a blood vessel in his eye and feared the onset of blindness.

But all this was merely the prelude to the biggest, and oldest, row of all. That December Pamela's daughter, Miranda, was due to marry her fiancé, Martin Davies, whom she had met during her Oxford years. Since the room she had been renting from a friend would be needed a month or so beforehand for a younger sibling, she asked her mother if she could come and live at South Street in the run-up to her wedding day. Yet again, Sir Arthur became hysterical and vaguely threatening.

'I am quite certain that to share your tiny flat in your present tired state,' he wrote, '... and simultaneously work for me and look after me, as you have so nobly done for so long ... would be too much for you.'

Most reluctantly, he said, he would have to discharge her from his service and find someone else to do his typing. In desperation, he even offered to rent a furnished apartment for her daughter so that she would not come between the two of them.

But, to Sir Arthur's amazement, Pamela stood her ground: Miranda came to stay at South Street after all. Like a jealous elder child, the eminent historian took this development as a personal slight. He complained that he could hardly be expected to fend for himself, as well as work on his new book – a biography of Samuel Johnson – without her constant care and assistance.

'You are impossible,' she told him at one stage. 'Why aren't you content to stay put and grow old gracefully? You ought to be sitting in the Close, relaxed and benign, patting the heads of your non-existent grandchildren.'

But Sir Arthur merely shrugged.

'How dull,' he replied, before rushing out of the door – either to a secret assignation or for tea with the new bishop; he never did say. When Pamela finally told him that she could no longer cope, he almost relented.

'All right,' he huffed after a long pause. 'I'll take myself off to a health place.'

It was as close as Pamela ever got to her 'clean break'.

7

Some months prior to Sir Arthur's departure for his health cure, he and Pamela had been invited to a small London drinks party by their mutual friends, the Berrys. Except for their annual trip to Lord's, intimate social gatherings of this kind were generally the only occasions that the pair appeared in public together – though the historian was careful to leave the precise nature of their relationship implicit. In later years Pamela would recall how he would invariably walk into a room slightly ahead of her, as though they had arrived separately. He always said, in relation to business matters, that he liked to 'keep his options open', and he seemed to apply the same principle to other aspects of his life too.

For this reason, it was quite understandable that another of the guests that evening had imagined Sir Arthur to be romantically available. Lorelei Robinson was a flamboyant, thrice-married divorcee whose real name was Joan. Immaculately dressed and coiffured, she lived in the largest mansion on Chiswick Mall, Said House, where she was competently looked after by a team of live-in staff. Like many women of such phenomenal means, her age was impossible to discern, though a figure between fifty-five and sixty was widely mooted. Prior to the party, she had told her hostess that she was on the lookout for

'Number Four' – and Margaret Berry had clearly thought the historian to be eminently suitable.

It was not so much of a betrayal as Pamela would later imagine. Her old friends had, by this time, come to realise that her relationship with Sir Arthur was somewhat damaging and dysfunctional for them both. In the space of three short years, they had seen the shy countrywoman withdraw from social life and become a mere cypher of an older, controlling man. Sir Arthur, meanwhile, was beginning to look notably tired and decrepit – his old secretary, Susanna Hoe, thought him to be 'wretched' when she saw him during this period. By a strange irony, the Berrys followed the same dubious logic as Anne in supposing that everything would be solved if he simply met a woman who could manage his complex requirements. Lorelei was envisaged as being exactly what Pamela had once been to both Barbara and Alwynne: a saviour who could 'keep the show on the road'.

The new woman, however, needed remarkably little help and encouragement. Throughout the party she hung on Sir Arthur's every word – throwing her head back and laughing at his slightest pleasantry – while Pamela was forced to endure a stage-managed tour of the family's impressive collection of hunting and shooting prints. The siren signals of Lorelei worked a charm: one bystander recalled the historian being completely 'mesmerised' by her performance. At the end of the evening, the enchantress gave him an extravagant kiss goodbye and then hung back slightly, as though she wanted to be invited to dinner. Sir Arthur murmured something to Pamela about her joining the two of them for the evening but was predictably met with a blank response. The younger woman had already taken an intense dislike to an individual whom she would soon dub 'the kissing lady'.

There matters might have rested. But a few weeks later, while on one of his exploratory visits to Salisbury, Sir Arthur stayed at the Berrys' country house, Compton. By a strange turn of fate – or design, as Pamela later suspected – it so happened that Lorelei would be visiting too. Most painful of all was the fact that the younger woman had arranged for her lover to stay with her old friends in the first place. Yet it was not until her daughter's wedding at the end of the year that she became aware of these furtive developments.

Still furious over her decision to house Miranda at South Street, Sir Arthur had only agreed to attend the church service, not the ensuing reception. 'I am not drinking your ex-husband's champagne!' he had fumed.

After sitting incognito at the back of the college chapel, Christ Church Cathedral, he made a rapid return to London, where he had promised to take the mother of the bride out for dinner once her duties were complete. She arrived late and exhausted, having just undergone the most momentous twenty-four hours in the life of almost any woman of her age and generation. But her thoughts quickly turned to the movements of her wayward man: she wanted to know where he had been the previous evening, while she had been staying with Miranda at the Randolph Hotel.

Her companion did his best to come clean: he had been with Lorelei. 'After all,' he kept saying with a note of indignation, 'I had to return her hospitality. It was too bad she had friends coming in for drinks. I just went along and then stayed on to dinner with her.'

'*Alone?*' asked Pamela, accusingly.

'Yes,' he replied, 'but I was back by ten.'

Everything, then, was primed for Sir Arthur to spend substantially more time with 'the kissing lady' after his departure for Champneys luxury health spa on 11 April 1974. Unbeknown to Pamela, he had been liaising with her in the preceding days, suggesting dates when she might like to come and spend time with him during breaks from his *Life of Johnson*. Although she would ultimately prove fickle in this commitment, as in so many others, the pair would see a great deal of one another over the coming months, including another weekend together at the Berrys' straight after his return. It seemed, finally, as if the historian had found his heart's desire.

'During these last weeks,' he would shortly write to his new lady-love, 'the precious memory of which will haunt me till I die, you literally carried my life and my soul in your dear hands. And all the tenderness and generosity which you gave me, Darling.'

Yet Sir Arthur was never a man to burn his boats. While simultaneously wooing Lorelei, he continued to reassure Pamela.

'Everyone else is dull and second-rate after you,' he wrote from his retreat. 'You always said,' he went on, 'you wanted me to be whole and single-hearted, and now, when you no longer want it, you've got it, hook, line and sinker.'

He said that he was tormented by her unhappiness, and his alleged powerlessness to comfort her: he protested that he could not be in more agony if he were to be 'crucified upside down'. In another letter, he told her that he loved her 'infinitely more than anyone else in the world' and that, in spite of their recent rows, he believed that they could still be 'happier than we have ever been'. It was, however, no use. Not even a desperate plea for sympathy by describing the unpleasant effects of his colonic irrigation – 'enough poison came out of me yesterday to sink a ship' – would persuade Pamela to respond, or even pick up her telephone. Something told her that all was not as it seemed.

In her mind, the most substantial threat was still Alwynne. After failing to persuade Sir Arthur to end this relationship at the time of their move to Salisbury, Pamela had taken the bold step of writing to her directly.

'I think I have some idea of what the sale of the South Pavilion ... means to you,' she tried, 'and I am also desperately aware that you must feel that I am the person who is going to benefit by it all.'

Protesting that she 'never liked "taking"', she said that she had come to terms with the fact that the two of them were going to need to cooperate.

'I know how infinitely more practical and efficient you are,' she continued, '... [and] that, about the garden, compared to you, I know very little and wouldn't dream of wanting or venturing to alter an expert's plan in any way at all.'

Yet there was an underlying note of warning too.

'I think perhaps I made a mistake in choosing not to come to the South Pavilion again this summer,' she concluded, '...but I fully understand how ... it would be much easier for you if I didn't, in the same way as it would be for me in settling into Myles Place.'

These brewing tensions were another reason why Sir Arthur had elected to remove himself to Champneys. As Pamela was painfully aware, the retreat was just a short drive from Alwynne's farmhouse, and it was clear that the old companions would be seeing something of one another during the historian's two-week stay. Only to his separated wife was Sir Arthur entirely open about this reality. When she offered to collect him from Beaconsfield railway station, he apologised that his other muse already had this in hand.

'I feel it would be rather ungracious and ungrateful of me now to cancel,' he wrote diplomatically.

Alwynne's additional services included fetching him clean clothes, mending his glasses and even arranging for a young lady from the health farm to do his typing.

'I still had not fully grasped,' wrote Pamela in later years, 'his desperate need to be near one woman or another.'

But perhaps the most surprising feature of Sir Arthur's exile was that he was engaged in yet another herculean writing assignment. For as long as he had been a professional author he had dreamt of writing the life of Samuel Johnson.

'[He] was,' ran a typical sentence in the introduction, 'a Falstaff in rich humour and appearance, a near-saint in goodness, a man of transcendent courage who overcame almost superhuman difficulties, an intelligence more comprehensive and balanced than almost any other of which we have record.'

It did not seem to matter to him that no fewer than four biographies of Dr Johnson had recently appeared, including popular works by Christopher Hibbert and Peter Quennell. Nor was his elbow stayed by the reluctance of his publisher, Collins, to underwrite the project.

'The use of my large fan list,' Sir Arthur was forced to write to his editor, Adrian House, '... can give the subscription the same start as *The Great Duke* and *Jackets of Green*.'

Not even when Mr House and another representative of the firm warned that the sample chapters were somewhat 'wearisome to the reader' and marred by 'inaccuracies and repetitions', did he relent:

throughout the spring and summer of 1974 he wrote a staggering 2,000 words a day. He said that he would be able to get the first of his prospective two volumes, provisionally entitled *The Ascent of Parnassus* and *The English Socrates*, completed in time for the Christmas sales.

Sir Arthur's rationale for selecting Dr Johnson was clear. The two men were, even more than the historian's previous subjects, ideally matched. Whether it was their relentless pursuit of acclaim along the hard road of English letters or their dogmatic and unflinching conservativism, there were parallels between the writers which transcended the centuries. Sir Arthur would make much of these similarities – but he was more cautious when it came to the good doctor's curious relations with women. While he accepted that Johnson's 'highly passionate nature' made him a somewhat demanding husband, he believed that the 'Great Cham' had always been 'chivalrously devoted' to his long-suffering wife, Tetty – or at least, he had obeyed her stricture that he could lie 'with as many women as he pleased, provided he loved her alone'.

At no stage did this latest biographer come close to anticipating the modern thesis that his predecessor had been a bigoted hypocrite who tormented himself with sexual fantasies before, in lonely old age, finding happiness at the mercies of a literary dominatrix, Mrs Thrale. Indeed, it was Sir Arthur's considered opinion that his hero's pleading and suggestive letters to that Streatham housewife were 'an essential part of the English cultural heritage, as the Psalms of David and the Proverbs are to the Hebrew'.

There is no doubt that Sir Arthur placed his own letters to Pamela in the same category.

'Oh my dear estranged Pam,' he wrote from his rest-home cabin, 'whom I love so deeply, I am so terribly sorry for all my folly and unkindness ... I could scourge myself for my folly.'

He said that the sight of her at the railway station before his departure had made him feel like one of 'Christ's disciples ... when He suddenly appeared beside them after his Crucifixion.'

When, a few days later, he heard that his publisher was not going to rush out the Johnson biography after all, he expanded on the theme of death and redemption, even suggesting that he had attempted to take his own life.

'I'm going to try very hard [to finish the book],' he wrote, 'partly because I feel if it is the last thing I ever write, it will be a worthwhile thing to have done because the subject is so great and my own unhappiness makes it easier for me to understand what I am writing about ... and partly because writing is my lifeline and without it I should break down completely and do something insane as I nearly did this morning.'

Referring to his setbacks with his correspondent as much as with his publisher, he continued: 'I don't like accepting defeat, and as I'm now finally defeated in the thing that matters most to me – and utterly humiliated with it – I feel I must somehow meet the challenge of defeat in the only way I can, not for fame or success, but, at the end of life, for the mere sake of refusing to give up altogether and to go down at least fighting. And even if it can only be published as a fragment I feel I've already written enough of it to make it worthwhile.'

Pamela could hardly fail to be moved. And yet the theatrical element was never far away. Besides the fact that Sir Arthur was simultaneously writing cheerful letters to Anne about his afternoon strolls with Alwynne and her new dog, Fenny, he would soon admit to writing for effect. Rereading his letters from Champneys later that year, he wrote conceitedly to Pamela: 'They amount in quantity to several months of *ILN* articles [his newspaper column]! and in quality, well to the nearest to great poetry my inadequate Muse can get, and you wouldn't be worthy of literary occupation let alone love, if you didn't!'

Yet Sir Arthur relied on more than literary prowess in his assault on Pamela's heart: he could use a battering ram as well.

'Can you wonder,' he scrawled with reference to her plan to sell her flat, 'that faced with such callousness towards me and irresponsible behaviour, I feel bitter and doubt altogether your love for me?'

By 16 April, Pamela could withstand no more.

> Boaz [she wrote in semi-capitulation], unfortunately for you and for me, I believe, despite everything, I am still in love with you.
>
> I think you are absolute hell to live with but worse hell to be without. I find you exhausting, bewildering, uncertain, secretive, stubborn and more than a little mad. I can hardly believe a word you say; you are untidy (except when washing up), mind-changing and time-absorbing. Your procrastination exasperates to screaming-pitch. You wishful-think. You hurt and you are a runner-after-of-other-women. But you are absolutely wonderful when it comes to two things: writing books and going to bed.

These final qualities were enough. When, some months later, Pamela reread the final pages of his wartime epic, *English Saga*, she wrote of her renewed love and admiration for the author. She said that the passage in which he had stated that a man, like a nation, could 'learn from his mistakes ... [and] raise his stature by self-regeneration' seemed particularly apt in the context of their present difficulties. By the summer of 1974 the pair had resumed their former intercourse, shuttling back and forth between Mayfair and the Cathedral Close as if practically – though still not quite – man and wife.

But just as Sir Arthur's victory seemed complete, he forgot his own lesson. Without consulting Pamela, he invited Lorelei to join them for a small dinner party at Rutland Gate. This was perhaps his biggest mistake to date. Despite assuring the younger woman that the evening would be fun and relaxing – he had even engaged a professional chef to relieve her of her usual catering duties – everything seemed destined for disaster. Not only did the cook fail to materialise, forcing Pamela to don an apron as usual; it was also clear from the moment of Lorelei's intentionally tardy arrival that the evening would be anything but restful for the reluctant hostess.

Shown upstairs by Mrs Chalkley, the 'kissing lady' appeared in the library, carefree and serene, clasping a designer handbag from which protruded the head of a very small dog – Jomo. To the amazement of the silenced on-lookers, this unexpected guest was carrying between its teeth a slim volume which was dutifully presented to the host with a peal of laughter. Jomo was then required to perform the same trick with a small bunch of flowers for Pamela.

'Only a woman,' the latter would recall long after, '... could fully appreciate the feeling of nausea which rose inside me.' Lorelei had staked her claim.

The next day Pamela received a prompt letter from her latest rival. 'You were so wonderful to rescue a planned dinner party about to fall apart through the cook's indisposition,' she wrote, 'and with your capable, expert hands produce the most delicious dinner and lovely evening to be enjoyed by all.'

This was enough to raise Pamela's hackles, but the lacquered effusiveness was soon to get a good deal thicker.

'A four-legged [friend] with built-in black dinner jacket,' she continued, '... Jomo sends a big lick of love and thanks.' She said that she hoped they would 'meet again very soon'.

Over the coming weeks Lorelei would be the source of countless rows between Pamela and Sir Arthur. Disappearing for long stretches of time between taking his former secretary out to literary soirées and military parades, he became increasingly vague about his precise whereabouts. When he vanished for forty-eight hours on a top-secret visit to – he said – Cheshire, she was forced to go round in person to Rutland Gate to collect his post. Here she was surprised to find a letter on the post-mat in the same delicate handwriting as the note recently dispatched to South Street. Although she resisted the temptation to open it, she demanded upon Sir Arthur's return that he reveal the full extent of his infatuation with the Rhine maiden. Once again, he tried haplessly to reassure her.

'No one can light a candle to you,' he wrote in yet another begging letter, 'or come anywhere near you.' But this time it was useless: she saw straight through his defences. After venturing into his chaotic piles of rough workings and unpaid bills, she even discovered that he had been writing smitten poems for his new beloved. One of these began: 'The light of evening, Lissadell.'

This time, Pamela said, she was leaving. For good. She dispatched a long, bitter letter to Sir Arthur outlining all her hurt and frustration and anger. She never wanted to see him again. So certain was she of this that, for once, she did not bother to keep a copy of her letter. But that was not all she forgot: she also overlooked the historian's deft skill in the art of emotional blackmail.

'I can't believe,' he responded angrily, '... you of all people would walk out of a professional commitment without due notice ... I must ask you to continue working for me till the end of the month, and to do for me what I cannot ... which is to wind up the arrangements I made for your benefit as well as mine in Salisbury.'

Lorelei, too, was brought into this rear-guard action.

'I could never,' she wrote in another letter, '... cast one shadow of sorrow on another person.

'Please believe this,' she went on, 'and please talk to me if you should wish, because I understand so much more than my masked face and shielded heart gives me credit for.'

After inviting her for tea at South Street to discuss the situation, Pamela received another letter from Lorelei.

'Arthur is a great wonderful person, yet a man,' she wrote, 'and all men are selfish, even though they do not realise it ... they all want their "penny and their bun" ... it is prudent to understand.'

Within a few days, Pamela found herself, once again, watching the Eton vs Harrow match at Lord's, laughing at the historian's jokes and entertaining his well-heeled friends.

Sir Arthur very nearly succeeded in this remarkable double act – but not quite. He made a fatal mistake in allowing his two principal women to keep up a regular line of communication. Early on 1 August, Pamela learnt from Lorelei that she was expecting their mutual friend at Said House later that evening. It would only be a matter of time until Sir Arthur would have to give her some reason why he was unaccountably indisposed.

Pamela played an unusually cool game, dutifully typing up his latest chapter on Dr Johnson without allowing even the smallest hint of suspicion or recrimination to show. Then, around five o'clock, Sir Arthur let out a heavy sigh and said that he was much too tired to go on.

'You look as if you could do with a rest as well, Pam,' he continued, in the most considerate tone he could muster. 'I think I'll take myself off to Pratt's' – one of the seven gentlemen's clubs to which he belonged.

His typist said nothing for a moment, then launched into her tirade.

'I cannot feel under the sort of obligation you expect,' she wrote shortly afterwards, 'I no longer wish ... to be a penny or a bun ... If you need your self-respect as a man and someone who is "good for you" ... you must remember it applies the other way round.'

Sir Arthur had to concede that he had been caught out. But, as ever, he was not going down without a struggle.

'I feel not the slightest resentment,' he wrote, 'even though I know that so much of what you have believed ... and imagine is not true.' He said all that remained for him was 'love for you and all you are and have been to me'. He said that her 'dramatic disappearance' had come as a heavy blow which would cause him untold hardship and inconvenience. 'Even my dining clubs are ... shut up for the next few weeks,' he added self-pityingly.

Ignoring the irony that he was still married to someone else, he hinted that there would be whispers in the Close if she did not return there with him. What would he say, he wondered aloud, to the bishop and a host of other local worthies who were due, as Pamela knew, to come for dinner with them over the coming weeks? Likewise, he asked her what he was to do about the collection of prospective house-keepers who she was supposed to be interviewing for him, not only for Myles Place but also Rutland Gate, now that his loyal domes-tic couple, the Chalkleys, had finally retired. The frontrunner, a Mr Hepburn, whom Sir Arthur only ever referred to as 'the little man', had been suggested to him by the 'nice rector at Down Street'.

'[He] is very "security-minded",' he told Pamela approvingly, 'and could do a lot of badly needed painting and maintenance work both here [at Rutland Gate] and at Salisbury.'

As was his custom, Sir Arthur combined these manoeuvres with further protestations of love.

'Believe me,' he wrote despairingly, 'I love you very dearly, and always shall, I know whatever happens and nothing can ever alter that.'

He sent her verses by a favourite fifteenth-century monk, as well as a stanza from William Cowper, both to the effect that suffering was only a prelude to eternal happiness. In the hope of facilitating this transition, he offered her £100 in arrears of wages, and also said that he would dedicate the second volume of the Johnson biography to her.

'It would comfort me a great deal,' he wrote.

When these – to him – heavy enticements failed to move Pamela, he again called upon Lorelei to bolster his efforts.

'I cannot sit back,' she wrote, 'and see both you and Arthur com-pletely destroying yourselves ... Please, Pam dear,' she went on, 'do not be jealous of me, for I am only desperately trying to hold together, for you, the sad broken pieces that Arthur has been reduced to these last bewildering few days ... one can never know, in this life, when

God will strike and take away ... and whoever is left would be filled with remorse for the rest of their days.'

But Pamela would not relent.

'There seems no happiness in hanging on to a man,' she wrote from her tiny Mayfair roof garden, 'whose affections seem to be straying.'

Comparing herself to all the women in Sir Arthur's life, going back over fifty years, she continued: 'It maddens me to think ... that given a bit more luck, rest and fair-weather, I could probably have coped with your *ménages* just as well or *better* than most.'

She said that while she had once thought she could even be friends with 'the others', this had been a mistake. Like the historian's principal mistress during the 1930s, Monica Abel Smith, she was no longer prepared to share her man. If she could not be first lady, she would have nothing to do with the president. She would set him 'free' – just as he always said he wanted.

Determined to 'put an end to the thing', Pamela dropped off a farewell note to Sir Arthur at Rutland Gate and hurried to Salisbury to collect her belongings.

'It seems as if it's over, doesn't it?' she wrote. She said that she had known this ever since the 'more respectable' Lorelei had appeared on the scene but would nevertheless remember with gratitude 'the un-respectable part of the last three and a half years'.

When she arrived at the house shortly after midday, she did not open the shutters but immured herself inside in the hope that she would at least be able to pack up and leave the following day without attracting undue attention.

English Cathedral Closes, however, are not remarkable for their lack of curiosity. Already known to the entire environ as 'Mrs

Minniver', it was hardly surprising that she would be called upon by a concerned neighbour.

'Do please join us for lunch,' the verger's wife asked the following morning, 'or else I fear you shall not have any.'

The brief visit was turning into a long weekend. In accepting the invitation, Pamela had forgotten that she was racing against a Svengali: Sir Arthur was already en route to Myles Place. While she exchanged pleasantries with her hosts over their Sunday roast, he was passing through Woking, Basingstoke and Andover, as the looming shadow of the cathedral beckoned. No sooner had she said her farewells, having politely declined the trifle, than he was getting into a taxi at Salisbury station to commence the last leg of his journey. He pulled up outside the house just as she put her last items in her bag and prepared to dial for a local cab.

The door swung open.

'You,' she said from the top of the stairs.

'Yes,' he replied, uncertainly, 'I got your note.'

He made her tea, which they drank in silence on the back terrace. Pamela had already missed the five-twenty train that she was hoping to catch.

'You'll stay tonight, won't you?' he said at last. 'I nearly killed myself trying to catch the train to get to you. When I saw the shutters were closed, I was afraid you had gone.'

Once again, in spite of herself, Pamela was somehow persuaded. Like many women in her position, she was always willing to accept the notion that everything was her fault. She did not return to London for another week, during which time Sir Arthur himself made a forty-eight-hour round trip to the capital to take Lorelei to a Promenade Concert at the Albert Hall. His justification for this unwarranted digression was that 'Old Joan' – as Pamela now called her – had offered to drive a Polish cleaning lady, and himself, down to Salisbury the following day. The historian consoled Pamela by saying that he had only been forced back to the other woman because she had refused to interview 'the little man' and all the other candidates he had shortlisted for the position of his housekeeper.

The three of them arrived at Myles Place, rather awkwardly, the morning after the concert. As Lorelei had never been to Myles Place, the tour of the property was naturally conducted by Pamela, who knew her way around the antique furniture and inconveniently situated bathrooms as well as any hired broom. Though she tried her best to disguise the irregularity of the set-up from the bewildered applicant, her efforts were not helped by Sir Arthur and Lorelei. All through the cold salmon lunch which she had reluctantly prepared, the pair flirted like lovesick teenagers: while the historian had 'eyes for no one but Lorelei', the latter 'seemed to use her own eyes with great effect on the only male present'. At the end of the meal the visitor declared that she could not possibly cope with such a situation. The house was, frankly, a warren of clutter and intrigue.

Pamela felt much the same way. After Lorelei and her cleaning lady had returned to London, she went to sit alone in 'Cowslip Farm', a large field on the outskirts of Salisbury that she had inherited from her beloved father, A. G. Street. Remembering his sage advice about walking away, a thought flashed through her mind: '*To hell with A. B.'s evening meal!*'

But escape was never easy. Over the coming weeks she was yet again left in a state of total confusion. The principal reason for this was Sir Arthur's continued evasiveness, especially about his feelings towards her.

'Dearest,' she wrote to him towards the end of August, 'if you feel, as I'm pretty sure you do feel, that there *is* no hope for you and me, it would be kinder not to give me even a glimmer.' She said that she would try to fill her life 'as you want Alwynne to', and that she was going to take herself away on a short holiday to give herself time to think everything through.

'I would always ... "come back" from wherever I was,' she wrote with unintended significance, 'should you find either that I was the person you most wanted to look after you ... or if you needed ... nursing.'

Sir Arthur could not have been more understanding.

'Of the past,' he wrote the following day, 'all I can remember and ever shall is the sweetness and dearness of you and all you did for me ... all it means and always will mean to me.' He told her that he, too, would come to her in time of need, and that he would do all he could to help her write his biography.

'Why don't you let Collins see what you have written about me,' he implored, 'and allow me to tell them about it ...?'

When she secured an interview with C. P. Snow later that summer, there was another pang of regret, tinged with unspoken jealousy, from the historian: having escorted her to the basement office where the novelist conducted his affairs, he told her that she could not possibly go and work *there*. In a further sentimental touch, he offered to let her keep the little wooden mascot, 'Bear', that he had, shortly after their relationship began, exchanged for a lucky silver horseshoe of her own. The trinkets were, like themselves, supposed to be star-crossed lovers, clinging together in a cruel and uncertain world.

In her desperation, Pamela even imagined that Lorelei might be able to help. She called her up at the start of September to get answers: Was Sir Arthur in earnest about his recent protestations of love? Was she still looking for 'Number Four'? Did she think it would be a problem for her to go away on holiday for a few weeks to clear her mind?

Lorelei was happy to assist. Asking Pamela to dinner in Chiswick, she could hardly have appeared more sisterly. Only towards the end of the meal did she deliver her mordant blow.

'You probably don't know this,' she said, having consumed most of the bottle of wine they had shared, 'but Arthur recently asked *me* to marry him!'

Despite quickly adding that she had not accepted, the situation was beyond Pamela's comprehension.

'In any case,' the hostess continued casually, 'I told him he would have to get divorced first.' They both knew that she had triumphed: game, set and match.

Pamela did not quite remember how she reached home. Her head was a chaos of bitterness and resentment. She had a longing to throw a volume of *English Saga* at Sir Arthur – or to do something far worse. As soon as she was back, she dialled the secret number he had given her shortly after their first meeting. She poured out her anger. He listened quietly, for a while. Then he flared up himself: Was it not *she* who had walked out on *him*? Why could she not accept that he loved them both in separate ways? Did she really believe a woman like Lorelei would live with him in the Close *without being his wife*?

This last comment was the unkindest cut of all. After all Pamela had been through – the work, the letters, the pledges to solicitors, Anne, Alwynne, Lorelei … Barbara – this was the end. At last she knew exactly where Sir Arthur placed her in his hierarchy of affection. For almost a week she refused to communicate with him – even about 'that idiotic little man', whom he was still desperate for her to appraise. Still, however, the historian fought his corner.

'Lorelei was just an episode,' he told her once the dust had settled. 'Could I come round and see you? Couldn't we "start again"? Let me take you out to dinner.'

When these advances were rebuffed, he told her that she should refocus her energies on becoming an artist, and, to this end, sent her a biography of the painter Dora Carrington, who had killed herself after a failed romance with the writer Lytton Strachey.

'I was afraid,' replied Pamela with some concern, 'you might be likening her to me.'

In another letter, the spurned lover told her that, even though she was reluctant to tell him of her holiday destination – Madeira – he wanted to see her off, like old times.

On the appointed day, Sir Arthur appeared at South Street with a taxi. As they headed out towards the docks, he held her hand and told her that he was going to change his will in her favour. He said that the suddenness of their parting did not change his feelings towards her, or his gratitude for all she had done for him. He was sorry for everything that he had done or said to hurt her: his offer to 'start again' remained. And he mentioned that he wanted her old house-keeper, Mrs Down, to come and work for him at Myles Place; she had refused to work for the new wife of Pamela's ex-husband.

By the time they arrived at their destination, Pamela had told him where she was going and felt almost prepared to take him back. Then he admitted that he had forgotten to bring any money and would need to borrow £5 to get home – a loan, recalled Pamela, 'he never did repay … actually.' It was, she thought, the final humiliation.

Once aboard the ship, Pamela tried to make sense of her conflicting emotions. It was a rough crossing, but while many fellow passengers felt ill and retired below decks, the weather somehow suited her defiant frame of mind. By the time she arrived at Reid's Hotel the storms were behind her, but as she tried to sunbathe, her doubts began to surface. Then, to make matters worse, Sir Arthur's letters and telegrams started to arrive.

'Darling,' he wrote in one of these communications, 'make the best of your little holiday and don't waste it worrying about me.' He told her that he was sleeping with her lucky horseshoe in his pyjama pocket, and that he hoped 'Bear' was 'doing his duty for his old Master' too. Without blaming her exactly, he revealed that since her departure his biography of Dr Johnson had foundered completely.

'The truth is,' he confessed, 'I attempted something beyond what is now left of my powers … *Sic transit gloria mundi!*' – thus passes the glory of the world.

Pamela did her best to console Sir Arthur without throwing in her hand. 'Are you *sure Johnson* is a non-starter?' she replied. 'I'm so sad to feel I failed to help over this as much as I (according to you) really did help over the others.'

Sir Arthur told her in another one of his letters that he had enjoyed a 'disappointing but rather sweet few hours' flirtation' with the Hollywood actress Jessie Matthews on his last visit to Madeira in the 1930s. Pamela fleetingly wondered whether anything similar could happen to her but quickly realised the impossibility; she simply could not get Sir Arthur out of her mind. Although an accommodating couple asked her to share their table in the hotel dining room, and welcoming strangers seemed more than willing to chat with her on the terrace overlooking the harbour, somehow it wasn't remotely the same. Even the casual advances of one of the historian's friends, recently commenced in London after their meeting at Lord's, meant nothing to her. She was most definitely a 'one-man woman'.

It was in this state of mind that Pamela was awoken by the telephone on the fourth day of her holiday. The receptionist said that there was a long-distance caller on the line. She put her through.

'Pam?' crackled a female voice. It was Lorelei. 'I was trying to get you all day yesterday ...' she went on tentatively.

Pamela felt her brain spinning into overdrive. *Oh, God,* she thought, *what has happened?* She heard herself asking if everything was all right with Sir Arthur.

'He's all *right*,' returned Lorelei cautiously. 'But he's not too good. He fell downstairs yesterday ... nothing broken, but, well, I know he's missing you and he's all alone in that big house.'

While she was careful not to instruct Pamela to return, she said that she was rather doubtful if she could have him to stay at the present time, and no one else was likely to be available either.

'All right,' said Pamela, sitting up with a start, 'I'll fly. I'll cable you if I get a flight.'

Thanks to the prompt action of the hotel's manager, Pamela had recovered her passport from the shipping office, booked a flight and was in the air by ten thirty. Changing planes at Lisbon, she found herself untypically jumping the queue for the luggage trolleys and pushing fellow passengers aside in her battle to make her connection. At six o'clock the same day she was back home.

As soon as she entered the flat, she dialled Lorelei's number.

'Oh, Pamela,' she answered with affected composure. 'I've only just told Sir Arthur about your return – I really didn't want to worry him.'

Pamela could hardly breathe for anger.

'It's probably best you give him a call yourself,' continued the other woman, 'he's just off to dinner with his publisher. He's *so* much better today.'

Beside herself with rage and bewilderment, Pamela put down the receiver and then phoned Sir Arthur. He seemed annoyed that Lorelei had called her up in Madeira. 'I'll come over,' he said, reassuringly, 'on my way to the Connaught.'

He arrived with a bowl of fruit. 'I was afraid you wouldn't have a thing to eat,' he said, handing her this modest friendship offering.

They looked at one another uncertainly for a moment. But before she could say anything, her visitor said that he had to hurry: could he, he asked confidently, come and see her tomorrow? Maybe later in the week they could go down to Salisbury together?

Hardly awaiting an answer, Sir Arthur took up his hat and set off for his meeting with Mr House.

Pamela flung herself down on her bed and wept. She was back in the spider's web.

8

The closing months of 1974 were among the most painful and tor-turous in the entire saga of Pamela and Sir Arthur's love affair. Like a military commander enveloping enemy forces, the historian found ever more ingenious ways of closing all means of his willing victim's escape. An integral part of this stratagem was, unwittingly, Pamela's former housekeeper at Yarnbury Grange, Mrs Down. No longer pre-pared to work for the new Mrs McCormick after David's remarriage that autumn, she had asked her old mistress if she could help her and her terminally ill husband find a suitable position, since their applica-tion for a council house had unaccountably been lost by the author-ities. Albeit with certain misgivings, aware of the potential clash of characters, Pamela suggested to Sir Arthur that he might offer them the basement of Myles Place as a stopgap.

It was as if all his prayers had been answered. As soon as the couple were safely installed that October, he wrote happily to Lorelei: 'Pam has been busy moving her devoted former cook and gardener hus-band into the basement flat. I think this is giving her a great deal of happiness and reassurance ... for nearly a week we haven't had any-thing to differ or argue about – a state of affairs which hasn't existed for three years.' Another rivet had been added to the chain.

The strongest tie, however, remained the prospect of marriage. Ever since his separation from Anne three years previously, Sir Arthur had hinted to Pamela – notwithstanding the letter he made her send to her solicitors – that this was his ultimate goal. It was partly on account of this understanding that Pamela had allowed her incredibly loyal and morally conscientious housekeeper to come and work in Salisbury at all. But no sooner had this been brought about than the historian threw further problems in the way.

That autumn Harold Wilson had narrowly defeated Edward Heath in the second general election of the year and there were fears, in the most reactionary circles, that a revolution akin to the Attlee years was shortly to follow. Sir Arthur played this for all it was worth.

'It wouldn't be much good marrying just now,' he told Pamela casually one morning: 'New legislation would make it financially very difficult.' Dumbfounded, his companion just stared at him. She realised that – once again – she had been tricked, and told him so.

But Sir Arthur could always rise above other people's problems. Frequently leaving Pamela to take care of Myles Place and his new retainers, he continued his peripatetic life, staying with Anne on his way to Rutland Gate or Chiswick to see Lorelei, then on to Buckinghamshire to call on Alwynne for a few days, before being driven back to Salisbury when he was ready to be looked after by Pamela again – Alwynne had even bought a new car to make this curious figure of eight possible. Although Pamela tried her best to return to South Street, she felt obligated to look after Mrs Down, and on occasion she was even persuaded to resume her role of London hostess.

'I'm lost with admiration for the wonderful dinner party,' wrote Lorelei shortly after one of these rather uncomfortable get-togethers.

'You were really wonderful and everything looked so beautiful, yourself, your flat, the table, and once again that spellbinding mousse.'

When Christmas came, Sir Arthur told Pamela openly, for the first time, that he would have to telephone each of his women to give them his best wishes – an operation that took well over an hour. It was, yet again, all too much for Pamela, who not only paid for these conversations but could hardly avoid overhearing them, as he was a guest at her flat. Unable to rationalise why she tolerated this sort of behaviour, she began to think of herself, as much as the others, as one of the historian's 'floating doters'. She told him that she felt taken advantage of, and that his refusal to marry her was rooted in social snobbery. Not untypically, her correspondent turned the tables.

'My first feeling of shocked horror,' he scrawled in response, 'was one of indignation that you should have supposed me such an unspeakable cad.'

Throwing the blame for his failure to marry her on her complex divorce proceedings from David, he told her that far from thinking her 'socially inferior', he considered her 'far superior to myself or anyone ... one would have to go back to Jane Austen or Walter Scott's heroines to find your like.' Moreover, as the daughter of A. G. Street, was she not also the 'Crown Princess of Wiltshire'?

The sheer energy required to maintain this level of intrigue would have broken a man less than half Sir Arthur's age; he was to turn seventy-six in February. But the effort was starting to take its toll.

In a letter to Anne that winter he described himself as a 'walking corpse' on account of 'the strain and the pains of the last few months ... [and] all the absurdities of my domestic and other problems'. He said that she alone gave him the 'peace and happiness' that were 'in rather short supply' in his present life.

After making a flying visit for her sister's funeral shortly thereafter, he spoke of being in 'great pain, chilled and exhausted'. He said that his health had been partially restored by her 'great care and feeding', which reminded him that although their marriage had been 'the greatest disaster' that could have befallen her, it had nevertheless 'proved for me a very great and wonderful experience'.

He was equally grateful to learn that she was now prepared to endure what she called the 'horrid sordidness of a divorce' – but naturally he did not mention this to Pamela. Both he and his wife understood that he was still seeking a match with Lorelei, whom Anne described, in the same letter, as a 'kind and healing' companion – not forgetting 'the loving Jomo' too.

The whirligig finally broke on Tuesday, 4 March 1975. That afternoon, as he was rushing out of Myles Place on his way to see Anne, who was then to take him for dinner with Lorelei in Chiswick, Sir Arthur tripped on a loose paving stone and collapsed in a heap on the pathway. Mrs Down, who was alone in the house at the time, knew at once that she would have to call for an ambulance. But the question of who else to telephone was less obvious. From her first day at the property, she had taken a dislike to Sir Arthur and his secretive ways. Having witnessed at first hand the breakdown of her previous employers' marriage, and having secretly sided with Pamela, it seemed to her a case of 'out of the frying pan and into the fire'.

Despite her reluctance to cause Pamela further anxiety, Mrs Down realised she would have to call her. For once, however, the unhappy mistress of Myles Place was out enjoying a life of her own: after

meeting Christina Foyle and her husband at Sir Arthur's birthday celebration at South Street two weeks previously, she had been invited for
an evening with the influential literary pair at their London home. It
was not until eleven o'clock that Mrs Down finally got her on the line.

'I'm sorry to have to tell you,' she began.

Pamela braced herself for tragic news about Mrs Down's husband,
Charlie, now in the last throes of cancer. But the information that
followed was somehow harder to process.

'Sir Arthur has fallen down the front steps. He was hurrying to
catch a train to London. They think he's fractured his pelvis. He's in
Salisbury Infirmary.'

Pamela packed her bag and prepared for another long stay in Wiltshire. But before leaving to catch her train the following morning, she
managed to get Sir Arthur on the telephone. To her amazement he
seemed quite calm about his injury; it was mainly the inconvenience
of being bedridden and the alleged inadequacy of the doctors and
nurses in the private wing of the hospital that were aggravating him.
Always neurotic about his health, he only trusted his homeopathic
doctor, Dr McCready, and was evidently dissatisfied by the service
and conditions provided by more conventional practitioners.

'They dope one up with so many things,' he would complain to
Anne, 'that one feels silly.' Though the nurses were 'very kind', he
deplored 'their awful habit of constantly making the bed, which hurts
like billy hoe'.

What he most wanted, he continued in the same letter, was a
muted companion.

'I wish I had a dog here,' he wrote, 'or even a little mouse to feed
with crumbs.'

After making similar complaints to Pamela, he told her that he had a delicate task for her to undertake before her departure. He wanted her to go round to Rutland Gate and tell 'the little man' that his services were no longer required. Despite the testimonial from that congenial rector – and the fact that he possibly had no other home to go to – the patient had become distrustful of him and wanted him out of the property that very day.

Worse was to follow. Having undertaken this most distressing of tasks – she took a friend with her for moral support – and travelled down to Salisbury Infirmary, Pamela was confronted by the sight of Sir Arthur, sitting up in bed, remonstrating with the hospital staff about his 'incarceration' and lack of adequate care.

Calmly turning to his visitor with one of his effortless key changes, he greeted her warmly and thanked her for discharging her duties as promptly and efficiently as he had expected. Now, he said, he had another task for her. He wanted her to go back to London straight-away to install a Mrs Tongue at Rutland Gate.

'The house mustn't be left empty,' he said with sudden urgency. 'Anything could happen … squatters … fires … burglaries … untold trouble with the insurance people!'

This new housekeeper had been recommended to him by Alwynne, and was, he said, sure to prove far more reliable than 'the little man' had been.

Forever wondering why, Pamela undertook this latest challenge and was back in Salisbury to peel Sir Arthur's grapes the following day – the skins reacted badly with his digestion, he always said. By this time Pamela was concerned that Anne had not been informed of the situation. The difficulty was where exactly she was to stay. For

Myles Place, despite its size, had few bedrooms, especially since its owner had, for Alwynne's sake, converted one of them into a 'music room', complete with an out-of-tune piano which she alone could play.

Sir Arthur saw no dilemma: Anne was going to visit him the following day and then return to Weybridge. To Pamela, such a proposition seemed – under the current circumstances – quite ludicrous. Only now did she realise how upset Anne was by the failure of her marriage. The two women had not seen each other or corresponded since the latter's departure from Rutland Gate in the spring of 1971. Resentment had stagnated and festered. In a curious aide-memoire, written during those difficult first months of separation, Anne had detailed each of her rival's incursions.

'Pam rang to say she had left her husband and was seeking a divorce,' she wrote on a loose sheet of paper. 'I invited her to my house,' the text continued, 'she said that when she felt stronger – she was looking awful – she would like to work in some voluntary capacity and questioned me about hospital work.'

Anne then chronicled how her husband had chanced to enter the room at that precise moment and had subsequently insisted that they invite the singleton for dinner on Christmas Day.

'She talked mostly with Arthur,' wrote Anne of that occasion, 'and was no help to me in entertaining Lord Goddard.'

After her husband's subsequent evenings with Pamela in the new year, she confronted him about the situation. She wanted to be sure that her own presence was superfluous before making way for the other woman. The Rubicon was apparently crossed when she dropped her husband off at Marylebone station on Sunday, 7 March 1971, so that he could go and stay with Alwynne.

'This is the end,' she said with the engine still running. But it was never quite that easy with Sir Arthur.

Unaware of these curious proceedings, though also strangely familiar with them in her own case, Pamela left a note at the hospital inviting Anne to come and see her after her visit. If either of the women thought how strange it was to be repeating their tea of four and a half years ago, their roles now practically reversed, neither of them said so. Avoiding recriminations, they agreed that Anne, as Sir Arthur's wife, should come and stay at the house for as long as she wanted. Pamela felt sure that the necessary arrangements could be made in advance of her stay.

'Would it be possible,' suggested the older lady in a subsequent letter, 'for me to p.g. [i.e. be a 'paying guest'] with the Downs [in the basement]? Otherwise I should like to be put up at the smallest nearby pub …'

While Pamela was adamant that Lady Bryant should be spared any such indignity, she had not envisaged having to manage the rest of the fold in like manner. To the bewilderment of herself and the rest of the Close, the entire troupe descended on Myles Place over the coming days: first Lorelei (known to the neighbours as 'the golden one'), then Alwynne and finally Anne herself. Each of these women revealed something of their characters by the way in which they approached the vexing issue of living quarters. Pamela, who naturally had first choice, simply remained in her small bedroom in the top-floor flat; Alwynne agreed to come for just one day, so that Anne could use her room – but only if she consented to using the cupboards in Sir Arthur's bathroom instead of her own. Lorelei, meanwhile, casually took up residence in the master bedroom, as though to the manor born.

For Pamela, the next few days proved intensely harrowing. Years later, she would liken them to 'running about in a confused never-ending battlefield, while the cause of all the trouble sat in bed in Salisbury Infirmary, issuing contradictory orders.' These commands included having the main bathroom converted into a bedroom, complete with his private telephone line, so that he could conduct his life and affairs without the inconvenience of having to mount his large four-poster each night.

Upon his return from hospital on Good Friday he was lifted into this temporary dwelling, where he lay, like Jean-Paul Marat, surrounded by a strange combination of writing and washing paraphernalia: pictures and portraits on the green-patterned wallpaper, books, periodicals, his telephone, library steps, a rocking chair, old toys, quantities of rusted razor blades which no one was allowed to remove, a camp bed and a small electric bell for 'summoning whoever was available to come running'.

The complex dynamic in the house was further strained by the fact that Anne was, on her return, suffering from severe bronchial asthma; Pamela considered it madness that she had reappeared in such a condition. Unknown to her, however, this had been at Sir Arthur's own instigation. Fearful of his former secretary's eruptions of indignation and resentment, he needed his separated wife's presence as a buffer to protect him during his convalescence. For the younger woman, however, this only made matters worse: it now fell to her to prepare meals and carry them upstairs for both the invalids under her care – Lorelei, despite her repeated offer of 'help', was no use whatsoever in this regard, and, somewhat predictably, needed scarcely less attention than the patients. To make matters worse, in the midst of these dramas, Charlie Down finally gave up the ghost. Other than the inconvenience of his widow going away to mourn her loss in the company of her relatives, no one at Myles Place other than Pamela seemed to notice or particularly care.

Such a situation could not endure. Now barely on speaking terms with Sir Arthur – who was evidently pleased to be reunited with Anne – Pamela felt increasingly like a servant in the household; a feeling that was only heightened by the historian's repeated offers of monetary payment for her services. Taking her refusal of his bounty as an indictment, he told her that he would not allow her to post his letters unless she took his proffered cheque. This resulted in a farcical scene shortly after Easter, when the man of the house insisted on attempting to shuffle to the postbox himself. Aroused by the ensuing commotion, Anne appeared on the landing in her nightdress and hurried after him clutching her car keys. Not long after Anne had delivered him back, Pamela tore the cheque up in his face and walked out of the front door – for good, she said.

For some weeks the fractious pair were incommunicado. Ever since being bombarded by silent calls – which had proved, after having the line monitored, to be from Alwynne – it was now a rule at South Street that Pamela did not answer the phone without being certain of the caller's identity. At length, Sir Arthur desisted.

'It being useless,' he had written during an earlier period of 'banishment', 'and too hurting and humiliating'.

But one Sunday towards the end of May, when he knew she would be particularly lonely, he tried again. She answered. Before she could say a word of protest or even hang up, he blurted out his question – 'Do you want "Bear"?' It was a masterstroke.

'Yes,' she choked, adding in her head: *'I want that little wooden bear beside me ... almost as much as I want you!'*

The mascot was accordingly wrapped in one of Sir Arthur's hand-kerchiefs and lovingly placed in a special wooden box. For maximum effect, he then arranged to have this precious cargo personally delivered to South Street – by Anne. She arrived a few days later and was invited in for dinner. Once again, Pamela hardly knew what to say or how to act, but her visitor put her at ease by murmuring, as she passed over the container, that they were now 'sisters in distress'. Then she delivered something even more surprising: she revealed that she was getting a divorce.

'It's what Arthur wants,' she said quietly, 'and I think I ought to give him his freedom.' She said that they had come to a very amicable agreement and, although she would 'never love anyone else', she admitted that she was 'not really cut out for marriage'. Both women implicitly understood that Sir Arthur was now going ahead with his plan to marry Lorelei, as painful as that would be for the younger woman.

'Pam,' said Anne by way of commiseration, just before leaving, 'Arthur is a very *hurting* man.'

Another distressing month passed. Despite having found a new part-time secretarial job to keep her mind occupied, Pamela still had too much time alone in her flat. Matters were not helped by the fact that her principal writing task – her most pleasurable pastime – was to complete the 'authorised' biography of the cause of all her woes. Her pocket-diary entries for the period reveal, once again, her worst fear about leaving Sir Arthur's stable.

'Overwhelming depression,' was all she wrote for two consecutive days in June, followed by more 'depression', and, then: 'I wonder if I am going to make it.'

Perhaps with a bit more time and fortitude Pamela could have 'moved on'. She had always refused to see herself in the same light as the broken, clinging women who littered the pages of Sir Arthur's life. But, almost unconsciously, she was taking on some of their characteristics. Not only did she guiltily come to realise that she was drinking more heavily than usual, she also felt an inexplicable compulsion to resume her former burdens. As she would write of Anne: 'There was in her character a deep need to serve a cause, a desire to go out and work in a leper colony, to devote herself to those in need.' Now it was her who needed to be needed. Or, by her own account, she simply wanted information. She would later write:

> For once having been caught up in the vortex which A. B. created life, even on its periphery, became incredibly dull and often very lonely. After the initial relief at not being continually under pressure, after one had had time to get some sleep, go to the hairdresser, write a few personal letters and generally do all those things which recharge one's batteries, one invariably found oneself once more ready and anxious for the fray. What was A. B. doing? How was he? Who was he with? Our life, with all its vicissitudes, had become almost inexorably bound up together ... One had become *so* involved.

It was, then, unsurprising that she accepted Sir Arthur's invitation to dinner when he unexpectedly telephoned at the end of the month. Everything about the offer and acceptance was redolent of their first 'date'; only now he proposed to take her to an upmarket Italian restaurant in Mayfair, the Bistingo, rather than the modest Polish restaurant on the Brompton Road. And just like that early encounter, Sir Arthur was noticeably shy and deferential in his demeanour. He seemed reluctant to give anything away, speaking mainly about his progress with Dr Johnson, though occasionally asking with concern about her own life too. Only towards the end of the meal did he drop his bombshell.

'Lorelei has another man,' he said with finality; they were engaged to be married. There was another one of those deafening silences that had long characterised their meetings. Would she, he asked, take him back?

She did. But, once again, the terms were his.

'I may not love you as much as you wish me to love you,' he wrote half-apologetically, 'but I love you a very great deal; and love, like bitterness and resentment, is a thing that snowballs; the more of it there is, the more it grows – and the same is true of the reverse.'

He said that it gave him great pleasure to be able to resume their meetings and correspondence – though he left unsaid the even greater pleasure he presumably derived from their physical relationship, which was soon to be resumed: he had once joked that her 'skills' in the bedroom far surpassed those of the 'ladies of the night' who sometimes accosted him as he returned home through the Park Lane underpass.

As a means of demonstrating his affection and gratitude, he offered to pay for her to complete a course of art lessons at either the Slade School of Art or the London Polytechnic. '[The Hon.] George [Bruce, Honorary Secretary to the Society of Portrait Painters] would tell you which would be best,' he added discerningly.

Though an improvement on his previous offer to underwrite her painting so long as she remitted ten per cent of any sales to him, he remained both encouraging and strangely proprietorial. He assured her that, whether as artist or writer, she would soon achieve the fame that her 'intensely and rightly ambitious nature' so craved.

'You will never be happy,' he continued, 'till you can lose and forget yourself in the exacting but healing joy of depicting, with pencil and brush, God's and man's world in which you find yourself.'

Declaring that she was 'potentially a much greater artist' than himself, he would, shortly afterwards, praise one of her quick sketches of 'Bear' as being 'better than Rembrandt'.

'You will need no adventitious aids,' he concluded in his letter, 'to the place in life which is rightfully yours – as a very great woman in your own right.'

Still, however, mundane considerations stood between Pamela and this irredeemable Promised Land. In July, Sir Arthur accepted an offer from 'a nice oriental gentleman' for Rutland Gate and, shortly afterwards, asked her to go round to the property to oversee the removal of his possessions. It was awkward, he said, to leave Myles Place, where he was still being attended to, on an ad hoc weekly rota, by Anne and Alwynne. However violent his past disagreements with Pamela had been, the one thing he knew he could rely on was her total moral integrity in matters of administration and finance. Even so, such a delicate and important task could not be completely delegated, and Pamela would recall, long afterwards, receiving 'hourly instructions' throughout the fourteen-day ordeal during which she camped in the house, alone but for visits from a concerned relative and also Mrs Chalkley, now living happily with her husband and married daughter in Harrow.

The debris left behind once the removal people had done their work was prodigious. Attached to his possessions almost as much as to his female acquaintances, Sir Arthur had scarcely thrown anything away since purchasing the house in 1942 – he did not even discard old biros in the belief that 'they might come in handy for *something* ... poor dears, helping to stick things up in the garden, perhaps?' As a consequence of this eccentricity, Pamela was left to decide what to do with a staggering array of items: dusty brown papers, files, books, a seventeenth-century duelling sword, old clothes, memorabilia and 'strange unaccountable objects of doubtful shape and antiquity'. Like Mrs Pepys, Pamela was not too squeamish about disposing of such oddments. A company specialising in private refuse collection was duly engaged and, one day towards the end of August, she found herself giving a tour of the property to a representative of this firm who laconically declared that he had 'never seen nuffink like it'. Only by throwing vast quantities of miscellaneous rubbish out of the windows directly into the back of the small truck parked on the pavement below could the operation be completed in a single day.

Pamela wisely kept the details of this procedure to herself. But her reticence was not only to avoid Sir Arthur's rancour: it was also to spare him from her own. For, in the course of deciding what to throw away, she had discovered a most compromising document. It was the draft of an extremely long letter written to Lorelei on 15 October the previous year – shortly after she had returned early from Madeira, when their fraught relationship appeared to be back 'on'. The screed began by detailing his satisfaction about Pamela's role in settling Mr and Mrs Down into his basement, before moving on to his imminent trip to the City for an evening with his political dining club, Grillion's:

I can't say I feel at all like it while the thought of London without you is almost more painful than I can bear. Everything in
my past and present life pales into nothingness compared with
those days when all my hopes and being centred on one dear
being – You – and those moments: our dinner at the Botanical
Gardens and walks beside the Serpentine, Harrow and Hamp-
ton Court and the Promenade Concert, our dinner at Salisbury
and our walks with Jomo … Lost things they are to me for ever
… which seem the only reality and everything else a dream.

Then he delivered his peroration:

Please, my Darling, don't take your friendship away from me,
unless its existence hurts you. I could not bear to lose that.
After all, it was because it was so precious, even essential to
me and [illegible] that last summer I suffered what I did, and
it would seem ironical now, when Pam is far from jealous, that
we shouldn't be able to write or see each other. The day is going
to come when God will have taken one or the other and why
should we anticipate it? For I cannot believe after all your goodness to me, that you are indifferent to me and my love for you
… Vivid days … Loneliness … What I owe you.

After reading through the confused, deceitful document several
times, Pamela could hardly hold back the tears. The line about her
being 'far from jealous' particularly struck her as duplicitous – 'Pam
would have been *viridian!*' she later added in a footnote. For now, she
decided merely to keep hold of the evidence and say nothing.

Never had she been more unsure of what to do or where she stood with the man she still, unaccountably, loved with all her heart.

———

Throughout the latter half of 1975, Sir Arthur continued to attack the modern world in his monthly newspaper column. Disgusted in equal measure by the 'bullying' trade unions and the inaction of a series of 'timid and over-submissive' governments – leading inflation to reach almost twenty-five per cent – the historian looked back with nostalgia to the Victorian age, when national prosperity was unhampered by the working man's desire for such trifles as 'cars, television sets, washing machines, holidays in the sun, sweets, ices ... [as well as] drink, smoking and gambling'. 'For the truth,' he wrote, 'is that human beings are only at peace with themselves, and therefore contented, when they feel they are giving more than they are taking, not because they are compelled by others to give, but because they want to, and take pride and satisfaction in the giving.'

During the very month that Pamela was clearing out Rutland Gate for him, he railed against the 'stay-at-home idlers and venture-nothings ... the petty-minded, small-time, curmudgeonly, grudging militants ... [and] the state-assisted vandals and layabouts of our "permissive" society'.

Other criticisms by the historian also tallied with his belief that an Englishman could hold two contradictory ideas at the same time. He was, for instance, one of the most 'progressive' conservative thinkers on the issue of race, having once written an admiring foreword to a biography of Paul Robeson, and also regarding 'mixed marriages' as a solution to racial divisions; but he was also opposed, in the early years of mass immigration, to 'an influx ... of men and women of alien race, accentuated by strongly marked differences of pigmentation and mould of feature, as well as of habits and beliefs'.

And while he endlessly proclaimed his faith in Britain's future, he wrote scornfully of the 'unkempt, unhygienic, tramplike and brutalized' youth of the day. Once – and only once – the assistant editor of the *Illustrated London News*, Nicolas Wright, attempted to tone down some of these contrarian opinions by altering the text. Such an intervention, however, could never be tolerated by the star columnist, who viewed all his writings as sacrosanct.

'He was far too grand to visit the office,' the veteran recalls. 'His "copy" was delivered like tablets from the mountain and woe betide anyone who tried to change it any way.'

It was no easier for Pamela to correct the man himself. Unchallenged for almost seventy years, he was singularly incapable of making even the smallest concession for someone he allegedly loved. Yet this was not how he saw it. When Pamela declared that she would no longer come down to Myles Place unless it was as his wife, he all but accused her of selfishness.

'*My darling*,' he wrote in fury as he made his way to Alwynne on 14 September, 'you are so unyielding in your beliefs and attitudes.' Repeating the claim that he would have married her in 1971 – 'so long as it did not involve you in surrendering ... what was absolutely essential to your future security' – he argued that he had already suffered both 'in purse and reputation' for her sake. 'If only you could bring yourself to realise at least this,' he wrote, 'it would transform the whole situation between us and make possible that feeling of secured and unbreakable love and trust ... without which marriage would be for both of us a tragedy.'

Pamela hardly knew what to make of these protestations. If Sir Arthur had suffered in 'purse' it had not been for paying her a regular salary: he could only mean the purchase of Myles Place – his own home – or the small monthly payments he made to Anne as a return on her lost investment in Rutland Gate.

'Reputation', however, was another and certainly more important matter. He would return to this theme in another letter that autumn, in which he spoke of the 'public obloquy' he faced as a result of their connection. But, she wondered, what could he mean? Other than preparing dinners for him and his guests in the capacity of 'private secretary', her existence had been a strangely closeted affair. Unlike Sir Arthur's old friend and neighbour in Salisbury, the moralising Conservative MP John Cordle, who had just settled down to live with his children's nanny – thirty-five years his junior – the historian's name seldom appeared in the gossip columns or scandal sheets.

The central problem, as Pamela saw it, was Sir Arthur's feelings towards Anne. For all his womanising and reluctance to provide adequately for her financially, it was clear to her that he did genuinely worry about the effects of a final separation upon his wife. And neither of them could be blind to the fact that, since agreeing to divorce Sir Arthur, the older lady's state of mind had deteriorated badly. That Christmas she checked herself into a nursing home, where she was closely watched by her long-term psychiatrist, and in the new year she announced that she was joining Alcoholics Anonymous. Tired of Sir Arthur's typically guarded version of events, Pamela wrote to Anne herself to ask if she could come and see her in Weybridge. She wanted, once and for all, the truth about the long-delayed divorce.

The meeting proved surprisingly friendly. Anne seemed rejuvenated and completely at ease with the situation. She told Pamela that agreeing to a divorce was 'the most sensible thing I have ever done – *Arthur is hell to be married to!*' She said that no one would be more pleased than herself if the younger woman agreed to 'take him on' and look after him in his dotage, preferably as his wife.

It seemed to Pamela that this might, after all, be her fate. But she remained disconcerted by the fact that Anne and Sir Arthur seemed to be spending more time together than ever since agreeing to part irrevocably . The hectic merry-go-round of the historian's 'floating doters' was fast escalating into an almost unending cycle of misery and worry. This was not helped by the fact that Anne's AA meetings were held in a hall conveniently near South Street.

Years later Pamela would recall how one particular week that winter, Sir Arthur left her flat 'exhausted' on a Sunday night, then caught the train to Buckinghamshire to visit Alwynne – calling her up 'constantly' once he arrived – afterwards to be driven on to Salisbury, returning to Alwynne's farmhouse on Wednesday, before being deposited back at South Street on Thursday to take Pamela to a folk dancing festival at the Albert Hall. The following day, the two of them entertained Anne for lunch at the flat, after which Sir Arthur walked his wife to her AA meeting. On the Monday, the historian took his hostess to a function at the House of Lords, before returning to South Street, where Anne was waiting in her car to drive him back to Salisbury.

It seemed fanciful to Pamela that such a man was intent on going through with his divorce and then marrying her. But Anne tried to

Bryant at the height of his fame, c. 1950.

Bryant working at Myles Place, Salisbury, shortly after his move to the Cathedral Close in 1973. Visitors to the house said they could come and go without him noticing.

Bryant and his second wife, Anne, shortly after their marriage in 1941. Although childless, the pair were united by a common love of dogs, including Jimmy (pictured), who would later be subjected to biographical treatment by its famous owner.

Pamela at the time
of writing Bryant's
biography in 1979.
© Barry Swaebe

Pamela and David McCormick at Yarnbury Grange, Wiltshire,
shortly before their separation in 1970. Despite attempts to 'keep
up appearances', the couple had become increasingly estranged
since their marriage at the end of the Second World War.

Best of times: Pamela and Bryant at a literary party
in March 1979. © Desmond O'Neill Features Ltd.

Worst of times: At a party the following year, the
day after Bryant had informed Pamela of his secret
engagement to Laura, Duchess of Marlborough.

The historian at work in Pamela's flat around the time of their engagement in 1976.

Pamela during a brief reprieve from hosting Bryant, c. 1979. Her neighbour below often complained of stormy encounters when he visited.

Pamela on her roof terrace, c. 1980

Lorelei Robinson with her fiancé Max Turner at a private view of paintings, December 1978. For much of the decade, Bryant was besotted by this glamorous lady, who was known to his neighbours in Salisbury as 'the golden one'. Reproduced by kind permission of Hearst Communications.

Bryant's lifelong 'muse' and companion, Alwynne Bardsley, who he met while lecturing in the 1920s.

Laura as a young woman in the 1930s. Prior to her marriage, in 1973, to the 10th Duke of Marlborough (who died within six weeks) she had been married to the 2nd Viscount Long; the 3rd Earl of Dudley, and a wealthy socialite rumoured to be the biological son of the Duke of Kent. Bryant hoped to be her fifth.

Bryant reading Edwardian love letters in Laura's garden, June 1980.

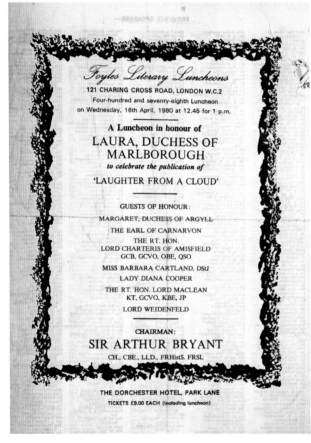

The invitation to the party celebrating the publication of Laura's memoir, *Laughter from a Cloud*. Within eight weeks of this first meeting, Bryant and the novice author would be engaged.

Hugo Vickers looks on, c. 1980

All the images on this page are reproduced by kind permission of Hugo Vickers.

Laura on court, c. 1980

Bryant listens sceptically to the Labour Prime Minister, James Callaghan, at a City lunch to mark his 80th birthday in February 1979. To their left, Harold Macmillan and the Archbishop of Canterbury, Dr Donald Coggan, reminisce.

James Callaghan, A.B. Macmillan, Archbishop of Canterbury

Luncheon, February 17, 1979

Vintners' Hall

Seating plan at the Vintners' Hall.

Celebrating with Sir Arthur Bryant (centre) were (from left) Rt. Hon. Mr. James Callaghan, Mr. Jan Collins, Sir Denis Hamilton, Mr. Harold Macmillan and the Archbishop of Canterbury, Dr. Donald Coggan.

80th birthday celebrations for Sir Arthur Bryant

Bryant shares a joke with Sir John Gielgud at a literary party, March 1981.
© Desmond O'Neill Features Ltd

Bryant on one of his last
outings to clubland before
his death in January 1985.

Alwynne outside her
Buckinghamshire
farmhouse, c. 1983.

persuade her otherwise. 'It is just because we are divorcing,' she reassured her, 'that we now get on so well.'

During the actual week that their divorce was granted in February, the two of them stayed, alone, at Myles Place; Pamela – yet again bewildered by the turn of events – preferred to remain in London. She was determined to stick to her commitment not to go to Salisbury again unless their relationship was regularised.

The announcement of the divorce did create the small ripple of adverse publicity that Sir Arthur had feared. 'He was granted a decree under the "quickie" procedure,' smirked the *Evening News*, 'under which neither party has to attend court.' But the details of his separation from Anne could not be guessed at, even by the most imaginative of tabloid journalists. Pamela felt that, at long last, Sir Arthur was going to ask her the vital question.

She waited and waited – in vain. Instead, the first piece of news to flow from Myles Place after the announcement of the divorce was that Sir Arthur was going to spend the weekend with Lorelei's sister-in-law, Lady Louise Stockdale – the only other guest, Pamela quickly discovered, was to be the 'kissing lady' herself. It was a bitter blow. It seemed that Lorelei's engagement had been broken off, and she was once again in the offing for Sir Arthur's hand. After another huge row on the telephone – the issue of Miranda staying in the flat had also recently resurfaced, with Sir Arthur threatening 'never to set foot in the flat again' should this come to pass – Pamela told him that, as far as she was concerned, their relationship was now truly over. She was going to focus on her writing.

For weeks on end Pamela devoted every spare moment to various literary projects such as starting a novel, continuing with her 'portrait' of Sir Arthur and composing magazine articles. The success of one of these Fleet Street offerings, appropriately entitled 'Walking Away', proved just the tonic she so badly needed. Subtly drawing on her own recent experiences as well as the earthy common sense that was her father's trademark, the article was both amusing and informative. On Friday, 28 May, she heard from Mr Jack at the *Sunday Times* that, even though they rarely printed unsolicited pieces, they were going to use her article in that week's issue – and he wanted her to write for them again. It was a revelation.

'It suddenly makes everything different,' wrote Pamela in her diary. 'Can be alone.' She had taken a bold step towards freedom.

But Sir Arthur was not going to let go that easily. Writing to her from his garden easel, beside his latest muse – a 'little, loving, mewing' stray cat he called 'Pussums' – he made a final attempt to win her back.

'Dishy dear,' he wrote, employing another one of the many pet names he had given her, 'despite your reproaches and my exasperated ... reaction to them, I love you very deeply and tenderly.'

He rehearsed, once again, his justifications for not marrying her in 1971 – her 'completely irrelevant letter' to her solicitor; the slowness of her divorce from David and her attempt to commit 'financial suicide' by offering to give up the flat; her insistence that he was not to ask Anne for a divorce, and so on. What was new, however, was Sir Arthur's confession that he would have been compelled to marry her even if he had ceased to love her.

'It never seemed to occur to you,' he explained, 'that, if our position in the Close was invidious or disapproved of, it would be considerably more damaging and professionally harmful to me as a public man with a particular "establishment" image.'

In confusion, he even claimed that, 'in the social conventions of today', it would have been quite permissible for them to have lived there together, as he had originally envisaged, without any public scandal or inconvenience – 'just like John [Cordle] and Terttu [the nanny]'.

Yet again, Pamela felt helpless, friendless and emotionally distraught. She wrote a long reply to his letter, mostly to correct his inaccuracies but also to accept that, to some extent, her own character 'weaknesses' had contributed to the failure of their relationship. Seizing upon this opening, Sir Arthur called her up immediately. He sounded worried – desperate, even. He told her that he needed her to come down to Salisbury at once. It was a matter of grave importance, he said.

Pamela was there by teatime. Sir Arthur welcomed her into the house with his enigmatic grin but scarcely a word. He took her by the hand and led her into the garden. Here, beside a pile of broken pillars which he called 'the Temple', and witnessed only by Pussums, the historian got down on one knee and asked Pamela to marry him.

9

In accepting Sir Arthur's belated proposal, Pamela had every reason for contentment. After years of disappointment and broken promises, it looked as though – just like Sir Arthur's secretary in the early 1940s, Dinah – she was finally going to achieve 'her life's biggest hope'. To dispel any remaining doubts, her 77-year-old *beau* wrote her a detailed 'letter of intent' to take with her back to London the next day.

'My darling,' it ran, 'I will try very very hard to make you as happy as you so richly deserve to be.'

Conceding that he was not 'much of a catch', he said that at least he could offer her 'a home in the place that you love', which he swore would automatically become hers upon his death. Only a passing reference to his other 'affections and obligations', gathered during his 'muddled and unsuccessful life', struck a somewhat discordant note.

As always, it was these nebulous 'others' that most concerned Pamela. Within a few days of their engagement on 6 June, Sir Arthur told her that he would need some time to 'prepare' each of them for the news – a level of secrecy that was compounded by the fact that he had not offered her a ring; he told her that he wanted her to choose between receiving one and having her portrait painted by his favourite Italian artist when he was next in Britain. He estimated that it would take at least two months – including a weekend in Norfolk with Barbara – to disseminate the happy news, after which they could marry straightaway. In the meantime, he said, they were only to tell Pamela's daughter, Miranda, and their increasingly disapproving housekeeper, Mrs Down.

But even this proved unsatisfactory. For one thing, during the heatwave that immediately followed their engagement, Sir Arthur now had the perfect alibi for being alone with his various women. First priority naturally went to Anne. Having recently moved into a small flat at Sussex Mansions on the Old Brompton Road – just around the corner from the Polish restaurant where Pamela's troubles had begun – she gladly hosted her ex-husband in the 'quiet spare room at the back' which had been designated specifically for this purpose. The pair then travelled down to Salisbury for a dinner party hosted by some of their old friends who, in confusion, simply presented Sir Arthur's ex-wife as 'Anne Bryant'. Their bewilderment would have increased significantly had they been aware that their distinguished guest also had a fiancée kicking her heels back in London.

Anne, however, had no intention of clinging any longer to Sir Arthur. In one of her saddest and most moving letters to him, written just before agreeing upon a divorce, she thanked him for a long stay at Myles Place:

> I have loved it, every minute of it – the leisure, pleasure, whisky in the sunset evenings – all. But it isn't my life. It is your life with, I hope, Pam to help you as, I told her yesterday, only she can. It's all there for her and you both have so much

to share in common. And it's time that I now went back to my own life and try to set it in some sort of order before the winter sets in.

She now wrote to the prospective bride in a similar vein:

'To my mind there is no one more suited than you are to help Arthur [she declared], who I found to be a particularly demand-ing person.

Everything had to be done his way, here now and at the double. And he doesn't seem to me to have changed much since I first knew him, getting on for forty years ago.

And I know that this will mean much self-control for you and, possibly, a good deal of frustration. But you will be repaid if you can succeed in making him happy, since, as all we dis-carded women know, he is the most lovable and generous of men. There are many moulded in common clay but only one Arthur, one Harrow, caddish, utterly lovable Arthur.

Over the coming days and weeks, as Sir Arthur continued his strange pilgrimage, Pamela received several more such letters and phone calls. Whether or not it was really reassuring to hear, in another letter from her predecessor, that Anne was now enjoying a 'cosy, sex-free, non-demanding relationship' with her ex-husband was somewhat unclear.

'I felt Anne to be more and more of an all-forgiving mother to Arthur,' wrote Pamela in later years, 'and would have been like a mother-in-law to me.'

More promising was the news from Lorelei that she would shortly 'fade from [their] lives'.

'Very soon now,' she continued in her letter of congratulations, 'you will be able to relax into the life you so deeply wish, and for which you are so suited and talented.'

Even Alwynne, the most obsessive of all Sir Arthur's loves, said that she knew Pamela would take good care of 'the precious possession'. Only Barbara preferred to keep her counsel.

It was all too much for Pamela. With Sir Arthur endlessly making excuses for going ahead with his complex arrangements – dinners with Lorelei, weekends with Anne and Alwynne in Salisbury and Buckinghamshire, and, in the course of a single week, wandering off with both her own and Mrs Down's address books – there had seldom been a time when Pamela had been more isolated or perplexed. The historian even insisted, albeit unsuccessfully, on inviting Alwynne to accompany them to Lord's that year. Yet whenever Pamela complained about this strange sequel to their engagement, he protested his innocence with as much force as ever.

'My sweet, passionate, impatient, intense, intolerant, proud, consumed with anxiety, ardent, apprehensive, but utterly adorable Pam,' he wrote following one such row, 'thank you for the happiness we shared last Sunday and on Monday and Tuesday until the evening's tragedy and again this morning.'

Reusing a favourite line about treasuring every 'moment which God had offered' them, he saw no reason why these passages of 'peace and happiness' could not be sandwiched between visits from the rest of his troupe, and for some weeks Pamela made a valiant effort to accommodate this request.

The trouble was that Sir Arthur pushed his margins too fine. One particularly distressing Saturday, Pamela cancelled a visit to Salisbury at the last minute because, contrary to their agreement, Alwynne had stayed the night on Friday and had even prepared the historian's lunch in advance – an undertaking which Mrs Down, who was the informer on this occasion, had also planned to make.

'Boaz,' she wrote in the wake of this farce, 'it's a well-known thing that two women can never amicably share a kitchen ... [and] I've explained before I don't like working on a rota system and I especially don't like arriving within an hour of someone else's departure.'

It seems probable that Mrs Down was not her only pair of eyes in the property – Pamela was often accused of being 'too friendly' with domestic staff – as she would also, at the end of August, chastise her non-committal fiancé for asking the head gardener, Mr Barrow, to water Alwynne's beds and borders in defiance of the ongoing hosepipe ban.

As ever, Pamela's firm commitment to her principles – including not staying at Myles Place until they were married – only served to rile Sir Arthur. In response to the comment about the illicit watering, he wrote that, far from nourishing his rare tobacco plants 'at the expense of society', he had actually – 'like Ferdinand in *The Tempest*' – personally slopped buckets up from the river, and had even begun preserving his bathwater for the same purpose: 'So there!' More philosophically, he informed her that they could only marry if they accepted one another's 'defects' and 'maddening faults'; in his case, a 'fatal craving for romantic love' combined with a tendency to 'idealise any woman' who returned his affections. He attributed these characteristics to 'never having had a sister' to ameliorate the effects of his 'solitary, repressed childhood'. It was for Pamela, he went on, to reflect on her own 'childhood-induced taboos', which now threatened – due to the nature of her divorce settlement – to relieve her ex-husband of all his financial obligations to her. Only by seeing these matters from the other's point of view, he implored, could they proceed with their plans:

> I have a very romantic nature [he confessed], and, where love is concerned, there is no limit to what … I want both to give and receive, or the trouble I will go to for its sake, so that, even when the flame of passion and romance has long ago died, anyone I have loved deeply and been loved by, whether alive or dead, I have found I continue to love with tenderness and devotion and to do whatever I can to make them happy.

'Couldn't we, my Darling,' he concluded rather hopefully, 'as a pre-requisite to marriage, make a new start? If the will is there on both sides – as it certainly is on mine! – it shouldn't take us long.'

But this confession did nothing to revive Pamela's flagging spirits. 'Oh Boaz!' she responded in frustration, 'to me it doesn't seem a case of the eternal triangle, but more like a very *unusual* quadrangle and, at times, quintuple!'

Nor was this the only stumbling block that Sir Arthur presented. A more serious one had already arisen, rather typically, in connection with a part-time job that Pamela had taken, about a year previously, with a paper merchant called James Heard. The historian had often teased her about this position – he liked to refer to her new employer as 'Mr Seen and Not' or simply 'Hurdy-Gurdy'. But he now proposed that, even though she had handed in her notice at the time of their engagement, she should continue working for him until October, when they could go away on their honeymoon – to Madeira. He said that they could get married 'next week' if only she would agree to this scheme. Yet, once again, Pamela could not understand: were they to spend over two months apart in the aftermath of their wedding?

Matters were quickly made worse by Sir Arthur's strange idea that his fiancée should personally invite Alwynne to make use of the upstairs flat at Myles Place – the one that had originally been intended for herself.

There were innumerable rows such as these throughout the summer – by letter, on the phone and in person. The situation was so bad that Pamela's neighbour below – dubbed 'the Wife of Bath' by Sir Arthur – would often enquire what exactly was going on above, and she may even have interrupted one particularly stormy encounter with some sharp thrusts of her broomstick.

The argument in question took place in the middle of July, when Sir Arthur was staying at South Street for Lord's. Already sensitive about his plan to include Alwynne, it only took a comment from Sir Arthur about David's unwillingness to pay for an increase in the service charge for Pamela to explode with pent-up anger. She could not believe that, alongside all his other possible reasons for not marrying her, she could now add the cessation of her ex-husband's financial obligations.

Turning the tables once again, Sir Arthur warned, in a subsequent letter, that it was no certain thing that these 'repeated quarrels and outbursts' would end once they had married and that they should, accordingly, postpone the wedding indefinitely. He told her that he wanted to get married – but 'happily' – and that the 'wild accusations and jealousies and suspicions' of the past weeks had left him 'utterly shattered ... as though I had been shell-shocked'. 'I have reached an age,' he continued, 'when I am just longing for peaceful love and quiet. And I need it so much and am so lost for lack of it.'

Yet Sir Arthur remained full of plans. After his letter about his 'very romantic nature', he suggested that they go through a 'trial period' of living together before committing themselves any further. When Pamela pointed out that this was, in effect, simply a return to the status quo ante, and that she could hardly be held responsible for rows instigated by his curious way of life, the historian returned to the offensive. He wanted her to return to being the 'dear, gentle, sensitive, adorable and intensively capable child of genius' that he had fallen in love with, rather than the 'resentful, bitter, intolerant, jealous, sanctimonious and slightly crazy Edwardian school mistress' she had lately become.

As a means of highlighting this dichotomy, he reminded her that it had been *her* who had 'moved up the sofa' while he read from his book, *The Lion and the Unicorn*, causing him to do 'all sorts of rash and foolish things ... as no scolding schoolmistress ever could have done'.

In a further bid to regain the initiative, he made several additional marriage proposals over the coming months, as well as offering to pay for the trousseau that Pamela had rather too optimistically arranged to have fitted and made. Always, however, the historian avoided mentioning any precise dates. His desperation to keep her at his side, at whatever cost, was almost palpable.

It was testament to Sir Arthur's shrewd diplomacy that he returned to South Street for Christmas that year. But by the start of 1977 it was clear to Pamela that their relationship remained without any fixed purpose or goal. Part of the problem was the ambiguity of her own position. While she certainly wanted distance from her intermittent lover, she continued to have strong feelings towards him, and – most importantly – the town in which he had so intelligently chosen to make his new home. When a suitable house once again came up for sale in the Close, she told him that she was considering putting in an offer: an action which would have, as he well knew, required her to sell her valuable London property. This brought home to Sir Arthur exactly what he stood to lose if he mishandled the situation.

'If you do,' he fumed in response, 'we'll *never* marry!'

Shortly afterwards, he was back at South Street to celebrate his birthday, as well as to work on another book – a series of short biographies of 'Great Men'. The stay had, in part, been facilitated by his suggestion that they return to the little Polish restaurant where their romance had started so that they could 'plight their troth' once again. But as soon as Pamela had finished typing up one of his chapters, he calmly proposed that they go out to the theatre instead.

As a result of all these disagreements and misunderstandings, Pamela began to ask herself whether Sir Arthur 'really was more than a little mad'. Or was he, she wondered, like Pavlov? 'He seemed to condition people,' she recalled, 'into expecting something and then just as they were about to receive it, he took it away from them. There was something sadistic, something psychologically very wrong.'

As she would put it on another occasion: 'He seemed to get hold of women at their most vulnerable, make them fall in love with him, turn them into willing slaves, treat them disgracefully, feel sorry for them and then do some kind of rescue act.'

There were clearly reasons why Pamela put up with this pattern of ill treatment. Besides her dreaded fear of loneliness and depression, she could not easily forget the exalted position Sir Arthur continued to command in the highest literary and social circles. It was an ace that he was always ready to play.

'Remember,' he had long ago written to his younger brother, Philip, 'that nearly everyone in this world is a snob ... Use it for all you're worth: only be careful not to let them know you're using it!'

While Pamela was a notably difficult person to impress in this regard, Sir Arthur made every effort to put his old maxim into effect. At various junctures over the course of his rough wooing he allowed her to pour the tea for such distinguished acquaintances as Stephen Tennant, Sir John Betjeman and Cyril Connolly. Tennant, who lived near Salisbury, had even been invited to pass judgement on some of Pamela's sketches: they were, he said, on a par with those of Jean Cocteau.

Similarly, Pamela had been grateful for her introduction to Christina Foyle and her husband Ronald Batty. 'Miss Foyle', who hosted frequent 'literary luncheons' at the Dorchester Hotel, had taken a liking to Sir Arthur's latest companion, especially on discovering that her mother's maiden name happened to be Foyle. Pamela would soon become a regular sight, along with the historian, at the top table of her coveted lunches, and from time to time would reciprocate by arranging dinner parties at South Street attended by some of the literary luminaries of the day. Before long, the fledgling author started receiving invitations to Christina's lunches in her own right, and the pair would occasionally attend dress shows at the fashion house of the bookseller's couturier, Peter Lewis-Crown.

It would have taken a willpower far beyond Pamela's to exchange such gratification for a lonely London life. And Sir Arthur knew exactly which buttons to press, especially when it came to exploiting Pamela's self-confessed 'guilt complex', repeatedly telling her that his entire life and work would become impossible without her ministrations. After seeing him once carry on happily with his writing when an electric toaster burst into flames besides him, she accepted that he certainly did need 'looking after'.

Sir Arthur was fortunate that, at this delicate crossroads in their relationship, he had the perfect means of winning Pamela back. Having been invited by Westminster Abbey to contribute an essay for the Coronation Programme in 1953, he was now asked to deliver the annual 'One People' oration in honour of Queen Elizabeth II's Silver Jubilee. With some of the old urgency, he persuaded his former secretary to fall in line with his complex arrangements, coaxing her down to Salisbury in mid-July for a long weekend to work on his text, as well as liaising with Anne, Alwynne and even Lorelei about a suitable seating arrangement for them all in the Abbey.

But, as always, Pamela soon felt intensely frustrated. For one thing, upon her arrival at Myles Place on the Saturday before the oration – which was to take place in only two days' time – Sir Arthur handed her a huge bundle of unsorted papers and told her that he wanted her to go to the tax office and investigate an overpayment he appeared to have made. No sooner had this familiar administrative burden been discharged than her host announced that he had invited some distant cousins to the house the following day. Not until after these guests had departed at 5pm did the historian finally get around to his pressing task. His method of composition was all too revealing of his new working habits. Insisting to Pamela that the text was already 'in his head' he instructed her to cut out lengthy chunks from his books, which they then stuck into the gaps between the passages that he dictated, extempore, specially for the occasion. The entire operation was completed by 10pm, when the veteran retired to bed with his habitual 'night tray' – prepared by Pamela – consisting of a thermos flask, jelly, fruit and biscuits.

Despite all the complications of getting Sir Arthur to Anne's flat, and then to the Abbey, the next morning, the solemn occasion could hardly have been bettered. To a hushed audience of Labour cabinet ministers, distinguished royals and the idle curious, the patriot spoke for almost an hour about England's past and future. Quoting Swinburne's poem 'England', he began by asking if it was still true that 'come the world against her; England yet shall stand'? 'I, who am no prophet, politician or social reformer,' he continued, 'can only answer it as a historian. Our past made us ... *we must go back to the past to find an answer.*'

While the address was generally received favourably, at least in Conservative circles, one or two discerning critics of his own persuasion feared that he had overdone it slightly. 'What they really want,' wrote Lord Clark in connection with one of his popular television documentaries, 'is a sort of Arthur Bryant script, and I can't do it ... It is so much *not* my line.'

The performance was all the more remarkable for the fact that Sir Arthur had learnt, just a few days beforehand, that he was suffering from bowel cancer. The unpleasant symptoms of this condition had been manifest for many months, not least to Pamela, who had been worried by his detailed descriptions of his ailments; but it had only been with the greatest reluctance that the historian had agreed to see a specialist – as late as the weekend before his oration he was still writing enormous letters about his medical history to his homeopathic doctor, now retired and living in Ireland. It was, as much as anything, Sir Arthur's outwardly casual attitude towards his own mortality that forced Pamela to return.

'It's probably nothing,' he had told her at the Authors of the Year party in March. 'Let's wait and see.' Now it fell to her to save him.

Sir Arthur was not ungrateful. Almost as a second prize to the longed-for marriage, he gave Pamela, along with his solicitor, Gerald Reyburn, limited power of attorney, promising that everything was going to be arranged to cause her the least inconvenience should anything go wrong with the operation. This was made easier by the fact that most of the other women in his life were not minded to interfere: after patching things up with her fiancé, Lorelei was off the scene, while Alwynne was prepared to hold back for the greater good. Barbara, meanwhile, appears to have moved to Rhodesia, where her son had recently been convicted for the murder of his wife and children. Only Anne, on this occasion, was going to assist. Just before she drove from London to begin the 150-mile round trip to take her ex-husband and his former secretary to the Fitzroy Nuffield Hospital, Bryanston Square, there was, however, a final complication. A large chequebook made out in the name of Eddie Birchenough had, a few days earlier, arrived at Myles Place. Batting away Pamela's suggestion that they send it back by return, the historian furiously told her to lock it away in a drawer – he would not be paying postage for the bank's careless mistake.

But, like the polyps in his rectum, the chequebook should not have been ignored. Barely had the operation been completed than Pamela received a call from Sir Arthur's bank. The manager sounded extremely anxious. Sir Arthur was heavily overdrawn – and the sums being taken out seemed to be increasing by the hour. It was just the sort of complication that Pamela had feared when she signed the necessary documentation to take power of Sir Arthur's finances. Some dishonest clerk, she presumed, was drawing money from the account by forging her signature. Although she went to see the patient every day at the hospital, she felt it was impossible to raise the matter with him at such a delicate time. Anne, meanwhile, who had asked to stay with her at South Street, simply 'didn't want to know'. Only after many sleepless nights, telephone calls and letters did the bank realise the mistake and accept responsibility: one Eddie Birchenough had accidentally been sent Sir Arthur's chequebook and was merrily using it to buy everything from yachts to penthouse apartments. Not that this fast-living gentleman was entirely to blame – for reasons known only to himself, the historian always insisted that his name did not appear anywhere at all on his chequebook.

As if such anxieties were not already enough to contend with, the day of Sir Arthur's operation proved equally fraught. Pamela and Anne spent an agonising evening together at South Street, wondering why the procedure was taking so much longer than expected – '*What on earth can they be doing to Arthur?*' asked Anne at one stage. But thanks to the endeavours of the world's leading colon surgeon, Aubrey York Mason, it was only a matter of time before Sir Arthur was back in his private room, running up an enormous telephone bill. Pamela, who he had rung only minutes before the operation, was amazed that the hospital staff had ever managed to sedate him.

When she went to visit him the following morning, she was perturbed by how alert – and angry – he appeared to be. While the operation had been a great success, he railed about the inadequacy of the service. Refusing to take the prescribed antibiotics – 'That's what killed my mother and my brother!' – and equally disdainful of the ministrations of the 'tap-tap girl' (the physiotherapist), Sir Arthur was desperate to escape. A particular gripe was the way in which the nurses were constantly changing. 'Never see the same one for more than a minute or two at a time,' he fumed at one stage. '*What* this country has come to!' He said that he could not possibly spend any longer than, at most, two weeks recuperating. He wanted to get back to his books.

Yet again, it fell to Pamela to facilitate Sir Arthur's desires. By arrangement with the hospital, a young nurse called Honor, with whom the historian had forged a cordial relationship, agreed to return with them to Salisbury. Since Myles Place had been unoccupied since Mrs Down's recent removal to her long-awaited council house, Pamela headed down in advance to shop, clean and rearrange furniture in accordance with the master's wishes. Honor was to be installed in the basement with her husband, Peter, who had aspirations to write plays for television. The odd trio were deposited by Anne, who was also to stay on and evidently had no objection to the curious new set-up – during her recent stay at South Street she had confided to Pamela that she had allowed a 'strange youth' from Alcoholics Anonymous to take up residence in her flat. Only Pamela, it seems, foresaw trouble ahead: her unheeded warnings to Sir Arthur about his new retainers were vindicated when, early the following year, the pair precipitously absconded from the property – but not before smashing up all the furniture in the basement.

The days that followed Sir Arthur's return to Salisbury were among the most harassing that Pamela had ever experienced. 'It was,' she later recalled, 'like the time he fractured his pelvis, only more so.' All day and every day a stream of callers and 'floating doters' descended upon the property: 'The builder popping his head round doors as he came to fix electric bells or move beds, the doctor arriving on his daily visit, the gardener buttonholing me about his pension, someone bringing flowers, A. B. shouting, canons calling and Anne drinking cup after cup of coffee to keep herself going as she attended to A. B.'s every whim.'

Like the court of Henry VIII, everyone had some special task or function – and guarded their position jealously. Willing to do almost anything besides empty Sir Arthur's temporary colostomy bag – only Alwynne among the 'doters' would later be asked to help with this – Pamela remained the lynchpin of the entire operation, cooking and washing, as well as somehow managing to work through the invalid's backlog of correspondence on a trestle table in the 'music room'. At length, the visiting physician, Dr Collings, realising that she was on the point of collapsing, commanded her to escape back to London to recuperate.

It was not until after Sir Arthur's second operation in November – reversing the colostomy – that Pamela returned to Myles Place. Everything had now somehow changed. It was not merely that Anne and Alwynne had resumed their unholy rota system, nor that young Honor was becoming the dominant female. It was more than that – someone else was back on the scene.

'I was told quite casually by A. B.'s nurse,' recalled Pamela, 'that a Mrs Robinson had been there, that Lady Anne (as she called her) had given them all lunch, then retired to bed while Mrs Robinson and Sir Arthur had gone for a drive.' But this was not the end of it.

'On my second visit,' continued Pamela, 'I heard that Mrs Robinson had been there again.

'And finally,' she added by way of crescendo, 'I was given some even more interesting information to think about. It was that the nurse thought Sir Arthur ought to get away to the sun after his second operation and who, she was wondering, might go with him?'

Pamela was wary enough not to confront Sir Arthur with these revelations. She merely indicated her surprise that Lorelei had sent no flowers to the hospital. Sir Arthur was equally cautious in his reply: he assured her that this was only because of another 'breaking-off of her long and unfortunate engagement'. The poor lady, he suggested sorrowfully, was now suffering from a severe emotional crisis of her own.

Pamela did not press the matter any further. But she was increasingly annoyed by Sir Arthur's evasiveness; no longer did he make her visits to Myles Place seem quite so necessary or welcome. Though aware that the Rhine maiden was lurking somewhere at the bottom of it, she tried to give the historian the benefit of the doubt. Then his secret broke in the least probable manner. During one of her frequent conversations with Mr Reyburn about legal matters, the solicitor mentioned that he was now advising a Mrs Robinson professionally, and he understood that she would be going with Sir Arthur and some friends of hers to Reid's Hotel in Madeira in January. It was all fixed.

Pamela nearly dropped the phone. Then she remembered Anne's fateful warning: 'Pam, Arthur is a very *hurting* man.'

———

Sir Arthur's latest transgression was enough for Pamela to pack her bags for good – or, rather, to pack Sir Arthur's bags for good. In a series of blistering letters and phone calls, she outlined exactly what she thought of a man who could secretly arrange a holiday with a 'whirly bird' such as Lorelei to the very place he had promised to take her away on honeymoon, and, incidentally, the same place from which she had, three years previously, returned post-haste at the latter's instruction to nurse him back to health. Added to this betrayal, Pamela was incensed that the historian clearly seemed to believe that he was still welcome to spend Christmas with her at South Street before jetting off for his foreign sojourn.

'What you ask of me seems unnatural,' she wrote in response to this hopeful suggestion, 'against human nature and cruelly hurting. I am no saint. But am longing to devote myself ... to one man and wish, how I wish, that man wasn't you.'

Sir Arthur fought his case with all the energy that remained. 'My darling,' he replied, 'you are, and have long been, so cruelly unfair to me, and, in being so, have inflicted and continue to inflict so much needless suffering both on yourself and me.'

He swore that the only reason that they were not already married was that she had refused to assure him that she would cease to 'continuously upbraid' him thereafter. The tragedy, he explained, was that she resented 'the others' merely for stepping in where she herself had shirked her duties, especially during his second operation. He told her that he had been particularly hurt by a drawing she had done of Anne, Alwynne and Lorelei – 'who had virtually no part in it all' – dancing round his sickbed while she looked on 'indignantly'. Sugaring his protests with an offer of up to £2,000 to help with the much-disputed service charge for her flat, he claimed that Anne and Alwynne had only come to his aid when Pamela suggested, during one of her many hospital visits, that it would be 'silly, wrong and pointless' for her to keep coming if his affections lay elsewhere. It was, perhaps, the sort of trick his hated nanny, Sarah, used to execute to like effect.

And Pamela was no less resolute than that Edwardian governess in standing up to Sir Arthur. Excoriating him for attempting to 'justify the unjustifiable', she pointed out that, as she had done so much for him at the time of the first operation, any subsequent slacking off could only be used against her with the greatest unfairness.

'Boaz,' she wrote, 'you were too ill to notice, but I took that big operation very hardly, not to say conscientiously, and what with sitting with you all and every day (because Anne didn't want to do too much of that), then having her to stay with me for a week ... to say nothing of all that awful bank trouble ... [it was] a nightmare.'

She then chastised him for alleging that Lorelei was merely 'taking a turn at looking after me'. 'All I can say,' she went on, 'is that now everyone else has done the donkey work, for someone whose life is one long holiday to take you away in great luxury, is "*some* turn"!'

In the final section of her letter – or 'manifesto', as Sir Arthur often designated these missives – she chronicled the unhappy events of each of their failed attempts to marry, beginning in 1971, before categorically refusing his offer of financial help. 'I would feel "paid off",' she complained, 'at the expense ... of easing your conscience a little.'

Pamela then proceeded to clear out her spare room. In the years since she had known Sir Arthur, he had gradually turned this space into his own private quarters, filling all cupboards and wardrobes with his clothes and possessions. She now demanded that he come and collect everything, and further ordered that he provide her with a convenient date when she could send a removal van to Myles Place to recover her mother's furniture, which she had prematurely moved into the top-floor flat. Finally, it seemed, their romance was as dead as Queen Anne.

But Sir Arthur had not learnt nothing from his years of womanising. While a jilted love like Pamela might fulminate about his high crimes and misdemeanours, they would never truly leave so long as he retained hold of some prized antique or beloved trinket of theirs. To this end, he put up every kind of objection to Pamela's attempts to disgorge her mother's sideboards and cabinets – 'As all those heavy things,' he scrawled in a particularly contorted screed, 'will have to be carried by the removers right through the house ... I should prefer it to be when there is no longer any risk of wintery weather and after I have had time to buy dust sheets to cover the carpets and stairs to replace those which so mysteriously disappeared from the house 18 months ago.'

Even when Pamela forced the return of his spare dinner jacket and hole-ridden underwear by getting her daughter to deliver them directly to Anne, she admitted that she desperately wanted something back – the wooden bear that Sir Arthur had taken into hospital with him at the time of his first operation. With Machiavellian genius, the eminent historian first hinted that she could have it but later found a way to avoid going through with this parting. 'If you need him,' he reassured her with studied ambiguity, 'I could never keep him from you, whatever I may have said in the past in momentary anger.'

Combined with these manoeuvres, Sir Arthur was also prepared to give some concessions, or at least appear to do so. For reasons either connected to Lorelei's equally complex love affairs or Sir Arthur's notorious unwillingness to commit to anything, their holiday to Madeira did not in the event materialise. With relief, Pamela renewed her Christmas invitation, only to discover that Alwynne had now agreed to come and spend the festive period with him, swapping with Anne, who would be staying once again at a nursing home. In the event, Pamela took a room at the White Hart in Salisbury, juggling visits to Myles Place with Alwynne's plans, as well as the arrangements of her own daughter and son-in-law, who were staying with her ex-husband at nearby Yarnbury Grange.

Early in the new year, Pamela told Sir Arthur that while she felt a 'loneliness and emptiness' without him, they had been through too much already ever to start again. 'I just want to settle down with my dog and my things,' she wrote, 'to avoid becoming emotionally upset and to stop leading what seems to me at present a fragmented, unsatisfactory life.' But the historian made the most of this small opening, sending her several long letters explaining the depth of his feelings and how much he still depended on her. It worked: that February, on his seventy-ninth birthday, he was permitted to come and stay the night at South Street. History was repeating itself.

The difference, in Pamela's mind, was that now she was merely a friend and professional assistant. But almost immediately a further level of complexity was added by the news that Sir Arthur's publishers wanted her to complete the biography she had submitted to them at the time of their abortive engagement. They said they wanted the book to be ready in time for the historian's eightieth birthday early the following year. Quite why this project suddenly became so imperative was never entirely disclosed to the prospective author.

Only much later would it emerge that Sir Arthur had, at precisely this juncture, indicated to the senior editor at Collins that he was planning to shift his allegiance to Weidenfeld and Nicolson. 'I've committed adultery before,' he told Mr House during one of their lunches at the Connaught, 'but I am not going to commit bigamy!' He wanted to make a clean break so that his next book could get the full attention of what was widely viewed as the boldest, most commercial publisher of the day.

Pamela heard just enough reverberations of these negotiations to feel uneasy. It seemed odd, she told Sir Arthur, that her contract stipulated that the book would only be released if he remained with the firm. Knowing how little writing he had done of late, she was even more troubled by a clause which required her subject to bring out his own book to coincide with the publication. Over the coming months, under her exasperated direction, the veteran scribbler would flit between a variety of ideas, including: a gallery of 'English gentlemen'; a single volume history of England called *English Panorama*; a final instalment of his mammoth biography of Samuel Pepys, and a rehash of his recent work on the eighteenth century provisionally entitled *An Introduction to Dr Johnson*.

Had Sir Arthur dedicated himself to any one of these projects, he might have been able to honour his part of the bargain. But throughout the entirety of 1978 he wrote little besides interminable letters to Pamela, nearly all of which concerned the biography that she was supposed to be writing of him – a work, it quickly became apparent, he would have rather composed himself.

These difficulties came as yet another shock for Pamela. Having returned to Sir Arthur's life in what she believed to be a new capacity

– in March he had paid her to undertake some vital research about the Tichborne spoons – she was adamant that her undertaking was not going to be complicated by their previous emotional attachment. He assured her that her 'wonderful opening chapter' about his working habits while he was bedridden in 1971 needed no alteration from him. 'I could see in a flash,' he effused, 'how good the book is and is going to be. You need have no fears about it now.' The book was sure to make her famous – as well as himself.

'More than ever it seems to me,' he wrote after mulling it all over, 'brilliant and arresting … calculated to arouse interest in the subject … That I should feel this, even though it presents me as something of a figure of fun – like Sir George Sitwell! – is testament to its quality. Little or no pruning possible here.'

But, even at this early stage, it was clear that they were not entirely in agreement about the development of the biography. In the hope of persuading Sir Arthur of the necessity of including as much quirky, personal information as possible, Pamela sent him a newspaper profile of Sir Osbert Lancaster by his wife, the journalist Anne Scott-James, which detailed such matters as how the artist slept and what he hummed to himself in the bathroom.

'I am horrified at Lady Lancaster's article about her hubbie's revolting intimacies,' wrote back Sir Arthur, 'it made my stomach quite squeamish to read about them! Is nothing sacred nowadays? And to think that she must have been paid for these ghastly marital revelations! What would your father have said had he been subjected to something similar – or mine!'

Only a final sentence suggested there might be just a glimmer of hope: 'I read it with great enjoyment while eating my breakfast!'

The problems soon mounted. Inevitably the first great battle concerned Sir Arthur's amatory history – though not even Pamela could have envisaged that this would have cropped up as early as his infant school days. After, with greatest difficulty, persuading him to let her include a traumatic childhood experience, in which the future Sir Arthur had been locked in a cupboard in the assembly hall only to be released before the whole school with unmistakably sodden trousers, Pamela dwelt on his feelings towards a little girl who had pitied him. 'It heralded,' she wrote, 'a long line of similar occurrences as the years went by.'

The indignant historian replied: 'You're not writing a life of Rudolph Valentino, but a study of the work of an octogenarian historian!' The offending line was duly cut.

Excising the other women in his life was not going to be so easy. Of this necessity, Sir Arthur was forthright – he would not have either of his wives brought into the book. While this was at least in part to protect his irreproachable public persona, it was equally true that Anne was rather against the project.

'You've got letters, I suppose?' she asked Pamela, adding: 'So have I; suitcases full of them.' She told her that 'Lady Wavell wouldn't allow a book about her husband', and preferred, in deference to her ex-husband's wishes, not to appear in the biography at all. But she did not fail to see the funny side of these developments. When Pamela told her, jokingly, that if she was not mentioned in the book, readers might assume that the subject was 'probably a queer', she suggested that the author add a footnote: 'He is married – or was, as the case may be.' Only when Pamela passed on this idea to Sir Arthur did he finally relent and allow a sentence or two about each of his wives to be included.

And yet this was barely the beginning of the conflicts between author and subject. First and foremost, as Sir Arthur had indicated at the outset of their shared endeavour, was the importance of focusing on his work. The difficulty, in his view, was that Pamela – by her own admission – was not a historian, and so would be unable to write authoritatively about his numerous publications. He wanted her, for instance, to include long quotations from what he called his 'extraordinary' book, *The Age of Elegance*, to give some indication of his style at the height of his powers in the 1940s and '50s, as well as a few paragraphs of commentary to help the reader form the correct judgement of this magnum opus. This, again, was too much for Pamela.

'I can only really ever "write from the heart",' she wrote back. 'When you put words into my mouth I am writing from *your* heart ... and they therefore *stick in my throat!*' She hated the way he tried to present himself as a sort of 'historical robot' – or even 'the Archangel Gabriel'. 'One becomes so unsympathetic towards a character,' she complained, 'who simply writes and writes and has splendid reviews and, apparently, no failings.'

On several occasions that summer the pair played out these rows in the garden at Myles Place; one memorable Saturday, after Sir Arthur had told his biographer to 'shut up and listen', Pamela ran out of the house only to be chased across the Cathedral Close by her subject who called out: 'It would be such a pity ... we don't want the book *abandoned!*'

By this time, Sir Arthur's publishers were aware of the difficulties he was throwing in his biographer's way. One of the young editors, Robin Baird-Smith, duly travelled down to Salisbury in an attempt to stave off further meddling with the text: the book was, he declared, going to need to stand on its own merits alone.

The visit appears to have worked, for shortly afterwards the historian wrote to Pamela saying that he, after all, wanted her to focus on what she knew of him at first-hand; she could, he modestly suggested, try to do a 'short ... and arresting book like Lady Donaldson's book on Evelyn Waugh or yours on your father'. But almost immediately he returned to the importance of his writing and public life, bombarding her with flattering letters and reviews for her to include – as well as entire chapters completed in his inimitable hand.

'It is a well-written account by the Master,' she wrote in response to one of these insertions. 'Not by me.' To her it seemed incredibly disingenuous the way so much of this material focused on Sir Arthur's tireless public service. 'I am unhappy about all these references to honour and being honoured,' she continued, 'and "proud" wartime records and greatly admiring Cunningham and your hero, Trenchard. It somehow makes everyone out to be "too good to be true".'

Another issue was more personal to Pamela: all her friends would see straightaway that the biography was not entirely her own work.

'I can't be party to deceit,' she wrote, before turning her guns on another of the historian's doters. 'The book seems to slip more and more away from me,' she carried on, 'as if ... my "baby" were being passed into the hands of Arthur Bryant and Alwynne, who were superimposing themselves on it and bringing it up in an entirely different way than that which I would approve.'

Only by occasional concessions and a welcome vein of humour did Sir Arthur smooth out these difficulties. As he wrote in September: 'If only I could "pop off" by the middle of the winter, you and Collins could put in or take out anything you liked in the book, for I should no longer have any responsibility for what was in it!' He said that he had lately felt as though he 'was about to oblige!'

At length, with Sir Arthur still very much alive and kicking, the book was completed that October. While *Portrait of a Historian* was not exactly what either of them had envisaged, it was a more than passable work, and the publisher was pleased to go ahead with the printing, even though its subject had failed to produce his own book in time.

True to form, another potential calamity had been caused on the final weekend before submission, when Sir Arthur had wanted his biographer to rework a passage dealing with his various clubs. 'I shall have to resign from them all,' he had sighed down the telephone. Although he insisted that this could be amended without a face-to-face meeting, Pamela said she would prefer to come to Myles Place, as she was spending the weekend in Salisbury anyway.

'Suddenly I became aware,' she later recalled, 'as only, perhaps, a woman can be, of the real reason why he did not want me anywhere near Myles Place: Lorelei … was staying the weekend.'

In the face of Sir Arthur's furious protests, his unwelcome visitor walked up to the house to find him literally barricading the door. She handed him the relevant corrections before marching herself away again. The 'kissing lady' was not to be seen; nor was she told of this stormy encounter until much later. 'I imagine,' continued Pamela, 'she was still in bed in the room which used to be mine, but which was now more or less given over to Anne.'

Pamela saw little more of Sir Arthur in the lead-up to her book's publication the following February. While the latter was constantly offering her enticements, such as remuneration for hosting, at South Street, a panel of 'historical prima donnas' – himself, A. J. P. Taylor, Antonia Fraser and Ludovic Kennedy – for a meeting of the Franklin Mint's new advisory board, the relationship was barely lukewarm when the book's long-awaited due date finally arrived. Even Pamela's friendship with Anne had taken a battering, though for reasons that were not entirely clear to the younger woman.

During a particularly harrowing period dealing with Sir Arthur about the book, she had rung on his ex-wife's doorbell to enquire of his precise whereabouts, only to be told that she must know that he 'didn't like his movements being queried or disclosed', before having the door slammed in her face. As much as this came as a shock to Pamela, she felt partially relieved to have finally glimpsed the 'true and human Anne, who was much more understandable'. As with the similar scene at Myles Place, it was more than probable that her visit had been rather inconvenient, in a favourite expression, 'harem-wise'.

Sir Arthur was, understandably, not too discouraged by the appearance of a two-hundred-page book about his life and work – a long chapter entitled 'Years of Achievement' (his own idea), was especially pleasing. In a letter that was as revealing of his stays with Anne as of his own self-image, he wrote: 'I bore it away [from Collins] to gloat over ... [throughout] my solitary evening by Anne's electric fireside, reading it once more during the three hours till Anne returned from her missionary work to cook my supper.'

Beautifully bound in purple and gold, he said that he longed to tell her what a superb book she had written – 'A finer book even than your exquisite little masterpiece about your father (and that's saying a lot) and as near perfection as anything human can be.'

Even more pleasing for Pamela was the approval of her wide circle of friends and acquaintances, as well as distinguished individuals including Churchill's former private secretary, Sir John Colville, who had been the publisher's mystery 'reader'; the headmaster of Harrow, Ian Beer, and Sir John Betjeman. The book's publication also prompted her first communication with her ex-husband since she had heard, via her solicitor, that the new Mrs McCormick was seeking a divorce. 'She told me that the marriage had been a disaster from the word go,' the letter had explained, 'that her husband was extremely mean and had made a slave of her.'

David was, nonetheless, full of genuine praise for the biography. 'I congratulate you,' he wrote, 'I think you have written a very good book which will be well received. It is what it purports to be – a portrait of a historian with the sitter close at hand, and a very good portrait too!' He went on to say that his attitude towards her subject had been changed:

I know A. B. hates me. He must have only heard the worst, stirred up by solicitors. Even so, if he knew me better he would find little to interest him. I have felt very 'anti' him in the past because I felt you were giving him everything you had to offer, whereas he was withholding from you – in short he was taking advantage – but as a result of reading your new work I do now believe that he has given you something which probably makes up for the disparity I sensed, namely the privilege of knowing him as you have and do, the broadening of your thoughts and horizons gained through his company. For there must be very few men in England who could give you such gifts. He is

undoubtedly a great man, who has made a great contribution in
so many fields, a great poet and a great Englishman.

Only a passing, though well-intended, reference to the book being
most impressive for 'a half-educated girl' somewhat marred the overall effect. All were agreed that this was a new beginning; one which
might even herald a profitable line of 'high-brow' literary work for the
breakthrough author.

The book certainly received the publicity required for such a development. Lengthy reviews appeared in most national newspapers, the
palm going to the two-page spread written by Professor John Kenyon
in *The Observer*. Although this piece was rather light-hearted and
apparently 'angered' Sir Arthur intensely – even to the point of inti-
mating a libel action against the paper – it was apposite. The historian
was playfully described as an 'English institution, like warm beer,
fishcakes and wellingtons', who had written many wonderful books,
including one of the 'great historical biographies in the language' –
his life of Samuel Pepys.

What was less pleasing for Sir Arthur was the fact that so many of
his achievements were squarely placed in the past. Focusing particularly on his 'propaganda' histories during the war, Kenyon observed
that 'thirty or forty years ago', he had been 'the best known living
English historian', with the implication that he was now not to be
taken too seriously. Even more troubling for Sir Arthur was the clear
suggestion that his biographer was in on the joke. She was said to
have been 'affectionate and totally committed without being slavish
or awestruck'. 'The picture [she] conveys,' he went on, 'is at times
distinctly unflattering,' particularly with regard to Bryant's 'insanely

active' domestic life, as well as his unfashionable beliefs about such matters as capital punishment and the EEC.

'Great as was his respect for the Christian Church in the past,' the reviewer continued, 'he seemed to have no religious underpinning to his daily life.'

Sir Arthur's one relief was that the professor had been – along with nearly everyone else – left with no inkling of the true nature of the relationship between himself and his former secretary.

Rather surprisingly, Sir Arthur was far more relaxed about the book's most hostile notice, published in the *Sunday Telegraph*. 'Sir Arthur Bryant has been married twice,' the anonymous reviewer stated, 'for fifteen years to his first wife, and for thirty-five years to his second. These two women are both mentioned only once by name and twice in passing. The second wife is not even mentioned in the index, although her father is.'

The critic also pointed out that, despite his many patriotic masterpieces, Bryant had also written an extremely 'ill-judged' account of the rise of Nazism – *Unfinished Victory* – which had been published, with appalling timing, nearly four months after the start of the Second World War. While Pamela had only touched lightly on this in her book, she entirely shared the reviewer's complaint about her treatment of the historian's former spouses. When the manager of Hatchards, Tommy Joy, told her flatly that many readers felt 'cheated' in this regard, she could hardly disagree.

Whatever Pamela's private thoughts, however, she did not wish to go in for recriminations. She was going to enjoy *her* moment every bit as much as her subject. Not even the inevitable confusion and complications which ensued from their joint invitation to a celebratory luncheon at the Vintners' Hall the day after his eightieth birthday, attended by the nation's leading public figures – including the prime minister, James Callaghan, and the Archbishop of Canterbury, Dr Donald Coggan – was going to dampen her spirits. Contacted by her publishers about where and when she would like them to send a car, she had to admit that it was not precisely clear where Sir Arthur would be coming from. Despite some of the coldest February weather in a generation, serious industrial disruption and the fact that he was recovering from a severe bout of flu, the historian still planned to flit between South Street, Buckinghamshire and the Old Brompton Road in an attempt to share some of the stardust.

Only with the greatest difficulty – including calling Alwynne to tell her to 'stop thinking about herself' – was it possible for Pamela to persuade him to stay put. She told him that it would be reckless, if not impossible, for him to have lunch with the other woman on his actual birthday if he also planned to attend the large cocktail party she had arranged for him at South Street the same day. After conceding that he might be 'let off' if he could prove to Alwynne that he had a temperature, he exploded with rage when his hostess admitted that she did not own a thermometer, and neither, on enquiry, did the 'Wife of Bath' downstairs. In an echo of his ill-tempered reaction to Professor Kenyon's review, he screamed at her from his temporary sickbed: 'Women who live alone should be made to have thermometers by law!' It was only by agreeing to have 'lunch on the telephone' with Alwynne that the crisis was eventually resolved. 'Mostly,' fumed Pamela, 'at my expense.'

That still left the problem of how exactly Sir Arthur was going to be transported to the Vintners' Hall – and with whom – the following afternoon. Pamela refused to travel with him in the same car, provided by Collins, as she was aware that they would also need to collect not only Anne but also Alwynne, who had somehow managed to make it to London for the day: Lorelei, yet again, was on holiday with her fiancé.

'It is rather like the old conundrum,' Sir Arthur would later joke, 'of getting a fox, a goose and a sack of corn across the river in a boat for only two at a time.'

His solution, on this occasion, was to offer to take the Underground, so that the three ladies could use the publisher's car.

'Even such an important occasion as this,' Pamela would recall, 'evidently did not warrant the extravagance of a taxi.'

In the end, after much 'consternation' at the offices of Collins, it was resolved that Sir Arthur would travel in their car with Anne and Alwynne, while Pamela would arrive by taxi 'accompanied and splendidly supported' by her daughter, Miranda. Only later would Pamela realise that there was another, more important, reason why Sir Arthur wanted to avoid going with Anne and Alwynne.

'Somewhere along the line,' she wrote, 'A. B. managed to "lose" them.' When he arrived at the Vintners' Hall, 'the guest of honour entered, caught by a photographer's flashlight – *alone.*'

The ensuing meal was rich in praise for Sir Arthur. Proceedings began with a speech from the chairman of the *Times* newspapers, Sir Denis Hamilton, whose employers were hosting the party. Harold Macmillan, a fellow member of Sir Arthur's dining club, Grillion's, then rose to compare his many books to the masterpieces of Gibbon and Macaulay. There were even some small crumbs for Pamela, whose newly released biography of the historian was favourably mentioned by both Sir Denis and, in a short speech of his own, her subject himself.

Afterwards Sir Arthur was seen relaxing in the company of Sir John Betjeman, Macmillan, Callaghan, Dr Coggan, and a host of others, including the editor of *The Times*, William Rees-Mogg, whose usual duties were in abeyance owing to the printers' strike. While short notices did appear in several other newspapers, not all the coverage was particularly favourable.

'He's no Thucydides,' smirked the Regius Professor of History at Oxford, Hugh Trevor-Roper, to one waiting reporter.

Although no one had paid quite so much attention to Pamela, her pocket-diary entry left no doubt of her sense of relief and achievement. 'My day of days,' she wrote breathlessly, 'there'll never be another as long as I live … I am *grateful*, so grateful.'

After years of being invited to literary parties in the capacity as Sir Arthur's secretary, she was now in demand in her own right, just as her companion had foreseen. While this instigated a slight thaw in their relations, she was no longer – as Professor Kenyon had remarked – wholly committed. She could afford to be a little detached, a touch aloof. Certainly, she did not mind occasionally arranging a dinner at South Street for Sir Arthur and a selection of their mutual friends, but she was not going to attend public functions with him unless he dispensed with the 'whirly bird' and all the others. It was, in sum, the same old impasse that had forever dogged their unhappy relationship.

'What couldn't I say if I really let my hair down!!' she wrote to him before speaking about his life and work at the Ruislip Literary Society that summer. To this end, she had already begun typing out their correspondence in the hope that, one day, she might publish the full story.

'Even I,' she wrote in another letter, 'with my imagination, couldn't dream up a more lunatic household or a novel, at any rate not one that anyone would *believe*. I wonder what Dickens would have done with a saint, a sinner, a furniture-bashing couple, a Chinese gardener, an ageing rags-to-riches siren, a still more ageing and adoring yellow-hammer, to say nothing of a peripheral, letter-writing sledge-hammer, bashing out criticism on her typewriter!' For the time being, she said, she was prepared merely to use her experiences of the past ten years as the basis for a short novella. Gamely, he told her that he looked forward to reading whatever she chose to write about.

Then, quite dramatically, Pamela learnt that the 'whirly bird' had flown. This followed a long exchange of accusations between Pamela and Sir Arthur concerning the relative merits and demerits of the 'kissing lady'. 'You know as well as I know,' wrote Pamela on 23 August, 'and Anne and Alwynne (if they were honest with themselves) know, and half the Close knows (especially as she began staying when you had others in the house), that during Lorelei's not altogether brief visits, you spend most of each night in the spire bedroom and do not primly bid each other adieu on the stairs.' She told him that having his 'kind of reputation' might be all right at '30, 40, 50, 60 or even 70', but not at eighty – 'unless you want to get into the *Guinness Book of Records*'.

What Pamela had not bargained for was that Sir Arthur was now sharing these letters with his new first lady – a significant raising of the stakes since the estranged pair had, the previous summer, argued about Alwynne proofreading the drafts of *Portrait of a Historian*. Now, just a few days after her speculation about what was going on in the 'spire bedroom', Pamela received the most extraordinary letter from her rival.

'I have just heard of your constant tirade of the most fantastic lies,' Lorelei wrote. 'I had been sympathetic towards you recently,' she continued, 'having seen the violent and hysterical side of Arthur, so I realised what traumatic times you must have had, with your distorted imagination, and Arthur's likewise.'

Yet these were just the preliminaries.

'Orgies!!' she continued indignantly. 'You must be joking, and my rejecting Max [Turner, her fiancé] because I wanted a title. You must be joking too … Remember your life is not blameless,' the letter concluded, 'so people in glass houses should not throw stones. The new news for you is that I will never see or hear of Arthur again. Over and out, Lorelei – or, as you call me, Old Joan. You're not far behind!'

Pamela was stunned. 'I think her own imagination had become somewhat distorted,' she wrote long afterwards, 'but she was evidently very fussed about her "name", having hoped, as A. B. always did, that owing to her age anything could be "got away with".'

Yet the outcome was by no means entirely what Pamela had wished for. While an evil influence appeared to have been lifted, Sir Arthur was now alone and helpless, with no one – least of all herself – prepared to 'take him on' again. After telling him this quite openly, she was persuaded to contribute at least a modicum of assistance: he was, after all, now an incredibly aged man. Getting him to and from parties in London – as well as allowing him the occasional night's rest in the 'little eyrie' that he had long considered his own – seemed not such a great sacrifice. And there were, as Lorelei had cattishly suggested, small perks for her as well: at the Authors of the Year party the previous March she had been introduced, as the historian's biographer, to the Duke of Edinburgh, who declared that he was an occasional reader of Sir Arthur's column in the *Illustrated London News*. For all the angst, Pamela could not help feeling partially happy to return to the old arrangement.

It was not until the spring of 1980 that this uneasy equilibrium was put into complete disarray. Sir Arthur had, rather unexpectedly, been asked to chair a Foyle's Literary Luncheon to mark the publication of the autobiography of Laura, Duchess of Marlborough, whom neither of them had met. Grateful to have received a separate invitation from their hostess, Pamela was more than willing to accompany the historian, but it was clear that, owing to his ceremonial duties, they would be sitting some distance apart.

To help Sir Arthur with the brief speech he would need to make at the party, they both spent a few hours at South Street flicking through the Duchess's cheerfully indiscreet memoir, *Laughter from a Cloud*. While the historian was not quite as decided in his disapproval as Pamela – whose own copy would soon be filled with such marginalia as 'How *does* a woman with these legs get all these men? On pleasure-bent?' and 'How *could* you!' – he was by no means uncritical. 'I cannot remember whether he actually used the world "vulgar",' she would write, 'but he certainly inferred it.'

Sir Arthur stayed on at South Street for a few days after the party, conducting his business in his usual manner from her living room. Nothing more was said about the Duchess or her book. If anything Pamela's relationship with her wayward companion seemed to be on the mend.

'You have such an *intense* capacity for both happiness and suffering,' he had written to her on 12 April. 'It is this, I think, more than anything else that has drawn me to you and ... bound me to you.'

Writing, as always, on the letter paper she had specially designed for him some years previously, he also thanked her for her resumed secretarial work, and subsequently renewed an offer for her to put together an anthology of his writings, provisionally entitled, *The Age of Wellington*.

'You can always count,' he wrote sympathetically, 'on a substantial share of my royalties … in consideration of all your wonderful help over both *The Great Duke* and *The English Socrates* in the past.'

In moments of reverie, the lonely lady even wondered if she might not move down to the Close and pass out her last years either with or near to Sir Arthur.

On 10 June 1980, a mere eight weeks after the Foyle's luncheon, that daydream was shattered into a thousand pieces. Pamela and Sir Arthur were due to appear the following day at another one of these exclusive literary gatherings, but for some reason he had made no intimation of whether he preferred to arrive together or separately. Pamela was still awaiting this information when, at about 11pm, she heard the soft sound of something being pushed under her front door; evidently a letter retrieved from downstairs by a neighbour. Curious to know its contents, she climbed out of bed to find a thick envelope addressed to her in the historian's familiar handwriting. Dropping to her knees, she tore it open. At once she recognised the paper – or, more accurately, card. It was the back sheet of a packet of carbon paper; she knew them only too well. 'When re-ordering quote ref: 10L Finclean,' she read in block capitals on the reverse.

Spinning the document around, Pamela could just about make out the following text, scrawled with a blunt blue crayon:

Dearest Pam,

I am writing to tell you before it becomes known to others, that all the complications of my life have suddenly ended because since our meeting two months ago in the Crystal Room, Laura Marlborough and I have grown so fond of one another that we want to spend what remains of our lives together and marry as soon as we are able. I can only regard it as a kind of miracle that she should love me, old as I am, but we make each other so happy that I can only be very – and humbly – grateful.

It does not make me love the few I have loved and love any the less, than [sic] whom, for all our past estrangements, none is dearer to me than you. If the happiness which has so undeservedly and unexpectedly befallen me should prove a renewal, instead of a further breach of our ancient affection and friendship, it would add to my happiness – and, I believe, Laura's – whom I should love you to know.

Yours with my love as always,

Boaz

The shock was brutal. Years later Pamela would come to see the letter as merely a variation on a theme, but at the time, kneeling on the floor in her nightdress, it seemed to her a new and far more profound kind of betrayal. Was it the incongruous terms of endearment: 'dearest', 'with my love *as always*', 'Boaz'? Was it the slipshod appearance and grammar? Was it the painful comparison she could not help making with the other women whom he had asked to 'prepare' at the time of their own engagement four years previously? Or was it simply the quiet confidence that she was expected to share in the happiness which had 'so undeservedly and unexpectedly befallen' him? She could hardly decide. But all night she sat awake on the sofa thinking of how exactly she should respond.

Only Anne's tragic warning seemed to offer an explanation to the whole, bewildering situation: 'Pam, Arthur is a very *hurting* man.'

Part Two: Operation Duchess

1

Neither Sir Arthur nor Pamela had known much about Laura, Duchess of Marlborough, prior to the celebratory lunch for her book, *Laughter from a Cloud*, at the Dorchester Hotel on Wednesday, 16 April 1980. Exactly why Sir Arthur had been asked to chair the event had been a minor mystery to them both – the historian had only been asked by the hostess, Christina Foyle, at the 'eleventh hour', and had initially asked to be excused. As his first impressions of the book to Pamela had indicated, he feared that the *debutante* author had revealed more about herself than was necessary or wise.

The Duchess's life had certainly been full of incident. The product of a union between a nephew of the 11th Earl of Wemyss and an heiress of the Tennant chemical fortune, she had been born in 1915, during the premiership of her great-uncle, the Liberal politician Sir Herbert Asquith. Despite the tragic loss of her mother in childhood, she grew up in a charmed world of money, position and blue blood – it was nothing for her, as a young woman, to sit at dinner beside a cabinet minister or a governor general. Many of these individuals, as she suggested in her memoir, had been besotted by her. Not even the aged playwright George Bernard Shaw had been immune to her girlish charm – though, in that case, she pointed out, the romance had got no further than a series of bon mots from the Irish sage, including: 'To be healthy you must have loose boots and an empty bowel.' Subsequently she had married four times, most recently to the late 'Bert' Marlborough, from whom she derived her title, but who had died, unlike Sir Arthur, following an operation on his bowel, just six weeks after their wedding in 1972. Her other husbands had included a viscount, an earl and a wealthy socialite rumoured to be the illegitimate child of Prince George, the Duke of Kent.

When Sir Arthur first laid eyes on Duchess Laura, he was even more lovestruck than he had been in the case of 'the kissing lady', Lorelei Robinson.

'When I came into the Crystal Room at the Dorchester,' he later wrote, 'and saw you standing there with your eager, alert, almost electric expression, I felt rather as knight errants must, I suppose, have felt (not wholly disinterestedly!) when they sighted a maiden in distress tied up on a rock awaiting dragons!' Dressed in 'exquisite clothes like a princess out of a fairy tale', the historian would tell her that he had seen no woman so elegantly dressed since Lady Edwina Mountbatten – the same line he had once used to woo Pamela.

Sir Arthur's latest love, however, was quite unlike any of her predecessors. Although not far off her sixty-fifth birthday, she retained an almost childlike nonchalance about social norms and conventions. In her book, she fondly recalled how, as a young mother in the 1930s, she had bought herself a pet monkey from Harrods and taken it for walks in Hyde Park. In another revealing passage, she admitted that she had once surreptitiously dissolved some sleeping tablets into the whisky of a particularly tiresome gentleman. It was on account of these examples of her carefree self-confidence, even more than her physical appearance, which best explained her timeless appeal to the opposite sex. One favourite story, also recounted in the book, was of the time she had kept the Conservative MP Duff Cooper and an equally distinguished rival impatiently knocking at separate doors of her private railway sleeper.

Over lunch, Sir Arthur tried his best to play the role of avuncular elder scholar. He told his new acquaintance that her book had reminded him of Dr Johnson's satire on the vanity of human wishes, *Rasselas*, which he proceeded to describe in some detail. When this failed to provoke enlightened discussion, he brought their conversation down a few levels. Did they not, he suggested amicably, have a mutual passion? But before Laura could interject with one of her famous witticisms, Sir Arthur continued boldly: *dogs*. They both adored them: the Duchess's book had devoted more space to her two terriers – Russy I and Russy II – than to most of her siblings (one of whom had married the creator of James Bond, Ian Fleming), or to her only daughter, Sara, with whom she had had a difficult relationship.

So prized were these canines that Laura had even made a gift to one of them of the priceless Marlborough pearls. 'Bert murmured something about me being crazy,' she wrote in her memoir.

It had been owing to such eccentricities that the Duke's family had virtually disowned her. In the case of Sir Arthur, however, these fripperies were to become a source of amusement and admiration. Before departing with Pamela, he promised to send his new friend a copy of his little book, *Jimmy: the dog in my life*.

It was another masterstroke.

'I read it twice over straight away,' wrote the Duchess just two days after their meeting. 'I cannot ever tell you the pleasure it gave me – and I shall treasure it for the rest of my life.'

Whether it was through his portrayal of his own heroism in rescuing the stray creature from the cliffs at Boscastle in 1942, or his sad depiction of the friendless, starving animal, a strong bond was instantly forged between reader and biographer.

'It refreshed me in every way,' she continued, 'and helped me to forget two truly horrible letters from the Marlborough family ... saying I had "humiliated their father and mortified them and others" [as well as] even worse things which I will not bore you with.'

As a further signal of her trust and confidence in her new acquaintance, she passed on some colourful judgements of their fellow diners, notably 'that vast "shocking pink" figure of Barbara Cartland, looking like an over-plumed predator from another age ... [and] the hard, bitter eyes of the Argyll woman' – the famous beauty, Margaret, Duchess of Argyll, who had, long ago, been captured in an extremely compromising photograph with 'the headless man', produced at her divorce trial. She closed her letter with some admiring comments about Myles Place, as portrayed by Pamela on Sir Arthur's letter paper, before enquiring: 'Would you ever leave it for a weekend?' His presence, she indicated, would be most welcome at her country retreat in South Buckinghamshire, Gellibrands, any time he should like.

It was the sort of invitation that was simply too good to be true for Sir Arthur. But he was, at first, cautious. He knew from his recent experiences with Alwynne, Anne, Barbara, Lorelei and Pamela that any sudden change in his routine could be highly damaging to his well-being and that of his entire fold. And it was, moreover, potentially tricky that he had just insisted on Pamela coming down to

Salisbury for the week to clear his backlog of correspondence and begin typing his new book, *The Elizabethan Deliverance*. He stalled.

'Your dear letter,' he wrote from his garden early the following week, 'touched me so much that I am sending you this little interim note to let you know I have received it, lest you should think that my delay in replying meant that I didn't appreciate it: it has moved me *profoundly* – as did your book and meeting you.' He said that the demands of Pussums and the Virgin Queen meant he would only be able to write in more depth over the coming days.

Two days later, on Thursday, 24 April, Sir Arthur wrote Laura a much longer letter – though, once again, he said he would need more time to respond to her invitation. He repeated that he worried she might think he 'hadn't appreciated' her letter, when 'in fact it was all I could do to keep the tears out of my eyes when I read it'. He told her that he had been rereading her book with a newfound admiration, claiming to have now fully discerned her 'courage and genius'. 'An intense capacity for feeling,' he went on, 'which is also what makes you so lovable, and why so many have loved you.' With regard to her difficulties with the Marlborough family, he told her not to worry about the complaints of the 'Ugly Sisters', for she had written nothing in her book 'to which they ... could possibly take exception'. He promised to write to her at greater length over the weekend, before signing himself off as her 'devoted friend of a week – but of the rest of my life'.

Only the following day, however, Sir Arthur was presented with his first dilemma. By longstanding arrangement, he and Pamela were to dine with their neighbours in the Cathedral Close, John and Terttu Cordle, in aid of the cancer charity Marie Curie – Sir Arthur was going to read aloud to potential donors from his biography of Charles II. Just before leaving, Pamela casually mentioned that she had seen an amusing paragraph about Duchess Laura's book in the *Daily Express*'s scurrilous 'William Hickey' column. Knowing that he could hardly show any reaction – but also that such a barb would be intensely painful to his new beloved – Sir Arthur had to wait until he had walked Pamela back to the White Hart, where she was staying, and then presumably said goodnight to Anne, who was residing with him at Myles Place, before he could finally escape to his bedroom to make the necessary call. As it was now passed midnight, it was little surprise that this intervention was not entirely welcome. Sir Arthur was so confused by the gruff, masculine voice that answered the phone that he assumed he had dialled the wrong number. His first telephone conversation with the Duchess was embarrassingly brief.

'I must apologise for having rung you, so unmannerly, so late at night,' wrote Sir Arthur shortly after Pamela had returned to London on Sunday, 'but earlier that day I had seen a silly gossip paragraph in the *Express* which, with unspeakable vulgarity and misrepresentation, described your brave and noble book as "saucy", and it made me so angry that, fearing you might have seen it after one of your weary book-signing journeys, you might be upset and saddened by it.'

Blaming the tardiness of his call on his rush to get to his good cause, he said that he hoped his admiration for her book 'might possibly serve as an antidote' to the journalistic poison.

'And on the previous night,' he went on by way of additional explanation, 'rereading your book because I wanted to review it, I had read again those two harrowing chapters about your brother's illness and [her penultimate husband] Michael [Canfield]'s death and that later chapter when you felt life wasn't worth going on living.' He told her that her book should have been called *Tears from a Cloud*. Those squally manifestations, he said, were 'haunting' him too.

These outpourings crossed the Duchess's own letter, posted the same day. 'When you telephoned the other evening,' she wrote, 'I fear my utter exhaustion may have showed in my voice.' It had been, she explained, a frenetic week, with publicity trips to Birmingham and Manchester immediately following on from her book's official launch at the Dorchester. But she did not want Sir Arthur to worry, so pleased was she that he had seen 'the tears behind the laughter'. To put his mind at rest, she revealed that she and her third husband 'had both always loved' his books: her favourite being *The Age of Elegance*; his being *The Age of Chivalry*. Then she remembered that, almost a decade ago, she had been recommended by the assistant at her favourite bookshop, Heywood Hill in Mayfair, a collection of his journalism, *The Lion and the Unicorn*, which she had subsequently spent a weekend devouring in her nearby flat.

'It was the lovely gentle persuasiveness that made me not only read, take in and cling to every word,' she continued, '[but also] your wonderful prose.'

She said that despite her incessant loneliness, she had 'found comforting words again' about 'our England, however drastically it has changed'. After expressing her joy and gratitude that he – 'a great and world famous Historian' – had admired her book, she came to the point: '*Please* review my book in *The Times* or its literary supplement, or your own *Illustrated London News*.'

In a confused and misspelt final sentence, she remarked that 'any

one with your brilliant art of presentation and real perseptation [*sic*]'
could get any one of those publications to 'take a word from you'.

Duchess Laura's romantic availability was made especially clear
from something she had written across the back of the envelope: 'I
feel like your "Jimmy".' But just to make her meaning clear, she added
within that she had thought of Sir Arthur as 'her Knight' even before
he had first written to her. This was almost too much for the historian to handle. He had already decided that the Duchess must be
given his 'special additional telephone' number without delay; now he
declared that he had never received a more precious communication
in his entire life – 'Like that which interrupted St Paul's journey to
Damascus,' he wrote. 'If you ever do feel you want a little reassurance
on the telephone at any hour of the night,' he had written in his long
apology letter, 'and that I can give it you, please don't hesitate to ring,
for should you do so … I could think of no greater honour.' As with
his romantic breakthrough with Pamela in January 1971, he assured
her not to worry about the time – 'I work most of the night,' he added
in parentheses.

From the private telephone line, it was but a small step to poetry
and even more effusive praise of Duchess Laura and her book. Yet the
poet and sentiment for which the historian first reached, in the same
letter, were almost too shocking a self-revelation.

'Man's love is of man's life a thing apart,' he quoted from Byron's
Don Juan – "Tis woman's whole existence.' He told her that she had
'unwittingly' done him 'a great service' in giving him a 'release …
from an unavailing hope which had long vainly enslaved' him. A clue
of his meaning, he suggested, was to be found in 'the last nine lines of
page 137' of her book: a passage in which the Duchess observed that

'to be deeply loved is not so difficult but to love that person as much as they love you is as near perfection as one is likely to get'. He told her that her book was practically 'the most sensible and revealing' work 'on the nature of love and loving' that he had ever read.

As if to illustrate his point, he went on to hint at the complications that had arisen from allowing himself to be loved by the wrong women. 'Last autumn,' he wrote somewhat guardedly, 'having had so many domestic problems since my old married couple of 30 years had to give up through old age and death, I decided to run the house with two daily women – a mother and daughter who came in the morning but can't cook for me in the evenings beyond leaving a meal on a hot plate.' With no mention of the woman who had so recently departed from the Close, he said that he could now only rely on occasional visits from 'his noble former wife' and 'a faithful old flame of fifty years ago' – Alwynne. How different things would have been, he lamented, had he married a woman like herself. 'I think I could have been Prime Minister!' he wrote.

The arrival of Duchess Laura's letter on Wednesday sent the historian into further paroxysms of passion. 'My precious Laura,' he replied, 'no words can express what your dear letter meant to me this morning ... it does seem as though God has answered each of our prayers and needs.' But this was only the beginning of Sir Arthur's excitement. He went on:

> To be your Knight, my love, is the greatest honour that I could
> possibly have conferred on me – it is like having the Garter, only
> far better. Please God make me worthy of it – I will try so hard
> to serve you in any way you want, and I have added now to my

daily prayers for those I love, living and 'dead', the words, 'Pray
God give me grace and power to make little Laura happy.'

These effusions carried on to the next page, with an entire rendition
of Browning's 'Flight of the Duchess', culminating in the lines: 'With
the thrill of the great deliverance/Into our arms for ever more/And thou
shalt know those arms once curled/About thee, what we knew before/
How love is the only good in "the world".' Before thanking her for her
kind words about his prose writing – 'No one has ever written about it
with such discernment,' he opined – Sir Arthur declared that Browning's verses could have been written for her and her remarkable book.

It was somewhat ironic that, the very same day, Sir Arthur received
an unusually friendly letter from another one of his admiring critics
– one to whom he had, many times over, similarly pledged his allegiance. For while Pamela had often argued with Sir Arthur about his
tendency to send her what she called 'guilt money', on this occasion
– when her suspicion would have been most justified – she yielded.
Thanking him for a 'nice letter' and several 'ridiculously big cheques'
(totalling £36), she said that she would gratefully cash them so long as
he promised not to repeat such generosity 'for a long time' and would
then scale down any future remuneration to a 'more reasonable' level.

'In any case, Boaz,' she continued, 'I don't consider myself your
secretary ... I do what I do for you partly for old time's sake because
we once, before Lorelei, had such a good relationship ... and partly
because I so genuinely like to feel I am in some small way helping to
push you along: "pacing" is the word you once used!'

As well as wishing him well with his *Elizabethan Deliverance*, she
let him know that her own writing career was now starting to take

off, with rows of her revised edition of *A Portrait of Wiltshire* set up in Hatchards, and opportunities to appear on radio and even television beginning to present themselves.

But this reconciliation was ill-timed. The following Wednesday, 7 May, Pamela had agreed to let Sir Arthur work in her flat for a few days, so that he could attend one of his Grillion's dinners, staying each night with Anne, before heading out on Sunday to deliver a lecture on gardening at the home of Sir Ralph and Lady Verney in Buckinghamshire, from whence he would be returned to Salisbury by Alwynne. It was the sort of arrangement that had been working exceedingly well for Sir Arthur for a number of years, but he now risked it all by drawing Duchess Laura into his complex schedule.

'It has suddenly occurred to me,' he wrote to her in the lead-up to these manoeuvres, 'that if by any chance it would amuse you ... would you care to drive down to Salisbury [on Saturday] ... taking me with you and bring me back afterwards to either London or Gellibrands?' He told her not to worry about the amount of driving – 'it takes 1 ¾ hours from either London or Beaconsfield without hurrying' – and assured her that it would, in any case, be well worth her while. A friend of his from the Vintners' Company, he wrote, had offered to come and inspect some Regency pier glass that he was considering bequeathing them in his will.

The collision of all these schemes took place at Pamela's flat within a few hours of Sir Arthur's arrival the following Wednesday. Having spent the afternoon working through his letters and manuscript corrections, the pair began to discuss the idea of his former secretary taking a lease on another house that had recently come up for sale in the Close. It was a move that she had long wished for, irrespective of Sir Arthur, whom she had begun to see as a 'cuckoo in the nest', forever standing between herself and her ancestral lands.

'I felt A. B. was trying to weigh up the advantages and disadvantages to himself,' she recalled, 'should I come to live on his doorstep.' He said that it would be useful for him if she would continue to help him with his work, but this only precipitated the brewing storm.

'I want to be wanted,' wrote Pamela after his departure, '*but not just for work like a donkey!*' Unlike Anne – 'so much the best of the bunch from your point of view' – she could not act as 'willing chauffeuse/ London landlady and cook-housekeeper at Myles Place'.

'Perhaps Anne and Alwynne,' she went on, 'being of an older generation, are conditioned to doing what men want and are simply grateful for small mercies, but I'm not.' She said that she had been particularly appalled to learn that Anne had recently, having prepared the tea in advance, agreed to make herself scarce for several hours while Sir Arthur entertained some of their old friends, Lord and Lady Duncan Sandys.

In the course of this heated argument, Pamela came dangerously close to hitting the Duchess-shaped nail on the head. She fumed about his 'caginess and evasiveness' with regard to his weekend plans, 'first mumbling something about going to the Verneys', and then saying that he 'didn't know' what he was doing. 'Which always means,' she continued in her letter, 'you *do* know, but you don't want certain other people to know.' She told him that she was sick of being blamed for his 'strange, unsatisfactory way of life', which he conducted 'as if still in MI5', 'only … wanting to see one when it happens to suit'. The dispute reached fever pitch when Pamela refused any longer to cut Sir Arthur's hair – he had asked her to make him '*soigné*' for his forthcoming engagements. In disgust, the historian took up his papers and stormed from the flat, slamming the door behind him.

In fairness to Sir Arthur, his weekend plans remained typically confused, even at this late stage. After spending some days considering his offer to come and view his collection of antique mirrors, Duchess Laura had suggested that he put off the man from the Vintners' Company and come and stay with her at Gellibrands instead. Desperate to fall in with his new love's plans, Sir Arthur turned to someone he knew was always willing to do the same for himself – Anne. In line with her AA teaching of doing a good turn each day 'without being found out', Lady Bryant agreed to drop her ex-husband at the Duchess's door before returning, unacknowledged, to London.

While she made her lonely journey home, Sir Arthur was greeted by his hostess and a small menagerie of dogs, before being shown to his bedroom by two domestic servants, Pat and Jenny. Sensing his disappointment that his room was located some considerable distance from her own, the Duchess reassured her guest that he could contact her at any time using her internal telephone system.

After a simple meal, Sir Arthur read aloud a chapter from a favourite book – *The Happy Hypocrite* by Max Beerbohm – at the fireside, and then they went up to their respective rooms. Owing to the Duchess's state-of-the-art technology, the early night they had each promised themselves seemed almost alluring.

But the hotline proved temperamental.

'I am afraid you must find telephone conversations with me frustrating and maddening,' wrote Sir Arthur in her garden at 5am the next morning, 'as I find it so difficult to hear on the telephone and there is nothing more maddening than to be asked to repeat what one has just said.' He stressed that this was not, however, due to any sensory deficiency on his part.

'There is nothing wrong with my hearing,' he went on, 'only on the telephone or in a room where everyone is talking, words seem to get jumbled together.' He regretted that this had meant that her 'dear, deep, eager voice' had often 'eluded and escaped' him during their midnight conferences.

Sir Arthur had wanted to speak with her mostly of the past – both his own and his country's.

'My darling,' he continued in his dawn letter, 'I don't want you to think that I don't share to the full the pain and misery that you expressed … on the telephone about the destruction and shame of all the things we both feel about the England we were brought up to love and which matters more to both of us that anything else in the world.' He told her that his aim had always been to resurrect 'the dear, brave, honourable spirit of England … for future and happier generations'. It was, he said, a perennial source of 'consolation and strength' for him to do so.

Not that this was unconnected with his own history. Having evidently now told her something of Lorelei, he went on: 'I found the same a year ago in personal sadness and near despair when all my silly hopes and dreams of personal happiness after six wasted years of vain longing and waiting ended in total defeat, and I fell back on the only thing left to me – work.' Of the lady who allegedly made these labours possible, however, the historian remained silent.

Sir Arthur's amnesia was not unreasonable. As well as being doubtful of the current state of his relationship with his former secretary, he told Duchess Laura that, since their meeting, he had been transported back to a happier, faraway time. Reusing the same lines he had once used on Pamela, he told her – twice – that she had restored his faith in himself, and also that she had allowed him to forget, in his 'last years of decrepitude', how little he could offer her. Thanks to her, he continued, he was no longer the careworn, has-been historian he saw in his reflection, but 'the silly romantic boy of sixteen I once was, and have never wholly grown out of'. By way of apology for the excessive romanticism to which this gave rise, he quoted a line from his favourite dramatic work, *Peter Pan*: 'It's a sort of compliment, capin',' as Smee tells the pirate chief of a particularly attentive crocodile.

Before turning out her light, the Duchess had written her own letter to her guest. 'Arthur Darling,' it began. 'If I could but find the words at this late hour to tell you how you enchanted me yesterday – you are the only real GENTLEMAN in my sad befuddled eyes since Michael died.'

Anticipating the historian's own letter, she wrote that listening to his 'enchanted … voice and love of words' had given her the sense of being in a 'true fairy tale'; she was once again a 'shy, foolish … young girl'. But there was a note of caution too. She wanted to learn more about his 'secret life'. 'Unlock the doors,' she wrote perceptively, 'tell me all, I *will* understand, as you *seem* to read in *Laughter from a Cloud* so wonderfully more than I was able to express in words.'

By whatever means these messages were conveyed – either personally or via the trusted hands of Pat and Jenny – it was clear that the pair were now locked into the sort of epistolary dialogue so beloved of this particular historian. Only the evidence of Duchess Laura's next letter, written late on Saturday evening, suggests that her guest soon invited her up to his quarters.

'I left you alone tonight,' she wrote from the other side of the house, 'for you must ponder on your life whilst I must think on what has happened since your words and ever gentleness seduced me.'

Fifty years of beguiling men, however, had not been spent in vain.

'Something in me,' she wrote, 'says: "Laura be careful – you are fragile now, so much has taken the brave, thoughtless spontaneous [*sic*] away from your old self."' While she said that his stay had been pure 'bliss', she made it clear that she would not tolerate being simply another notch on his vintage bedpost.

'Poor darling Arthur,' she carried on, 'you say you have never grasped the nettle and found the sting at once vanish.' Like Pamela before her, she hinted that there could be a 'miracle ahead', but only if he would back up his words with actions.

'Perhaps,' she concluded, 'we could find *real* happiness and content, which I once had.' At present, she said, he was only 'Arthur darling' not '*my* darling'. 'It would not be true – alas.'

By the time that Sir Arthur had been driven back to Salisbury by Alwynne the following evening, he realised what he must do. Waking, as usual, before dawn, he poured out his emotions and longings to his new muse in his most direct letter yet. He told her that since their meeting at the Dorchester, he had found in his heart 'a certainty and assurance' that he had never previously known, and that following his stay at Gellibrands he now knew what he had 'never known before':

> That the woman I idolise and long for and dream of and want,
> is not just a fancy phantom of my imagination and of romance,
> but someone whom I *know* has all the qualities I need to

complement and mend my own character and deficiencies and whose own experience in life has fitted her to give me *everything* I so sorely need to help me in my tasks, life and work, and who, above all, and so miraculously, loves and understands me and my own need for love and understanding.

After continuing in this vein for a further fifteen lines, he came to it:

So, my Darling, if you still feel like Jimmy, wanting what he wanted ... [I am] utterly yours – now and forever ... I *love* you, want to *marry* you if you will have me, and *dedicate my life to you*, past, present and future, in whatever way and place you want it provided you will share it with me, for without you I should no longer want to live, little princess of love and compassion and courage that you are.

Duchess Laura's acceptance arrived three days later, during which time Sir Arthur had held a solemn 'Knight's vigil' in front of a new window in the cathedral: 'A symbol,' he wrote, 'of my love for you.' The words of her letter, he wrote, 'might almost have been dictated by my own heart, only put so beautifully, as only you, of all the people I have ever known or read can put it'.

With reference to what they had clearly been discussing on the telephone since his departure from Gellibrands, he spoke of his relief that 'the endless frustrations and waitings and disappointments and z-turns of the last seven or eight years' were finally over. There was also his first, cryptic reference to Pamela, whose 'bitter resentments over what happened nine years ago' were cautiously alluded to. But all these matters, he said, were irrelevant now. He was, once again, going to 'prepare' each of his past loves for what was shortly to take place. He had already started with Alwynne, whom he was 'striving to enable … to realise what a true and utterly noble person' had come into their lives. He told her that his impending marriage would not 'change or destroy, but if anything enhance, a deep affection and self-less love that has now continued for nearly half a century'. He was going to have the same conversation with Anne when she came to relieve Alwynne of her duties the following day, and he was confident of success. 'She has been like a sister to me,' he wrote, 'something I lacked and so much needed.'

It was not until the end of the month that Sir Arthur decided to 'prepare' Pamela as well. Yet, unlike his dealings with Anne and Alwynne, this difficult operation was done exclusively by letter. He told her – his 'dearest Pammy' – that their 'ridiculous and cruelly hurting quarrels' about such matters as why they did not choose to marry in 1971 had proved that things had ultimately worked out for the best. A life together as husband and wife, he declared, would have made them both 'absolutely miserable' – they would have, based on their latest rows, 'torn each other to pieces'.

But he still wanted her to think well of him. Whether she wished to see him again or not, he told her that he was going to present her with a 'substantial share' of his royalties for the long-delayed Samuel Johnson biography, and also returned to his plan for her to compile an anthology of his writings on the Revolutionary Wars, *The Age of Wellington*. He further added that he would still like her to come and live in the Cathedral Close, offering her to work 'with' him rather than 'for' him. Ten days later, without any further communications between them, he dropped off his happy news at South Street.

Sir Arthur had been prompted into this desperate action by the fact that he, Laura and Pamela were all due to attend another of Christina Foyle's 'literary luncheons' the following day. But if he had intended his letter to smooth over any difficulties, he was quite mistaken. Only to his mind could the presence of a past and present fiancée – and one of these his 'authorised biographer' – at the same literary party pass without event.

Ever cautious, Pamela arrived first. She asked their hostess if she knew about Sir Arthur.

'No,' replied Miss Foyle, 'is he ill?'

But before the historian's latest secret could be fully explained, the man himself arrived – slightly ahead of his newest companion, as Pamela tartly observed. He came straight up to her, beaming. 'He made a cursory introduction of Laura,' she recalled, 'to whom I had not been introduced at the previous luncheon.'

As calmly as she could, she asked him to hold her drink before surreptitiously sliding a letter into his top pocket; a reply to the one he had similarly dispatched to South Street the previous night.

The Duchess looked on, continued Pamela, 'half puzzled, half annoyed'. Then, as though to complete the picture of horror, the photographer who had arranged the jacket illustrations of *Portrait of a Historian* appeared. Jovially, Mr Swaebe demanded a photograph of that book's subject and author. The resulting image was as eloquent as anything the historian had ever written. Pamela, with her face drawn and eyes closed, appeared to be in the throes of extreme nausea; Sir Arthur, meanwhile, looked remarkably spry and content.

Before she could extract herself, Pamela saw the other woman slinking off alone to the bar. 'This time she looked more miserable than anything else,' she recalled.

Before leaving, Pamela went to offer her congratulations to the Duchess. It was an awkward exchange. Laura said that she hoped Pamela 'didn't mind' about the turn of events.

'I remember saying,' continued Pamela in her memoirs, 'that I did, but that A. B. and I could never make things work.' Her parting shot was double-edged: 'I'm sure you're cleverer than I am.'

Once out on the street, Pamela made her way to the Heywood Hill bookshop, where she purchased a copy of her competitor's 'wretched book', leaving the prospective bride and groom alone to read the letter burning a hole in Sir Arthur's breast pocket.

'Obviously the conventional, well-brought-up me wishes you every happiness,' this missile began. 'Obviously the real, honest, gut-reaction me is shattered, sceptical and cannot believe that an 81-year-old twice married, otherwise involved man who has known a thrice [*sic*] married, —?—year-old somewhat doubtful Duchess-of-the-world for only two months, cannot be marrying for anything other than somewhat dubious advantageous reasons on both sides.'

Complaining that she had suspected that he was 'up to something' – '*some thing!*' she gasped – for months, and chastising herself for bothering to buy him a special loaf in case he wanted to come over for tea after the party, she upbraided the historian for, amongst other things, not having the courage to break the news to her face. There were also some fairly hefty blows directed at his new companion – 'I must say I have to hand it to Laura. She knows how to get you cracking! *Two months!* But she has experience.'

Yet, as ever, beneath the fury and the comedy, there was an abiding note of sadness too.

'Poor Anne,' she added in one of several postscripts. 'Poor Alwynne, and maybe poor Lorelei.' She closed off by asking how he would explain his new arrangements to their mutual friends. 'Or does marrying a Duchess solve all previous social indiscretions?'

But the letter only served further to bond the happy couple.

'Pamela's letter is both cruel and bitchy,' the Duchess wrote the following Saturday. 'Her writing is both hysterical and unbalanced … She sounds so bitter and at the same time ridiculous.' She implored him not to be downcast. 'You need looking after and peace to work,' she continued, 'I will give you all that – plus my ever-lasting love, and will remain quite unperturbed by these foolish, selfish women.' She told him that he need only worry about Anne – everyone else could be left to take care of themselves. Nor did Sir Arthur need to make any apology or compensation to his past loves. Of vital importance, she said, was that he took a hard line on the little mascot he had often promised his former secretary: 'You must never give her "Bear",' she wrote.

'Listen to *me* sometimes,' the letter concluded, 'I really do understand jealous women – they are so tiresome.'

2

Even before these curious developments brought matters to crisis point, Sir Arthur had been irrevocably compromised. On only his second stay at Gellibrands, and just two weeks before delivering his fateful letter to Pamela, a most unexpected and improbable group of visitors had descended on the property to disrupt his amusements. Following a tip-off from a local informer, a dozen special branch constables had appeared late on Whitsun night to announce that they had reason to believe that the house was about to be burglarised by a 'highly dangerous' criminal gang. In order to make the necessary arrests, they asked for the Duchess's full cooperation, principally in the matter of allowing them to pass the entirety of the night holed up within the premises. As an additional service, they asked if she would let them admit the BBC film crew which they had brought along with them in the hope of preserving their successful operation for a grateful posterity.

Sir Arthur made it clear at the time that he was somewhat averse to this double intrusion, but he was already too much in the thrall of his hostess seriously to protest.

'The second or so you are seen,' the Duchess would later write, 'is when you quite rightly locked the Detectives out till you telephoned the local police [station].'

After allowing them into the house as a sort of public duty, the thwarted lovers were briefly captured as their truncheon-wielding guests surveyed the property, a motley collection of dogs yapping in their wake. At the time it was clearly understood by all parties that – whatever the reality – the two principal residents of the house were merely 'old friends': one a recently divorced constitutional historian, the other a bereaved aristocrat in mourning. And, as the suspected criminals never made an appearance, the footage was quietly consigned to the bowels of Television Centre, not to be broadcast until subsequent events had shifted the potential viewers' interest more than any of the participants could have envisaged.

For the time being, Duchess Laura was prepared to focus her attentions on private relations alone. Even before Sir Arthur had told Pamela of his impending nuptials, the noble lady wrote to each of her predecessors – not forgetting Lorelei – expressing a hope that they would reconcile themselves to the new situation, and even 'become friends'. But this was not merely a stratagem out of the historian's well-worn playbook: she was prepared to use her claws as much as her guile to secure her man.

Over the course of a long weekend at Myles Place in the aftermath of the abortive literary luncheon, she made as bold a claim on him as any woman since the advent of Lorelei. Her assessment of the pair of rivals she met during this brief encounter was shattering: she complained of the 'atmosphere that the pathetic, wicked Alwynne created', while even 'gentle Anne' came in for veiled criticisms – neither of these ladies had been able to prevent their 'perfect generous host' from being transformed into a wreck of 'exhaustion and unhappiness'. 'Perhaps she couldn't help it,' continued the Duchess with reference to Alwynne, 'and one must always forgive the frailties of all living creatures.' But she was adamant that her fiancé must ditch these relics of his past. 'Nothing can shake my love for you,' she wrote, 'but we cannot go on with this muddle.'

No less important for the Duchess was the immediate discarding of the 'unbalanced Pamela'. But this particular rival was not prepared to give up the fight quite so easily. In a series of blistering missives after the luncheon, she excoriated Sir Arthur for all his misdeeds.

'Oh Boaz,' she wrote after wading through the Duchess's tome, 'it's worse than I thought. You'll be her fifth!!!!!' She reminded him that she had loved him more than any of the others – and a part of her still did. It was because of this, she wrote, that she 'minded about you, your health, your writing, your way of life which was being talked about … [and] what many people would obviously call "making a fool of yourself".'

In the face of his endless protestations and flowers – which, like Anne in 1971, Pamela now demanded he cease sending – she made perhaps her most telling criticism to date. 'You simply endow us all with what you want us to have,' she wrote, 'put us on a pedestal and write love letters to us.' She then proceeded to play back various lines from the historian's vast back catalogue, including such *tendresses* as: 'I love and adore you'; 'I know my life can never be what it could and should be and what I want to make it, *without you*'; 'You are the most enchanting woman I've ever known and the most helpful and the sweetest'; 'I admire and respect you and like being with you [more] than any other human being I've ever known'; 'It would be utterly impossible for me to contemplate life with any other woman but you' – the list went on. While Pamela said that she would maintain a close interest in 'Operation Duchess', she was going to hide herself away in a bomb shelter as soon as the news went public. She prophesied that he would be 'keeping the gossips going' for a long while yet.

She was not mistaken. Just a week after her letter, the first of many satirical notices about the historian's latest love match appeared in the tabloids. 'Duchess Laura is really in Sir Arthur's good books,' chortled the diarist in the *Daily Mail*. 'They met only two months ago,' the anonymous author continued, 'at Christina Foyle's literary lunch to launch the Duchess's entertaining memoirs *Laughter from a Cloud*, which chronicled her extraordinary life.'

Spicing up the story with added revelations about the Marlborough and Wemyss clans, the journalist went on to explain how the event had been 'boycotted' by the Duchess's entire family – 'save her cousin Lord Charteris, the Provost of Eton' – who were supposedly aghast at the book's racy contents. It was a hint of the social hurricane that was shortly to gather around the affianced pair.

As Pamela was quick to allege, the article was the work of the Duchess herself. Not only was it the perfect means of settling scores with her own relations – as well as providing an excellent tonic to sales – the story was also the ideal way of putting pressure on Sir Arthur to hurry up with the formal announcement of their engagement. Like her predecessors, she had already discerned that he was a spectacularly difficult individual to manage – in one early letter she described him as an 'impossible ... petulant little boy' – and it seems at least conceivable that the story was a ruse to prompt him into action. It certainly started the countdown: as the journalist quipped, 'Miss Foyle successfully played cupid and the engagement will be announced next week.'

Undoubtedly the Duchess was playing her hand with consummate skill. Even the manner in which she spoke with the professional gossips suggested a degree of *savoir faire* that went far beyond the historian's outmoded devices.

'I really don't want to say much at the moment,' she was quoted in the article as saying. 'Sir Arthur is working on his new book, so I can't say when we'll marry.'

Had she been able to read the manuscript of that work, she might have been struck by the pertinence of her fiancé's brief retelling of the romance between Henry VIII and the mother of the first Queen Elizabeth. 'Accustomed to having his way in all things, he was also deeply in love – "stricken", as he put it, "with the dart of love" – with a femme fatale, Anne Boleyn, granddaughter of a rich London merchant, whose price was marriage.' The parallels were almost too exact.

And just like that historic love affair, both Sir Arthur and Duchess Laura firmly believed themselves to be in the driving seat. When the latter announced that she could not possibly move into Myles Place on account of its inconvenient size and want of suitable servants' quarters, the historian responded with a variety of schemes to pacify his new beloved.

'I had a letter this morning,' he wrote in one urgent screed, 'from the Deputy Director-General of the National Trust, Angus Stirling, who had already been spoken to about my request [for a stately home] by Lord Gibson, the Chairman of the Trust … who says there may be one in Berkshire … which could suit you.' Even more than his previous attempts to accommodate both Anne and Pamela with his life, there was no question that much of the money required for the purchase was to come from his new love.

It was amid these typically complex negotiations that the announcement of the pair's engagement appeared in *The Times* on Tuesday, 1 July. With a remarkable lack of self-awareness or human sensitivity, Sir Arthur now redoubled his efforts to take charge of the Duchess and her affairs, completely deaf to the warning signals he had already received. Just like his extraordinary interventions in Pamela's divorce proceedings almost a decade previously, he took up each of her personal and fiduciary problems without the slightest fear that she would perceive him to be in any way meddlesome or overbearing.

The most serious of Duchess Laura's immediate worries concerned the government's plan to construct the new M25 motorway within only a stone's throw of Gellibrands. Outraged that the proposed route would 'drive right across her little estate and almost through her garden', Sir Arthur fired off volleys of letters to the planning author-ities – and even to the Minster for Transport, Michael Heseltine – demanding that they reroute the causeway in deference to what he described as 'this blessed plot ... this little spur of England'.

After securing the Duchess a few extra metres of breathing space, he soon turned his attentions to helping her wriggle out of a £2,000 bill she had run up with an estate agent's for advertising the now unsaleable property. Emboldened by further successes in this direc-tion, Sir Arthur next threw himself into a bewildering array of additional troubles, including offsetting her tax liabilities and also extricating her from an insurance claim made by a fellow road-user.

'You kindly and public-spiritly stopped,' he wrote to another wit-ness, 'and together we examined the marks on the two cars which seemed very superficial.'

Scarcely less pressing, however, was Sir Arthur's attempt to receive, on Duchess Laura's behalf, compensation from Coutts bank for allowing her to provide a personal guarantee of £15,000 to a total stranger, one Hunt Kerrigan, who somewhat improbably claimed to have been a friend of her third husband's. As with his previous 'advice' to Pamela, there followed a series of letters, ostensibly from the Duchess, to a variety of the historian's contacts, most notably the former chairman of the bank, Sir Seymour Egerton.

'My solicitor has and wishes to continue suing Coutts,' one of these missives ran, 'on the grounds that at that date (1976) they contravened the currency laws.'

Under dictation, the Duchess pleaded with Sir Seymour to intervene on her behalf. 'My family and myself,' the letter concluded, 'have always banked at Coutts, so I find the whole matter both distasteful and very expensive.'

But after substantial quantities of paper had been exchanged between City conference rooms, Gellibrands and the Cathedral Close, it became clear that the bank would not be liable for failing to advise the Duchess against her generous though reckless commitment. All that had changed was that, as the bank had been forced into seeking 'expert counsel', the Duchess would now be liable for considerable legal fees on their side. The whole tangled tale was perhaps best summed up in the noblewoman's own words, scrawled across the large paper bag into which she wearily dumped the entire correspondence. 'My fight with Coutts Bank,' she wrote. 'Arthur's advice made things worse!'

Yet, once again, Sir Arthur remained strangely unaware of the tensions his schemes were placing on his delicate love affair.

'I won't let him take total control over me,' the Duchess told another gossip columnist shortly before the announcement of their betrothal: 'Nobody has ever taken complete charge over my life.'

Even in the matter of titles, the historian found ways of upsetting his heart's desire. No sooner had she told yet another journalist that she planned to style herself 'Lady Bryant' after their wedding than her fiancé wrote with another idea. Either out of a mistaken sense of duty to Anne or, more likely, to increase his own social status, he suggested that she remain known as the Duchess of Marlborough. 'For it is a proud title,' he wrote, 'to which you've every right, as much as any of that Churchill line, to bear, and it wouldn't humiliate me in the slightest degree ... for I should be so proud of you as being my wife ... that I shall always be on the point of busting!'

Retaining such titles was, he continued, quite ordinary in the seventeenth century when dowager duchesses had found it expedient to marry 'commoners'. In any case, he casually added, such an arrangement might allow them to avoid having to go through with the complications of a legal marriage, which would, under the law of the times, have serious tax implications for them both. At one stage he even proposed that he employ her as his *de jure* secretary since he could 'set the whole cost of doing so against tax ... which can be a considerable advantage'. It was as if he was reliving his previous sagas with Anne, Alwynne and Pamela – though without any evidence that he had learnt anything from those catastrophes.

By this time, the gossip columnists were working themselves into a frenzy. Through relentless dirt-digging and the increasing cooperation of the Duchess herself, these merchants of tittle-tattle fleshed out every particular of what had transpired in the Crystal Room – and after. The

Evening Standard's paragraph entitled 'Sir Arthur tells Laura he loves her' was closely followed by the *Express's* more historically minded piece on 'How Sir Arthur Wooed Laura'; an echo of a pioneering feature on the courtship of Queen Victoria by Prince Albert. These snippety stories spoke of the 'electricity' which had passed between the pair on their first meeting, as well as how Sir Arthur had bombarded his fiancée with copious love letters and bouquets. Nor were the newspapermen deaf to the farcical snobbery of the whole affair.

'I hope he has the right duchess,' one 'friend' was quoted. 'I once heard a speech he made in someone's honour, when he got the man's name wrong throughout.'

A slightly later piece smirked that the historian was, yet again, suffering a 'little back trouble of late'.

Tragically for Sir Arthur, the rise of all this adverse publicity had the effect of virtually killing off both of his ongoing love affairs. Most incensed of all was Pamela.

'It is all so horrid and undignified,' she wrote shortly after hanging up the phone on one of the relentless pressmen. 'You do not ever seem to care about any of us or what happens to us,' she fumed, 'only yourself and possibly the lady of the moment.'

It was small comfort for her to receive an impressive number of unsolicited letters from the other women in Sir Arthur's life.

'I am so very sorry it is not you,' wrote Lorelei in her first communiqué since the row about the 'spire bedroom'. 'This newspaper splash is so dreadful, harmful, and all rather sad,' she continued.

There was even a long apology from one of Sir Arthur's cousins, Aileen Ross-Stewart, whose knowledge of the historian's romances stretched back to the early 1920s, when she had herself been the object of his innocent affections. 'I do understand how you must feel,' she wrote, 'having been so close to Arthur for so long.'

She continued:

> He is in some ways a maddening person, and entirely unbeholden to anyone, and all his women friends have been quite wonderful to him, which is really more than he deserves! I know how you must feel with this last episode – and maybe it is just that – but I'm sorry there is gossip and criticism in London literary circles. Dear Anne must have known that her loving *support* for Arthur will always be just *that*, &, he will turn to her again, when (or if) he needs it & to you if you let him.

Aileen then shed some invaluable light on the origins of the historian's curious behaviour. 'In his youth he was spoilt by his mother as a budding genius and, of course, he has turned out to be just that!

'Anyway,' she concluded, 'there is something there to be loved and admired, in a detached sort of way by us all.'

As if to emphasise her own detachment from Sir Arthur's life, Pamela now renewed her demand for the return of all her furniture and possessions; items which had recently – without her knowledge – been moved into his rather insalubrious basement. But, once again, the historian stalled masterfully. He told her that, in the interests of security, he could not permit 'a firm of furniture removers unknown to me' to access Myles Place without his personal supervision – or hers. As he was currently staying with the Duchess in her flat at Portman Towers, just a short walk from Pamela's own, this would be somewhat difficult.

No less ingenious was the manner in which Sir Arthur bargained with their forlorn mascots, 'Bear' and 'Horseshoe'. While he said he was prepared to bring the latter round to South Street in person at a convenient time, he could not – as Laura had advised him – give up his 'mascot ... [of] more than fifty years'. 'This may seem ridiculous,' he went on, 'but during the fortnight I was ill here at the end of last month while desperately trying to finish my book, his presence helped to give me the courage I needed to go on.' In a further attempt to retain an option on Pamela, he sent her their usual tickets for Lord's but ended up going along to the pavilion all alone.

This unwonted isolation was exacerbated by Sir Arthur's simultaneous difficulties with Duchess Laura. Whether they were both staying at Myles Place or at one of the Duchess's own properties in London or Buckinghamshire, the besieged pair found innumerable ways to be at loggerheads, and not only about the merits and demerits of cricket.

One blazing July day, Laura complained that her guest had said 'stupid and hurting things' to her as they reviewed her share portfolio. While this may have, in part, been due to her considerable fortune – the words that had caused particular offence were, 'What use am I to you?' – it is clear that the Duchess was somewhat erratic in the management of her personal finances. To the historian's undisguised horror, he came to realise that the fiasco with Coutts had not been an aberration: a huge amount of her inherited wealth had been squandered in a series of misjudged investments and undertakings. As if to soothe Pamela's jealousy with this information, Sir Arthur explained, in another letter, that his new love was not as wealthy as she – and by implication, he – had imagined: she could not, for instance, afford to heat her swimming pool.

Shortly afterwards, on 8 July, he apologised to Duchess Laura for 'humiliating' her, and by the start of August, she was complaining that 'even Russy's bark' seemed to annoy him. Although she may have been troubled by Pamela's 'killing looks' when the latter came, with her daughter and son-in-law, on Sunday, 20 July to arrange the final collection of her goods from Myles Place, it was increasingly clear that the much-anticipated marriage was not going to happen.

Sir Arthur's obvious difficulty was how best to explain to both Anne and Pamela that this, after all, was to be the outcome of his endeavours. On his first telling his ex-wife about his latest marriage plans, she had apparently shown 'understanding and sympathy', only remarking that since their 'minds were made up' it would be best to get the wedding over with 'as soon as possible'. Now that those schemes seemed doomed, the historian was forced to invent a variety of reasons for returning to his former pastures. Alleging that Duchess Laura was physically unwell and that – not mentioning the sheer terror of being a passenger in her car – the 'long drives to Salisbury were too exhausting' for her, he now asked, on his fiancée's behalf, if Anne would be 'prepared to take me next time'?

'I would be very grateful if you would,' he wrote to her on 27 July, 'for I don't like to leave the house empty for more than a fortnight and I have so much to do once my book is finished.' As a final incentive, he wrote that he would 'love a couple or three days in the garden' with her and Pussums. This creature had, he added significantly, recently broken into his housekeeper's cupboard and helped itself to 'three basins of fish'.

What Sir Arthur could not tell his former loves was that the real source of his trouble with Duchess Laura concerned his pressure in the bedroom. Having so far failed to entice her to sleep with him, the historian made a final, desperate effort to consummate their relationship in the aftermath of the return of all the Street sideboards and dressers. For only two weeks after Pamela's brief return to Myles Place – a scene she thought worthy of a Harold Pinter play – the Duchess wrote Sir Arthur a long letter about his amatory advances. 'I could never marry you,' she wrote on 2 August, 'for alas sex is always on your mind.'

Even with her considerable experience of men, she could not fathom his 'constant worry of … wanting to be a young & virulent [*sic*] man'. Such behaviour had made her 'horribly unhappy'.

'I only too well know,' she went on, 'that I have shown it, & being frightened to just put my arms round you in a natural way without you wanting what I don't want … Surely we can remain more than friends?' she implored, before continuing: 'As for all the ridiculous things you said about making a fool of yourself – it's just rubbish.' Everyone would soon forget all about it, she reassured him. 'The dogs, Pussums and ourselves would go back to feeling relaxed & not under threat of change.'

Predictably, these words of wisdom did not deter Sir Arthur. His latest muse was heard to complain to a friend that, in spite of her strictures, he was 'always trying to come into her room', and on one occasion during this fraught period he even embarrassed her by falling to his knees and trying to put his arms around her – he said that 'if she rejected him, he'd die and that all his worldly goods were hers'.

A few days after this scene, the historian tried another tack: he told her that he was going to be less 'selfish' now that his book was completed:

For the sadness of the last week or so has made me realise two things: that to love you is its own reward and something I can no more help doing than breathing, and that it is for you to choose how much or how little of that love you need, for it is all yours to draw on whenever you have need of it, and the greatest privilege and honour I could have is to be your knight and serve you, as you wish and not as I wish, for to ask or even want more than that would be loving myself, not you.

To show what a new man he was, Sir Arthur proceeded to explain that he had arranged for his builder, Mr Robson, to deliver her a special birthday present on 10 August – a life-size bust of himself, along with a selection of antique furniture in which to store his papers.

'The ... ornate Empire side-table,' he scrawled in his letter, 'would I think look well in the entrance hall ... on the right of the door ... with the Georgian Secretaire Bookcase, if you approve, on the sitting room wall on the right of the door as you enter it, and the Regency Cabinet with the twelve drawers in the passage immediately beyond the sitting room door.'

As well as accepting these gifts, he wanted her to accompany him to a whole host of important-sounding functions that autumn: the Vintners' 'Swan Feast' in London; a judges' service at Winchester Cathedral, as well as the annual RAF Benevolent Fund concert to which he usually took Anne. In a slightly later letter, he compared himself to Doubting Thomas, swearing that he would never write to her again if she had really ceased to love him. Once again, the historian's blandishments struck home: during the penultimate weekend of August, he was permitted to creep into the Duchess's suite at Gellibrands and partake in his favourite non-professional activity.

Time, however, had done its work.

'What you took for the weakness of old age,' he wrote shortly after this disaster, 'was merely the utter exhaustion of trying to do the all but impossible' – that is, to complete his book in time for the Christmas sales.

'I can't expect you to realise this,' he went on, 'how could you without knowing what I had to do technically to achieve it?'

Added to the stresses of *The Elizabethan Deliverance*, he said that he was also mentally and physically fatigued by an oration on the prayer book which he was preparing to deliver in Salisbury Cathedral.

'I can only promise,' he went on, 'that I never will again [attempt sexual intercourse] unless you both tell me you want me to and I know that I can, as in the natural course of our living together it would happen inevitably if you ever wanted it.' He told her that 'however seldom it happens', sex '*is* something that seals and consecrates ... love'. Similarly, he would later agree with her that the 'male attitude about the act of sex as giving a man a sense of superiority and triumph' was wrong. 'It seems,' he wrote, '... disgusting and unnatural ...'

The historian's desperation for sympathy and understanding was almost palpable. 'I ... don't ... want to be looked after,' he went on in his apology letter, 'grateful as I am to those who have tried to do so. I want to love and be loved.' In a slightly later letter he promised that, if there was ever a next time, he would give her 'wonderful ... dear gift' his 'whole-hearted courtesy, total attention and devotion'.

But, as summer gave in to autumn, it became clear that 'looking after' was exactly what Sir Arthur required. To the amusement of the gossip columnists, the historian was forced to announce at the start of September that he was unable to fulfil his upcoming public engagements on account of the resurgence of his old back complaint. Prone on a little camp bed he had bought specially, he became dependent on the ministrations of 'matron' – as he now called the Duchess – just as he had been on Pamela almost a decade previously. There was, however, an additional variation to his treatment. His new carer insisted on using her limited medical experience – she had been a nurse during the war – to administer a daily injection of morphine.

'I ... could not help wondering,' wrote Sir Arthur's former secretary when she heard of these bizarre developments from Alwynne, 'whether she used aphrodisiacs.'

The jabs were not to be scaled down until the end of the month, when Sir Arthur's horrified local GP, Dr Collings, told him that the dosages were potentially life-threatening. Ever distrustful of conventional medicine, he had only sought this second opinion after collapsing in the middle of his oration in Salisbury Cathedral on 28 September – a shock outdone by his insistence on climbing back into the pulpit to complete his address.

Battered, bruised and broken, Sir Arthur now sought to return to Pamela. This was, at least in part, on account of his continued feelings of affection towards his former secretary.

'Dear Pammy,' he wrote just a few days after the mishap in the cathedral, 'if by any chance you're free on Thursday evening ... would you let me take you out for dinner, which I should dearly love to do?'

But there was a good deal of deception in his letters that autumn too. Most notably, he told Pamela that he had 'always known' that he would not marry the Duchess – even at the time of the announcement of their engagement in *The Times*. He told her that happiness had been 'a rather scarce commodity' in his life of late and implied that it was in her power alone to put an end to this sorry situation. It was as though the events of the past five months had never been: he even sent her a list of all the payments he had made to her during the previous tax year – some £300 – for such tasks as photocopying and typing, as if to suggest his unerring loyalty (Pamela, however, pointed out that he had failed to add up his own figures correctly). After weeks of similar lobbying, he persuaded her on Monday, 20 October to join him for dinner at 'our little place' – the Bistingo in Shepherd's Market. The romance had come full circle.

Pamela, however, remained cautious. While she was delighted to hear such pieces of news as the Queen's acceptance of his dedication of *The Elizabethan Deliverance* – 'It was a complete surprise to me,' gushed the author, 'as I had only posted an uncorrected proof copy on to Balmoral on Friday [requesting a reply before the text was sent to the printers three days later]' – Pamela saw no purpose in their getting back together.

'I cannot, *cannot*, *cannot* and *will not* be hurt again!' she wrote shortly after this latest olive branch. What particularly hurt, she said, was the feeling that she had been 'upstaged by a particular kind of Duchess' when she was herself 'as good as any Duchess – and sometimes better!'

'You seem to live,' she wrote in the same letter, 'such a strange, secretive, unconventional, hurting-to-others life, though cloaked by strangely conventional surroundings.'

Of scarcely less pain, she went on, was having to put up with all their mutual friends offering her gratuitous advice about how she should respond to Sir Arthur's infidelities, such as Christina Foyle's aside that she should never see him again – 'Is he a snob?' she had asked incredulously – and the comment of the veteran publisher Jamie Hamish Hamilton that the historian 'must have gone senile'.

'I can just hear you saying to yourself,' Pamela continued, '"silly, proud, self-righteous little so-and-so". But there it is. That's me and that, it would seem, is all I've got to fall back on (or anyone has) in the end.'

While she was ultimately willing to return to their old haunt for their reunion dinner, she was not going to be taken in by any more half-baked schemes – either their coffee-table book, or any of the other 'literary projects' which he was constantly dangling before her. Nor did she like his plan for her pregnant daughter to become the assistant secretary of his gentlemen's dining club; another one of Sir Arthur's transparently self-serving ideas. In the aftermath of their get-together, she told him it had been a 'mistake' to revisit the past, and the meal had, predictably, been overshadowed by rows – at one stage he had indelicately told her that Anne thought him 'mad' to see her again.

'Whatever happens,' wrote Pamela the following week, 'you really just go your own sweet (??) way regardless, don't you?' She told him that she was not prepared to be his 'sister/mother/secretary/platonic friend' like any of the others. She was going to focus on her writing – that little novel, she reminded him, in which he was to be the archvillain.

––––––––

Pamela was correct to suppose that all was not as it seemed. For one thing, the onslaught of Sir Arthur's latest batch of love letters had been provoked as much by the flight of the Duchess as by any residual feelings he had for herself. That winter Laura had taken herself off on two holidays – to Portugal and Spain – with a retired colonel, Alexander Frederick Farquhar Young, who was also vying for her hand.[1]

'Oh, my darling,' wrote Sir Arthur during this sad time, 'I was thrown into utter despair ... by your telling me ... that there was no longer room for me to share a bit of your London basket ... and that you were contemplating for a second time this winter going abroad for a prolonged jaunt with your sugar-daddy colonel.'

No sooner had she returned from the first of these escapades than the historian was bombarding her with his usual daily letter professing his undying loyalty and affection.

'My dear dear love,' he wrote to her only a week after his dinner with Pamela, 'I had felt earlier I was past being loved, and that I was no use to you ... but I think I do understand you ... little untutored

---

1 Hugo Vickers writes:

Colonel Alexander Frederick Farquhar Young, OBE, TD, DL (1903-89), a bachelor, Chairman of Redland Holdings Ltd, which specialised in roofing tiles, bricks, concrete and stone pipes, sand and gravel, hard stone aggregates and road contracting, later acquiring and merging with many other companies. Their turnover rose to £38 million annually. He lived in a lifeless house in Reigate – surrounded by rhododendrons and where as one joker mused unkindly: 'even the cat was stuffed and in a glass dome.' He liked to take Laura and at other times Loelia Lindsay out to lunch the Ritz, his weekly treat. He had a chauffeur, which appealed to them. Laura was consistently rude to him, which he appeared to savour.

... genius that you are, so like that little girl in the photograph in your book; and it's because I understand you and what you are that I love you so much and ... want so much to give you happiness.'

By the end of November this second string was proving more responsive to his tune: he wrote happily to the Duchess of the 'glorious' consummation of their mutual attraction during another brief stay at Gellibrands. For a few weeks the diplomatic revolution of the autumn appeared to have been reversed.

Yet, once again, events were moving too quickly for the historian to control. Having indicated the revival of his 'friendship' with Pamela to his neighbour in Salisbury, John Cordle, the pair had been invited for his annual pre-Christmas party in the Close. Awkwardly for Sir Arthur he had, just then, promised to spend much of the festive period with Duchess Laura; a plan which inevitably coincided with another demand from Pamela for him to cease all communication.

'Why, why, why,' she wrote shortly before travelling down to Salisbury to see some old friends, 'did you keep coming here with roses while she was away ... I suppose it is a sort of compulsion which makes you ... some kind of "woman-aholic".'

To avoid the inevitable storm, Sir Arthur resorted to a cunning plan. The first part of this stratagem was to tell the Cordles that he had only returned to the Duchess because Pamela had refused to marry him – an untruth that sent his former secretary into a further fit of anger when she found out from Cordle himself shortly afterwards. Sir Arthur then tried a little flattery, leaving a note at Pamela's hotel to say that, while he wished to abide by her latest strictures, he felt compelled to tell her that his old friend, the broadcaster Alvar

Lidell, had just made a recording of one of her biographies: either *My Father* or *Portrait of a Historian*.

'Whichever it is,' the subject of the latter of these books wrote, 'a work by one of the most perfect writers of English prose has been recorded for posterity by the most beautiful speaking voice in England.'

Returning immediately to Myles Place, he then telephoned the Cordles to say that, due to his backache, he would only be able to stay for long enough to read aloud a few pages of *The Elizabethan Deliverance*, in accordance with his hosts' wishes. The result was that, by a remarkable juggling act, the historian was able to arrive and depart from the party without ever having to breathe a word to Pamela – and yet also to find time to ingratiate himself with one Lady Burford, who insisted on driving him home; a distance of some two hundred yards. 'Simply another instance,' wrote the virago after this latest plot twist, 'of his astonishing ability to rake in the females when approaching 82.'

The next day Pamela marched up the driveway of Myles Place – ostensibly to deliver a silk tie she had bought as his Christmas gift – but found that 'the reputed invalid had flown'.

Having recently heard from Alwynne that the historian had taken up again with the Duchess, it was not difficult to establish his whereabouts. But, once again, Sir Arthur was able to dodge his private difficulties with a truly Napoleonic feint. For, just as Pamela wrote berating him for his elaborate pretences in Salisbury, he explained how he had – the day before Christmas Eve – travelled up to London in order to sign copies of his new book, only to fall into a snowdrift while crossing Green Park on the way home from his publishers.

'Without knowing that I had done so until a further X-ray,' he wrote, 'as a result of the extreme pain I've been in ever since, [I have now learnt that I have] fractured one of my vertebrae.'

Pleadingly he went on to suggest that he had passed the remainder of the holiday recuperating in his lonely four-poster – another exaggeration that Pamela was quick to check up on. Her investigations revealed that the historian had been seen cavorting once again with the Cordles, this time at their New Year's Eve party.

When Pamela finally phoned up Anne to ask how best to give Sir Arthur his tie, the older lady suggested, with studied calmness, that she leave it for him at the offices of Messrs Collins. The veteran added, without any hint of censure or approbation, that she had just deposited her ex-husband at the Duchess's London abode.

What neither of these women could have guessed was that Sir Arthur's Christmas with Laura was anything but restful. Even before Pamela had arrived in Salisbury to interrupt their 'love in', the Duchess had come to the same realisation as so many of her predecessors.

'You made me very unhappy at Myles Place,' she wrote on 6 December, 'I don't think you meant to – it was done more by habit than intent but no man but you has made me feel unwanted.'

She complained that he 'only had eyes for Pussums', and that her role had been confined to 'chauffeur & possibly to cook a steak in that cold comfort kitchen – not really a role that's made for me'. And for all his protestations of love and devotion, she spoke of an oppressive form of neglect. 'You call me your Treasure,' she wrote, '[but] that wasn't the way to treasure a Treasure? I can cook, clean & mend but I couldn't, and never have played Cinderella – unless I was certain my Prince was there – or would appear!'

Just like Anne and Alwynne before her, she also observed that she had come and gone from the property without him even noticing.

'I am used to being alone,' she ended, 'but it was worse to be cold & unhappy in your house of locks & bolts, no wonder I fled next door one evening – for even when I called – you were too engrossed to notice.'

It is not clear which of Sir Arthur's neighbours his guest had fled to that evening, but Duchess Laura was certainly not at the Cordles' party attended by Pamela later that month. In all likelihood she did not return to Myles Place after driving Sir Arthur back to London in early December. Instead, Sir Arthur was ferried between London and the Cathedral Close by Anne, who dropped her ex-husband at Portman Towers shortly before he slipped and fractured his vertebra: only the day before the accident, he had been seen enjoying a performance of Gilbert and Sullivan's two-act comic opera, *The Sorcerer*, with his latest companion at the Savoy Theatre.

The injury had hardly proved a happy start to their festivities, and the letters he and Laura exchanged over the coming week – often written while only a few metres from one another – suggests something of a nadir.

'Last night,' wrote the historian in one letter, 'after I had crept into your bed, longing to be with you … you had turned your back on me and for ten minutes or more were smoking and seeming deliberately to ignore me.'

As the Duchess began to see the advantages of a life free from Sir Arthur, the latter only became angrier and more possessive.

'I understand,' she complained shortly after Christmas, 'how you were able to lock up poor Jimmy if he wandered from your sight.' She told him that, although she was 'hard to frighten', she was always 'shocked by temper' and would only forgive him for the way he had spoken to her in one particular row, on Boxing Day, if he promised 'not to repeat that kind of behaviour' in the future.

Evidently, Sir Arthur's romantic insecurity had been a major factor in these altercations; but, in a strange echo of his disputes with Pamela, his nocturnal wanderings also contributed to their disagreements. The major row to which the Duchess had referred in her letter combined both these facets of Sir Arthur's personality.

'I don't want to excuse myself,' he wrote in response, 'but I really didn't know what I was doing.'

Having apparently spilled some ointment onto his night clothes at 5am, he explained how he had 'used up all the paper in that little hot lavatory trying to clean my pyjamas and then fainted on the floor with exhaustion'.

Matters had only worsened later in the day when he had struggled to come to terms with his hostess's plan to leave him alone in the flat while she went to see a friend.

'I was really in a kind of delirious dream,' he continued, 'with the sudden impulse to get up, dress, start tidying my room and packing my belongings, so that when you returned I could offer to be gone and leave you free of me.' He was particularly sorry for saying he would return the designer leather suitcase that she had bought him for Christmas; a rather more generous – and appropriate – gift than the tarnished medallion of Edward VII that had been his own offering.

Additional angst was caused by Laura's resumed matronly functions.

'The injection which you gave me,' continued the historian in his letter, 'so as not to upset my stomach went instead straight to my brain.' He told her that he did not blame her for this, 'having, in my weakness and love for you, allowed you and almost encouraged you to do so'. But he was now resolved to place his medical care in the hands of his latest 'quack' – one Dr Tigger – and, as a backup, the kindly GP who had already warned him against any more morphine injections, Dr Collings. What made this latter gentleman superior to most of his confreres was that – 'though not a research pioneer and genius like Dr Tigger' – he read Latin poetry at home with his Wykehamist son, and also showed close attention to 'the idiosyncrasies of medical experience … [as well as of his] patients'.

'[He] has developed greatly as a doctor,' he continued approvingly, 'studying his patient's personalities.'

Sir Arthur's only other balm that Christmas was the release of his book. Yet even this was bittersweet. While the responses both in the press and his daily postbag were largely favourable – he boasted to all of his lady friends of letters from Harold Macmillan and Harold Wilson, as well as a host of fellow historians, including A. L. Rowse and A. G. Dickens – it was not long before Sir Arthur was locked in another major row with his publishers.

On top of complaining to Mr House that not enough was being done to promote his latest publication, he alleged that the firm had reneged on a verbal promise to pay him, in addition to the emoluments for *The Elizabethan Deliverance*, an annual advance for the royalties of the many books that he was yet to write – or even agree on – with them. The result was, as he explained to the Duchess, that he now faced a 'crisis over my entire future work', and he waxed indignant about the 'incredible stupidity and meanness' that had led to this crushing disappointment.

By the new year, Sir Arthur's life was in as much turmoil as ever. Harassed by his various personal and professional anxieties, he told Laura that he was going to turn his attentions to writing three new histories of England simultaneously, with or without the backing of his current publisher – a single volume account, another in three volumes and a further instalment to complete the eight-volume series that he had set himself to in the 1950s. Despite proudly explaining that he intended to dedicate these works to her, his muse only wrote back to say that such a medley might prove 'a bit of a tangle to read through'.

Hardly less effective were Sir Arthur's desperate attempts to win back Pamela. In a vast letter chronicling the ups and downs of their relationship, the historian said that he had broken his 'rule never to speak to anyone else about anyone I had ever loved' in order to put John Cordle straight about the impossibility of their ever marrying. While he was eager to point out that she still, 'deep down', loved him, he explained that their relationship had – so far – failed because of her 'misconceptions' and 'unjust imputations' about his other women. Much of this he attributed to her 'inferiority complex' and her 'inner diffidence', which were themselves said to have resulted from a 'lonely, sensitive childhood and your awareness ... of the disadvantages in which you stood with your companions in the days when your father was having such a hard struggle as a young farmer.' Towards the end of the letter he attempted to appease Pamela by pointing out that he would have actually received 'fewer advantages' had he married either Lorelei or Duchess Laura instead of herself, since she was 'a kind of queen in Salisbury and South Wiltshire'. He hoped that, by putting this all down on paper, he would 'allay ... the ghosts which for so long have harassed and divided us'.

The letter – 'almost a book', as Pamela complained – did not quite have the desired effect.

'We have such totally different views about the past,' she wrote, 'and the rights and wrongs of it that our differences would seem irreconcilable.'

But the damage done by Sir Arthur's latest screed was negligible compared to the next tracer bullet to emerge from Fleet Street.

'Hurry, Hurry,' returned the 'William Hickey' column on 5 February, 'before it's far too late!' With feigned horror, the journalist remarked that everything seemed to have stalled for the 'frisky' historian and his Duchess.

'You will recall,' the piece carried on, 'how these Arthur Negus-style love birds met at Christina Foyle's literary feeding table last spring and announced their nesting intentions in *The Times* not long afterwards. Since then? Scarcely a peep on the subject apart from some distressing tittle-tattle about "cold feet".

'All coy Laura will permit herself,' the writer concluded, 'is "Nothing to say." Bridal nerves perhaps? Or is the whole thing OFF? One thing's for sure, time is running out.'

It was all too much for Pamela.

'Do you not think,' she wrote to Sir Arthur the day after rowing with this latest journalist, 'it would be courteous to issue another statement disentangling yourselves – if you are? – to prevent wretched discards like me from being pestered?'

Death, it now seemed, was all the historian had to look forward to.

3

Sir Arthur's intense sadness at the outset of 1981 was heightened by developments in the outside world. Nearly every letter and newspaper article he wrote during this time made reference to some new manifestation of Britain's decline – from the Brixton riots to the growth of 'trade union-aligned public servants' and the decline of 'honourable conduct and dealing' in society at large. Not even his admiration for the new Conservative prime minister, Margaret Thatcher, was unequivocal, and he would shortly set himself to writing a lengthy memorandum for her on the inadequacies of her monetarist policies. 'It is for Government,' he advised, 'to exercise the right inherent in all sovereign government to create and issue such money as is essential for its needs free of debt-charge, instead of continuing to borrow it at a prohibitive rate of interest through the banking system.'

It was this total dissatisfaction with the world as he found it that made Sir Arthur so obsessed with history in general and Duchess Laura in particular. Throughout their extensive correspondence, he had always been at pains to recall some aspect of her past which chimed with his own passions and experiences. In one letter he had speculated that she might have been present – in her capacity as the Countess of Dudley – at a speech he had given to the Birmingham business elite in the 1940s, while another of his scribbled notes included a stanza he had allegedly composed, decades previously, in the vicinity of one of her many former residences, Stanway House in Gloucestershire:

> *If I had pictures in my heart,*
> *I would engrave this lovely land,*
> *So in what place my soul was set*
> *The Malvern hills would ever stand*

Yet what Sir Arthur most prized about the Duchess was the opportunity she gave him to take one last, longing look at the vanished world of Edwardian high society. Though born after that watershed – a time when Sir Arthur himself had not yet started at Harrow – she knew all the prominent survivors of the early twentieth century with a familiarity which delighted the historian. While he might have sat on committees with many of these august individuals, or rubbed shoulders with them at parades and palace garden parties, he had only rarely been permitted to see them with their hair down. For Duchess Laura it was quite the reverse.

One of the most remarkable of these encounters had taken place the previous November, during the brief rekindling of their romance. Laura had arranged a lunch party for her old friend Lady Diana Cooper, whose late husband, Duff, had once sat in the Cabinet, as well as on the little stool outside her railway compartment. Now well into her eighties, she looked back without rancour on the past, and had progressed from 'reigning beauty' to acclaimed writer with a felicity to which the younger woman had clearly aspired.

There is only a passing reference to this 'happy lunch' in Sir Arthur's lengthy correspondence with the Duchess: he told her that the entire occasion had left him 'almost incoherent' with joy. But Clio, as the historian might have put it, has never wanted for ready pens. Through the muse's agency a young diarist and biographer named Hugo Vickers made up the quartet. He was to play Pepys to Sir Arthur's King Charles.

Mr Vickers had become close to Duchess Laura at the time of assisting her, at their publisher's behest, with the writing of her memoirs – so bad was her dyslexia that she was known to misspell common names. Since then, the pair had become almost constant companions, with the young author offering her regular advice in her dealings with the unsuspecting Sir Arthur. Upon their first, rather spontaneous, meeting at Gellibrands the previous June, Mr Vickers had taken a warm liking to this 'small, Dickensian figure' who had suddenly come downstairs for tea. 'Yet I felt very ill-read,' he continued, '[for] he can quote at length.'

After finding a mutual interest in the newly published correspondence of Enid Bagnold and the notorious philanderer Frank Harris, the veteran, some weeks later, asked him to undertake the very task that he had, so recently, offered to Pamela – an anthology of his works, *The Age of Wellington*. Owing to the Duchess's implicit trust in her young *consigliere* this was by no means disinterested. 'I felt like an elderly relative,' the youth wrote after the impromptu tea-party, 'whose approval was being sought.'

But Sir Arthur and Mr Vickers were not without a degree of mutual distrust. In several of his love letters to the Duchess the octogenarian referred to the younger man as her 'jester' or 'courtier'. Mr Vickers, meanwhile, could not help regarding the celebrated historian as something of a 'disappointment'. 'Laura … was full of stories,' he wrote after one of their private dinners that summer, 'about how Arthur Bryant's girlfriends were all chasing him & making his life difficult.'

'I keep forgetting,' he wrote a little later, 'that he is a very distinguished writer, a CH and a most successful author. I have seen him in another *rôle*.'

The luncheon with Lady Diana Cooper was the perfect opportunity for Sir Arthur to revert to his preferred guise. After greeting their guest – whom he had never met – with a bow and a wincing smile, he remarked straightaway that he 'thought her trilogy [of memoirs] the most enchanting books of the century'. This perfectly set the scene for the ensuing meal, during which Duchess Laura and her young friend were treated to a series of poignant reminiscences.

'He asked Diana if she had ever seen Queen Victoria,' the latter wrote. 'Oh! Yes, often,' the politician's widow replied, 'I remember that little black lone figure with the parasol.'

Telling her that he too, as a baby at Sandringham, had also laid eyes on the venerated monarch, he invited her to continue with her reverie. She told him that she distinctly remembered sitting on her father's shoulders to watch the 'unending parade of troops' at the celebration of the Diamond Jubilee in 1897. 'There were so many and from so many lands,' she went on, 'that it seemed to me they were all in fancy dress.'

As the Duchess's maid brought in the later courses, the elderly pair passed through the decades.

'Sir Arthur remembered the "last great military pageant",' the diarist continued, 'the funeral of King Edward VII.' Etched in his memory was the image of the new sovereign, George V, riding out from St James' Palace at the front of the procession. 'I can see him now,' the historian went on. 'The crowd began to cheer, but he raised his hand gently. This was not a day for cheering.'

Soon they had reached the 1930s.

'Diana happened to be at Westminster Hall the night the four brothers took up their vigil at the lying-in-state of George V,' wrote Mr Vickers. The mention of Churchill in the same connection was a painful reminder for Sir Arthur that, at that time, he viewed the future war leader as a troublemaker and a warmonger. More to his taste had always been Stanley Baldwin. 'Sir Arthur remembered [him] with deep affection,' continued the observer. 'He said that he didn't "scratch himself", as Diana Mosley wrote.' He claimed instead that his chief 'foible' had been 'that his tongue came out, licked the end of his nose, and went back in.' Fondly he recalled being with him and Queen Mary – George V's formidable consort – and hearing the latter remark: 'Well, this is a pretty kettle of fish, Prime Minister.'

Sir Arthur was in his element. So engrossed was Lady Diana with his conversation that she was provoked to remark, though not especially with her new friend in mind, that she had 'always loved rather unpopular people who others found difficult.' This appears to have roused Duchess Laura from her unwonted silence: she said that she had often been loved by such men – adding swiftly that she particularly had her second husband, Eric Dudley, in mind. But the older lady was not having any of it. 'Oh! darling,' she said with huge delight, 'he proposed to me years before he even met you!'

It was the loss of this kind of society that made Sir Arthur's parting from the Duchess especially difficult. Throughout the early months of the new year he wrote her an unending stream of lamentations and invitations.

'You are for me,' one of these ran, 'the wise and strong helpmate a man ... needs ... [and] also the living embodiment ... of all my romantic dreams and longings – the most beautiful, desirable, adorable, and spiritually and sexually exciting woman or girl I have seen in my whole life.' And, just like with Pamela, he tried to excuse his recent poor behaviour by referring to his hated childhood nanny, Sarah – 'a hysterical, neurotic, uneducated woman ... with a dark sallow face' – who had taken over from her older sister, Emma, when the child was four. 'The difference between the two sisters,' he elucidated, 'was that "Other Nan" was a darling loving creature who always seemed to understand, and Sarah never did, at least not me.'

But it was no use. For the first time since those distressing days in the Royal Mews, the historian was treated exactly as he had treated countless others: as an admirer to be seen only when convenient.

'I know you hate me going away to Spain,' wrote the Duchess shortly before her second holiday in March, '[but] I need it for my health, so don't be stupid & jealous – like you were last summer.'

At his lowest ebb, in the late spring, the historian even tried to surprise his lost love by paying for their own little getaway – to his old failsafe, Madeira. Yet not even this worked: Duchess Laura told him that he could not store his suitcases (packed by Anne) in her spare room in the lead-up to their departure, as she was expecting to see her military friend beforehand. In the wake of the ensuing row, it was decided that the historian's romantic holiday would, once again, have to be postponed indefinitely. His would-be travelling companion made it clear that she was beginning to find him something of a bore.

'You take yourself ... & everything too seriously,' she wrote at the time, 'and forget to laugh.'

The situation was anything but a laughing matter for Sir Arthur. When, shortly after her return from Spain, the historian persuaded the Duchess to let him stay at Portman Towers once again – there was no other way, he said, for him to attend a meeting about a new biography of Lord Alanbrooke for which he had been asked to contribute a foreword and an epilogue – he wrote her his most pleading letter yet. 'Please, my darling,' it ran, 'try to feel, as you must have done, when you wrote on that envelope nearly a year ago – that you felt like Jimmy.' He wanted her to remember that, whatever her feelings, his love and devotion remained unchanged.

> I want you always to feel free [the letter continued], as is your dear terrier-like nature – so that if you want me out of your life, whether for a time or forever you can feel free of me – but that I am, and always shall be, ready to offer you whatever you need of me. And, though I had wondered when you were away whether you ever would want me again, the dear terrier-like look in your eyes yesterday made me feel that you still need, poor thing though it must seem, all the love and devotion that I can offer, and I am so proud and happy to give you. God bless and keep you my dear.

Through such entreaties, Sir Arthur was able, periodically, to entice Duchess Laura to accompany him to public dinners, and even the Harrow School Speech Day and Songs. 'It's so dear – and brave! – of you,' wrote the historian after one of these returns to his alma mater, 'to be prepared to venture yourself among all the Harrow cads again on the day after our outing at the Swan Feast.'

Yet her sense of exasperation with her companion steadily increased. It seemed that whenever their relationship was close to being back 'on', he would push things too far, such as when he proposed bringing her along as his special guest to Lorelei's summer garden party that year.

'She wrote me the sweetest letter when our engagement was announced,' he implored, '... [and] I shall feel very wretched going alone.'

Further upset was caused when, during a brief stay at Gellibrands around the same time, the historian complained that the Duchess's housekeeper had made him feel 'unwelcome' after it was pointed out that he had left a trail of lemon juice all the way up to his bedroom. Yet this only forced his hostess to put the matter straight.

'All I said about the lemon drink didn't come from Jenny,' she wrote, 'they were all my own observation. I would be furious if she made you feel unwelcome, & I can't believe she did, in fact she would like to help you with your bags & packing but you don't want help.'

When the matter provoked another 'sad letter' from the historian, the Duchess wrote again. 'It makes me feel worse than ever writing about the carpets & mess, on the other hand these things are better out in the open, because I can't pretend it doesn't upset me ... I hope you will come & stay again soon & *try* not to *spill* things.'

Another reason why Sir Arthur's relationship with the Duchess continued to flounder was the rapidity with which the historian turned defence into attack. One of many instances of this less chivalrous side of his character was displayed barely twenty-four hours after Sir Arthur had again pledged her his undying fidelity.

'I don't think anyone has ever telephoned me *ever*,' she wrote in confusion from Gellibrands, 'in order to slam down the instrument ... Best forgotten,' she added generously.

There was, however, some logic to these seemingly unpredictable mood swings. They were most pronounced when the Duchess's actions threatened to embarrass Sir Arthur's public persona in some way.

'It's a great feather in my cap,' he wrote to her at the time of the School Songs, 'to be able to show my fellow Harrovians that anything so lovely came out of Eton!'

It seems more than probable that, just like Lorelei's summer party later in the year, the Duchess had openly doubted the wisdom of being seen together while they were, privately, still so divided.

Nor was it much easier for Sir Arthur to enlist his faithful reserve – Pamela. She had already discerned how he ranked his ladies.

'I suppose,' she had written the previous December, 'for you, only Duchesses are eligible for public dinners and Harrow Speech Days.' *Their* event had always been the Hatchards Authors of the Year party, but, once again, Pamela insisted that she was going to be attending in her own capacity as a feme sole.

'Boaz,' she wrote at the same time as accepting a £60 present on her sixtieth birthday in March, 'in the eyes of the world you are still an engaged man, even though I happen to know that Laura is abroad at the moment.'

What she particularly worried about was how their appearance at the party might set tongues wagging again. But there was no escaping Sir Arthur. As soon as she arrived, she was 'accosted' by him and enjoined to take up a position beside him on a nearby sofa. He implored her to forgive him for his various misdeeds and swore, once again, that his heart truly belonged to her.

While Sir Arthur naturally said little of this encounter in his subsequent report to the Duchess, it was equally important for him to conceal from Pamela what transpired following her departure from the 'VIP' couch. As he explained in his account, the vacant place was taken up by an impressive haul of grandees and potential doters.

'[Lady] Elizabeth Longford and A. J. P. Taylor,' wrote Sir Arthur, 'and [then] a whole succession of people ... descended on this decrepit Rip van Winkle ... until at the end I was joined by two of your chief bugbears, Jim Callaghan and Harold Wilson, complete with Mary W[ilson].'

And before the latter of these former prime ministers had declared that he had recently reread all of Sir Arthur's works (including two helpings of *Jimmy*), the trio were interrupted by a 'ravishingly pretty ... though rather intense' young lady who, seizing his hand, knelt at the historian's feet.

'Had I been able to hear a word that she said,' continued Sir Arthur, 'or had the remotest idea who she was or what she wanted – I might have asked her for her name and address in case you had become so committed to one of the Colonels that you wanted me out of your life.'

Notwithstanding these furtive developments, what prevented Pamela from completely extricating herself from Sir Arthur's life was his near total dependence on her for administration. She complained that scarcely a week passed without someone asking her to prompt him about one thing or another. These requests ranged from invitations to lunches with rich Americans to pleas for the historian to sign petitions relating to Britain's historic houses.

'I simply can't keep pace,' Pamela wearily complained that April,

'with all the people who think I am still your A. D. C. or something.'
In another letter she suggested he advertise through the Theological
College for 'the wife of an aspiring cleric' to act as his new factotum.
Unable to resolve the situation in this way, Pamela, for the first time,
now called upon the assistance of Anne. It was through her ministra-
tions that she overcame one of the many small crises of that spring:
the loss of an entire set of bookplates that a terminally-ill 'fan' wanted
Sir Arthur to sign.

'I shall write to Mr Davies,' replied Anne, 'that his bookplates,
regretfully, have got mislaid and suggest he sends a set addressed to
me. I shall then confront Arthur with them.'

It speaks volumes for the state of Sir Arthur's life and affairs that
even Anne was starting to find her ex-husband exasperating. Having
for years been willing to help coordinate his peregrinations – Pamela
once compared her to a mother dropping off her teenage son at
a party – she was increasingly tired and frail. Whether it was Sir
Arthur's excessive use of her telephone or his remonstrations about
various aspects of her housekeeping, hosting him at Sussex Mansions
was becoming something of an imposition.

In April, after seeing the announcement in *The Times*, she wrote
to Pamela congratulating her on the birth of her grandson, Rupert,
adding almost as an afterthought that Sir Arthur was furious with her
over the loss of two files of notes. 'I found both,' she continued, 'in
the first place I looked which was underneath his bed. He had looked
in the bed but not under. I think I am under suspicion for having
hidden them.'

In a later letter she described how her ex-husband had torn off his
dress shirt in a rage, accusing her of shrinking it in the wash. 'In my

stupidity,' she wrote, 'I hadn't realised a natural increase in his neck-line was a reasonable answer to the shrinkage in the washing of his shirts that Alwynne and I were accused of.' Enclosed in the envelope was a cheque for £17 to pay for a new one in the correct size. 'If I'm being a crashing bore – which I know I am,' she modestly ended, 'please just tear up the cheque and forget all about it.'

Amid such a characteristically muddled state of affairs, Sir Arthur once again became almost totally dependent on Pamela. Throughout the entirety of 1981 he worked tirelessly to repair the damage caused by the Duchess episode. Following a barrage of letters complimenting her looks, intelligence and – most effectively – writing abilities, he even persuaded her, for the first time since he had asked Alwynne to join them, to attend the Eton vs Harrow cricket match with him that July. Not insignificantly, Pamela's guest room also now came back into play.

'*Dearest Dishy*,' he wrote following one of his many stays, '*Thank you!* Thank you for your dear existence; for the generous hospitality and peace and comfort and temporary freedom from all the incessant calls and demands and interruptions that torment me everywhere else and, most of all, in my impossible home.'

Yet there were signs that the old strains remained.

'It is strange,' he wrote following another visit, 'that two people that have meant and mean so much to one another … can make one another so unhappy and subject one another to such terrible storms.'

The difficulty was that Pamela now had a more legitimate demand on her time and capacities. After becoming a mother, her daugh-ter Miranda had begun to suffer from severe post-natal depression, for which she would be hospitalised in July. Until a full-time nanny could be engaged, it fell to Pamela to look after her beloved grandson,

Rupert, on an almost daily basis. Everything in her life – from her writing to her dinner parties at South Street – was put on hold. So, too, was Sir Arthur.

As with his previous rows with Pamela about Miranda using the flat, this only provoked more resentment; but, on this occasion, Sir Arthur was less explosive in his jealousy. Either mellowed by age, or through sheer lack of understanding, the historian seemed almost to make light of the crisis. When she asked him to refer to her on envelopes as 'Miss Pamela Street' – the name she was now using as a novelist – he wrote back in amusement:

> Miss Street it shall be, and those who, like me, welcome any backward march of time, can only rejoice. But how disturbing to the over-righteous that, at the very moment you have elected to revert to your maiden status, you should be observed in public places pushing a pram containing a brand-new and far from self-effacing infant, so causing the censorious to put two and two, and more than two and two, together!

But Sir Arthur was evidently aware that Pamela's grandmotherly duties also made her more vulnerable than before. No sooner had the baby's paraphernalia been removed from the spare room than he had arranged for his own clutter to be returned. By his own account, he was an 'untidy, troublesome, paper-infested guest', and his resumed nocturnal wanderings only added to the overall sense of frustration.

'My neighbour below,' wrote Pamela long afterwards, 'objected to the *noise* he made, dropping books all over the place at any hour of the day or night.'

Although Sir Arthur tried to dismiss the complaints of this woman – now renamed 'the Suffering Warthog' – as vexatious, Pamela was inclined to take her side in the matter.

'On his bad nights,' she wrote, 'I couldn't sleep and he was constantly in and out of the bathroom pulling the [lavatory] plug until I thought he'd break the works.'

Once, he told her that, in the course of these struggles, he had suffered a heart attack, but Pamela 'persuaded him that he hadn't'. When Sir Arthur wrote instead to the Duchess, outlining all his various problems and disagreements with Pamela, she wrote back sympathetically but also guardedly: 'Some day you had better take me out to dinner again, these working suppers with Pam don't seem to cheer you up much!'

Clearly access to the flat – 'the acme both of beauty and comfort', as he described it – remained of vital importance to the historian.

'You haven't really got anywhere proper to "lay your head",' Pamela rather pityingly wrote, 'almost like the carol.' But with her altered family life, it was now getting harder to accommodate the historian at the drop of a hat. On at least two occasions that year, Pamela complained that he had virtually forced her to have him to stay because both Anne and Laura wanted a break. Ironically, the scholar-gypsy was fast to point out to his hostess that she must not allow her time and energy to be dissipated in grandmotherly duties.

'You must protect yourself,' he wrote after both he and 'Sir Rupert' – as he called her grandson – had enjoyed consecutive stays, 'at all costs from those who, unknowingly, rob you ... [of] that all-important creative work which I am artist enough myself to realise is now what really matters to you.'

Endowed with an innate 'sixth sense', the recipient of this advice was not unaware that Sir Arthur was, simultaneously, also pleading with Duchess Laura to let him back into her life – and guest room. 'Personally,' she wrote after her erratic guest had equivocated over coming to a dinner party she was hosting for the Foyles that June, 'I think the Duchess was at the bottom of it.'

But all was not what it seemed to Pamela. Firstly, the excuse provided by Sir Arthur was, on this occasion, essentially true: he had long promised to have Alwynne for two or three days at the start of June in order to replant the garden at Myles Place. The only details he left out from his explanation was that he was not actually going to be present for most of this time – he had been invited by the former High Sheriff of Hampshire to a party celebrating the lifting of the wreck of the *Mary Rose* – and it was likely that Alwynne would be leaving sooner than he claimed.

'I don't know whether Alwynne will finish her planting by tomorrow,' he confided in the Duchess the Sunday beforehand, 'but even if she does ... I don't think I can get through all I have to do ... so I don't think I shall be able to get up to Pam's dinner party in any case even if it's my only chance, if Alwynne goes, of a cooked dinner.'

The other reason why Pamela's theories were at least partially misconceived was even more important: Duchess Laura was starting to believe that the estranged pair should get back together. Only three days before the dinner party with the Foyles, Sir Arthur had once again called up Laura to find her otherwise engaged – this time she was happily watching *Dallas*; on another occasion she was recovering after 'playing backgammon' until 3am with the Hollywood screenwriter Ivan Moffat. In her subsequent letter to the historian she listed the 'ridiculous, long and utterly boring' things he had said to her while she had been trying to watch her programme.

'Alwynne's bedding out at Myles Place, and all your repetition of bedding down with various women over the years, a long unsatisfactory history – your work having been the only thing that ever counted, saving you from a pretty unhappy life!' She complained that he had become 'angry' when he said he 'need[ed] to be married' – the very thing that Pamela had so desperately wanted.

'You talk again like the very poor,' the Duchess continued haughtily, 'what you mean is you need a cook-housekeeper-secretary: quite a lot of asks, even in days of unemployment. Oh yes – this wonder woman must also drive and be attractive and be able to entertain & be as strong as ten horses!' She could hardly have had another woman in mind.

But Pamela was now busy with her own projects, most especially the novel she had been contemplating ever since the publication of *Portrait of a Historian* two years previously. She hoped that the freer medium would allow her to articulate the thoughts and feelings that had only been implicit in that 'authorised' production. No longer would she be bullied and browbeaten into making changes and revisions: this was to be *her* book to an extent that was virtually impossible in the case of the biography.

And yet Pamela had not reckoned on Sir Arthur's perseverance. Almost as soon as she told him about the novel, he began to interfere. While this was mostly well intended and encouraging, there was inevitably a sense that he was, yet again, 'muscling in' on her affairs. When her publisher suggested that she rethink her working title, *Change of Wife*, Sir Arthur was quick to step in with 'one or two possible suggestions'. He said that thinking up 'poetic or shorthand' titles had always been a great skill of his – a claim somewhat diminished by his recent idea to reissue *English Saga* as *All Our Pomps of Yesterday*. It was only in the lead-up to the book's publication in August that the author plumped for a title that made her purpose clear to the one person who really mattered: *Light of Evening* – a quote from the poem Sir Arthur had, long ago, written for Lorelei.

The parallels between fact and fiction were almost too perfect. Anyone who knew anything of Sir Arthur's private life could not have failed to see the historian's personality mirrored in the character of the philandering portrait-painter Alexander Dolan. Almost all the artistic deviations from truth simply made the story less incredible. Whereas Sir Arthur had made his advances on Pamela after writing a foreword to a book about her father and inviting her for dinner with a former Lord Chief Justice, Dolan meets the vulnerable housewife Sophie Brent in a doctor's waiting room.

'He's my mascot, child,' he says to her young son while brandishing a miniature wooden doll – a clear echo of 'Bear'. 'You can play with him if you like.'

After becoming Dolan's lover, and leaving her dull husband, the heroine of the story gradually discovers all of the artist's other women: a hairless cast-off who lives alone in a cottage near his country house; a disabled wife living in France; a garish American married to one of his 'sitters', and several other ladies whose identities are never fully revealed. The plot carries the reader through Sophie's initial rejection and ultimate acceptance of this extraordinary situation. The novel ends with her being called to the bedside of the dying Dolan. '*I wanted*,' he tells her, making room for her beside him, '*this.*'

It was perhaps on account of the 'happy ending' that Sir Arthur was so positive about the book when he was finally allowed to read the manuscript.

'I have never been left so wanting to know,' he wrote shortly before publication, 'what is in the next chapter since, as a boy of fifteen, in 1914, I read John Buchan's *Thirty-Nine Steps* in monthly instalments in *Blackwood's Magazine*.'

Still more flatteringly, he told her that the novel was on a par with anything by Jane Austen or the Brontë sisters, and would, eventually, be recognised as a classic of 'English civilisation' – so long as it survived.

If a part of him feared that the novel might herald his public unmasking, this was easily outweighed by the effect it had in bringing him back into closer contact with Pamela.

'It doesn't worry me in the least,' he wrote, 'that I should be thought the villain of it!'

Undoubtedly this sentiment was helped by the fact that, aside from a complimentary notice in the *Daily Mail*, the book did not receive excessive publicity: he told her not to worry about the 'shocking reviewing and publishing vacuum of today'. In any case, as he indicated in his earlier letter, he was confident that the story was not 'in the least repetitive of real experience, for it and the characters have a life of their own as all great creative literature has'. This did not, however, prevent him from signing himself off as one 'AD' – the initials of the anti-hero.

By the end of 1981, the problems in Sir Arthur's life appeared to be gradually resolving themselves. He had managed to persuade at least two of his former 'doters', Pamela and Anne, to have him to stay whenever possible, while even the Duchess was beginning to soften in her resistance; the rest of the time the historian was happy being cared for, often by Alwynne, at Myles Place, where he was busy rewriting the history of England. Although he was by now thoroughly out of touch with the younger generation of politicians, he remained a stalwart of his various dining clubs, and continued to display his wry sense of humour whenever opportunity arose. Early the following year he was seen gossiping with the disgraced former minister John Profumo at Grillion's.

'Having read my book [*The Elizabethan Deliverance*],' wrote Sir Arthur in a letter to the Duchess, 'he was avid to know whether that lady was a virgin. I explained that I had never shared her bed and couldn't have known, and even if I had, at my age it wouldn't have proved anything.'

Such candour did not prevent Sir Arthur dreaming of further Arabian Nights. Shortly before Christmas he sent Pamela her usual present along with an advertisement from the *Daily Express* suggestive of what she might like to spend it on – 'French knickers with a matching camisole top, trimmed with Leavers lace.'

'I thought they looked so pretty,' he wrote by way of explanation, 'and the lady depicted in them had the same lovely figure as you, that they looked as though they had been made for you.' It was as if her novel had made him even more brazen in his fantasies. But his former secretary remained quite impervious, writing back:

> I feel that if your readers … were to be informed of your 'other side' maybe it would be the book of the century – or all centuries – although I think it will be that anyway!! But dear Boaz,

I am too old now for French knickers and matching camisoles available in white, black, navy, coffee or *blackcurrant*. I am a rapidly-ageing, staid, conscientious grandmother who is attempting to grow old – albeit swiftly – in a graceful, orderly and organised fashion. I could wish that you yourself led a calmer, less fraught and peripatetic (Adrian [House]'s word) life, and that you were not constantly feeling the need to write ladies cheques with no appreciable return. I do say a very big THANK YOU, though, Boaz, for it will certainly be a boost to my pre-Christmas dwindling bank balance.

It was at precisely this juncture that Sir Arthur faced two further reversals. The first was to do with Duchess Laura's London flat. Following her complaints about the lemon juice and a variety of other mishaps with ink bottles and wicker chairs, Sir Arthur had insisted on giving her a cheque for £1,000 – at least ten times the bounty he had, usually unsuccessfully, tried to persuade Pamela to accept after their own domestic rows. But rather than ushering in a new period of quasi-connubial bliss, Laura simply used this money to knock down the walls of her spare room, making any future stays by the historian virtually impossible.

'I took the thousand pounds,' she explained disarmingly, 'because it is nothing, alas, compared to the damage to chairs and above all carpets ... I can't think of all the different things you spill but they *all* make indelible marks.'

And no sooner had the Duchess's builders set to work tearing down those walls, than another one unexpectedly came crashing down. Early in the new year, Pamela wrote to him with news of her old friend Sybil Scott, who was recovering from a minor operation.

'What she also told me,' added Pamela rather innocently, 'was that tomorrow night … there is a thing on television called "Thames Valley Police", in which she is sure she has seen you in some pre-publicity flash. I suppose it is connected with that thing you told me about when you first stayed with Laura?'

The reminder of that mad Whitsun night at Gellibrands struck him like a thunderbolt. For the first time since the BBC had aired a fly-on-the-wall documentary about King Juan Carlos of Spain, Sir Arthur took Anne's small black-and-white television into his bedroom, where he watched with growing horror as his personal life was exposed as never before. Suddenly the begging tone of his recent letters to the Duchess would not quite do.

'I want to … be of help to you,' one of these had ran, 'with [rewriting] *Laughter from a Cloud* … I would suggest calling it "The Beams of Love" or "To Bear the Beams of Love" after Blake's great poem.'

Fuelled by the return of satirical comment in the newspapers, Sir Arthur now wrote to his lost Duchess in a rather different vein.

'The very real and certain threat to my work … which I foresaw but failed to prevent has now happened,' he complained. No longer could he expect a fair hearing for his forthcoming books – 'something on which the whole future of England may depend' – since the press 'reptiles' had now written him off as 'a silly old "has been" making a fool of himself over a very fascinating and publicity-attractive lady'. In his anguish he was even 'curt' on the phone with the Duchess, who was left in no doubt that she was, to a large degree, responsible for this 'tragedy'.

Like Sisyphus, the historian was right back where he started; only older and weaker than ever before.

4

For some days after the broadcast, Sir Arthur neither toiled nor span. Alone, but for the silent carousel of Anne and Alwynne – 'the changing of the guard', as he called it – in a house overrun with cats, the historian wondered if he would even finish the one great task that still lay before him: a new history of England. It was to be his last battle.

The composition of this work had always been slightly confusing, even to himself. In an eighteen-page memorandum – 'On suggested ways to restore and develop a Literary Property' – written for his publishers towards the end of 1981, Sir Arthur valiantly attempted to explain how he intended to write a new book entitled *Set in a Silver Sea*, which would, if he could also rework several of his previous publications, complete the eight-volume history that he had started in the 1950s.

'Only with the completion last year of *The Elizabethan Deliverance*,' he elucidated, 'did I realise that I had only now to write one more volume ... to possess a complete and continuous eight-volume *Story of England* from B.C. to 1940.'

As an additional labour – which he described in a letter to the Duchess as a 'kind of herald and advertisement for my fuller history' – he also intended to put together a condensed version of his narrative, entitled *The Spirit of England*, to be brought out a year before the longer book.

Sir Arthur's publishers were not alone in questioning the wisdom of these herculean undertakings.

'Darling One,' wrote the Duchess from Gellibrands, 'I read your long memorandum to Collins with great interest & a certain sinking of my heart – what you intend to do is too much – no wonder you are a "Dormouse" except when writing!'

With as much pity and understanding as ever, she consoled him that at least the past was a happier place than the present.

'I'm always so glad,' she continued, 'that my dogs don't read news-papers or take any interest in television, in this way they remain care-free & in Russy's case Caddish, perhaps he went to Harrow in another world?'

Not even the recent wedding of Prince Charles and Lady Diana Spencer filled her with much hope – 'I shall be very happy when it's all over without some ghastly tragedy,' she wrote – while simmer-ing industrial tensions provoked her to declare that the government should deport all trade unionists 'to Moscow where they belong'.

Sir Arthur not only reflected these views, he internalised them. To his mind, his final books were both a swansong and a call to arms: a bugle call to awaken the entire nation from the doldrums. Pouring scorn on the supposed inadequacies of modern-day schools and uni-versities, he told his readers that he wanted to leave behind a history of his country for 'more than one generation [that] has grown up without being taught it'. When his publishers, again, implored him to avoid committing himself to any project – or projects – that they could not reasonably underwrite, he turned his guns on them instead.

'He seemed unable,' recalled Pamela long after, 'not to put obstacles in his way and then moan about fighting them.'

The historian told her that he was sickened by the 'conspiracy' against him and recalled with nostalgia the days when the former chairman of the firm, Sir William Collins, had boasted that he sold only three types of book: 'fiction', 'non-fiction' and 'Arthur Bryant'.

'I'm in the same wretched position I've been in for months,' he complained in another letter, 'of having to work at half a dozen things at the same time until I'm almost crying with frustration and no one can help me but myself.'

However much the world had moved on, the historian remained rooted to his past. The writing of his last books even provided him with the ideal excuse to reread his entire *oeuvre*; a task in which he clearly delighted.

'I've never looked at [many of these titles] since writing them forty or fifty years ago,' he wrote to the Duchess, 'and I've been staggered by how good the special passages I shall be using in this new book are ... but then I had genius.'

Nor did Sir Arthur neglect the little memoir of his dog, Jimmy, which had first cemented their bond. 'The most beautifully written book I have ever written or shall write,' he opined.

All day, and often all night, at Myles Place, he worked through the centuries, scissors and paste at the ready, regardless of the decay and chaos with which he was increasingly surrounded.

'The small hours of the night in which I love to write,' he wrote to Laura in the midst of his labours, 'are now squeezed like my hours of sleep, between struggling with sheets of paper, strewn with poor dying Pussums all over the bed, sometimes with bits of the *History* and at others with those interminable financial arguments and explanations I'm trying to make [for the Prime Minister].'

While she told him that she would gladly listen to any of his writings over the telephone, she was by no means uncritical. *'No more memoranda,'* she had written across the top of one of her recent letters.

Even the historian's soliloquies could sometimes get her down. 'I do think your St Thomas Becket chapter *is* a bit long,' she wrote a little later, 'before his poor "brains are scattered on the pavement".'

In a lighter moment she suggested they go to a topical new musical; one which Laura had recently been to see a portion of with her military friend – 'he had had enough' by the interval. 'You would be fascinated by "Cats",' she wrote, '... feline girls each dressed as a different cat who stroke, stare & ruffle the hair of the spectators ... I'm afraid your Pussums couldn't compete!'

While the Duchess offered escapism, Pamela continued to provide more material advantages for the historian. Almost every week during his busy summer in 1982, he invited himself to stay at her flat, where she was enjoined to type, wash and clean for him – cutting his hair and fingernails remained a particularly important undertaking. He told her, both subtly and through more direct means, that he simply could not manage without her and became almost delirious in his thanks for her assistance.

When he was locked in his battle with Collins over the release of *The Spirit of England*, he claimed that only through her support had he summoned the courage to slay the dragon.

'The peace and benison of the shelter you gave me,' he wrote after persuading the editorial directors to go ahead, 'gave me a victory ... And my eyes are full of tears of gratitude when I think of what has so suddenly and unexpectedly happened because of your goodness.'

Yet Sir Arthur continued to play a double game. At the same time as prostrating himself to Pamela, he told the Duchess that no one could 'hold a candle' to her, and endlessly pined for her lost love. In the same week as celebrating his eighty-third birthday at South Street, he wrote to tell her that their bond was 'like my love for Jimmy and Jimmy's for me'. 'You, my darling,' he continued, 'were my last romance in life' and he rhapsodised that he would never cease to love her, nor forget 'that lightning moment of mutual recognition in the Crystal Room which was not an illusion but something that mattered very much to both of us'.

At one point that spring, the historian attempted to bring his two most important 'doters' together, as he had always hoped. When the Duchess tired of his late-night monologues on the Black Death and the Hundred Years War, he suggested that she read Pamela's book on her father instead. As a means of relieving tensions, it was another masterstroke.

'I was much moved,' wrote the Duchess, 'and without knowing her I now feel I understand and also feel fond of her. You and Bear have taken the place of her father – she depends on and loves you – as I do. I really would like to meet her, strangely we have many things in common, although she is more practical than I ever could be.'

He had already sent her a copy of *Portrait of a Historian*, though in that case the effect had not been quite so good. 'You clearly wrote much of it yourself?' this latest reader discerned.

Pamela found herself, once again, reluctantly brought into these intrigues. With the Duchess's permission, Sir Arthur sent her a copy of the letter comparing himself with her father. This time, however, the historian overreached himself.

'In the *beginning* I might have thought so,' added Pamela in one of her indignant footnotes, 'not after I got to know A. B. He was so *very* different from dear old Daddy!'

And though she does not appear to have responded either to this missive or to a slightly more tactful one later sent by the Duchess herself, Pamela was constantly reminded that summer of the contrasts between the two most important men in her life. Whereas her father had been endowed with a natural empathy for other people, Sir Arthur seemed unable to comprehend that his many demands for favours could be intensely inconvenient and harassing. This had been particularly clear with regard to his repeated requests to stay at South Street – he could never understand why his hostess's daughter and grandson seemed to get preferential treatment. No less striking was the difference between a man who had prided himself on never telling a lie, and one who seemed hardly able to pass a day without trying to pull the wool over somebody's eyes.

'Nora Tarlo [aka 'the Wife of Bath' or 'the Suffering Warthog'] said she saw you in [the upmarket grocery shop] Hannell's yesterday,' wrote Pamela on 11 May. 'I didn't see how she could have as I thought you were home ....?'

Duchess Laura, too, was aware that Sir Arthur's accounts of his movements did not always correspond to reality. On one occasion during these months, he told her that he was spending the evening with his friends at Grillion's – 'A dozen prigs and bores (generally) whispering to their next-door neighbours over a bad dinner in a dingy room,' as Benjamin Disraeli described its nineteenth-century incarnation – but was spotted instead at the Hatchards Authors of the Year party at New Zealand House with his former secretary.

While Laura was annoyed to hear of this from her source, Hugo Vickers, she was by nature averse to confrontation, and was, in any case, now enjoying a secret dalliance of her own with a Swiss yachtsman named Hans de Meiss-Teuffen. Like their contemporary and mutual friend Patrick Leigh Fermor, this romantic adventurer had spent his long life traversing the globe, seducing beautiful women and inventing improbable stories of derring-do. In his 1953 memoir, *Wanderlust*, he explained how he had once skippered a yacht across the Aegean, while strumming, naked, on a mandolin. Unbeknown to Sir Arthur, this rival was now writing impassioned letters to their mutual love.

'Très chère,' one of these epistles ran, 'I had been packed away like a petrified piece of wood and [then] you ... came along, touched the petrified piece and it began to green again.' He told her that her 'current' had pushed his 'volt metre needle' to its very limit. 'Why, even now when only writing about it, the ... the ... well – let's call it the "needle" is oh oh! quite jumping and jumpy!'

One wonders what Sir Arthur would have made of these *belles-lettres*. Hans's considered view was that Colonel Young, at any rate, would not have been amused. 'What would be the Colonel's reaction (£&!!!),' he wrote, 'about Laura taking up with a b----y foreigner!'

But the Duchess was careful to keep Sir Arthur in the dark about these undercover activities. She knew enough of what he once called, in a letter to Alwynne, his 'Othello-like jealousy' never to disclose the particulars of what precisely she did when he was not at her side. The one occasion when, clasping a bunch of flowers, he had chanced to see her military companion emerging triumphant from her flat, there seemed no way to avoid a row other than to lock herself within. It was as if she had knowledge that, years previously, her visitor had accused his second wife of conducting an affair with a gardener at Smedmore House – only now the historian's imagination had every reason to run rampant.

For Hans's part, he was genuinely excited to be sharing the Duchess with Sir Arthur. A great history buff himself – 'Not for nothing did I show you our family tree which begins in 1225,' he wrote in one letter – he wanted to enlist the famous author's help with a novel he was writing, apparently on the subject of the intellectual grandfather of Nazism.

'PLEASE ask him if: a). does he know the book by Houston Stewart Chamberlain, *The [Foundations of the] Nineteenth Century*?' he wrote with reference to the notorious English 'philosopher' who had denied that Jesus was Jewish, 'and b). is there a book <u>ABOUT</u> Houston Stewart Chamberlain? ... PLEASE send me the title etc – or even better ask a bookshop to send it to me!'

Duchess Laura was wise to say nothing of either Hans or the abominable Stewart Chamberlain to Sir Arthur. She knew enough about him to tread carefully in matters to do with Germany between 1933 and 1945; and besides, she had no desire to cause further upset on account of her private affairs. Any pangs of conscience would have been soothed by the knowledge that the historian was simultaneously renewing his own ties with his other *amores*, notably Alwynne, who had issued an 'interdict' shortly after her first meeting with the Duchess.

'I cannot give you the *whole* of my life and capacity for loving,' pleaded Sir Arthur in a familiar screed, '[but] *I could no longer cease to* love, and love deeply and permanently, those I had been in love with in the past, including, of course, most of all Monny [Abel Smith], you and Anne.'

By such contortions, it was possible for the pair to return to something of an even keel during the months when the Duchess's attentions were more focused on her sailor-love.

Only a short time after the close of that adventure, in the summer of 1983, Alwynne sent Sir Arthur several confidence-boosting letters which he proudly forwarded to Laura, whose feelings he evidently hoped to trammel along similar lines. One of these missives – to 'the great big wonderful you' – heaped praise on his latest works.

'Goodness what a stupendous brain that shiny pate of yours conceals,' she wrote. 'You are a brilliant historian who can make history "tick" for the masses … Waggy wags from Fen [her dog], huggy hugs from "moi".'

In a sense, Sir Arthur had never been happier. While he may have been tired, alone, forgotten and often extremely unwell, he was never idle.

'I have a notion,' wrote the Duchess at one stage in their relentless discourse, 'that you, my darling, having worked so hard all your life, rather like the spartan life? Am I right? Or is it just you've been unlucky with servants?'

When rows over flats and dreary telephone monologues threatened to shatter their new-found tranquillity, Sir Arthur was just as capable as ever of fighting his corner, particularly with regard to the Duchess's ever-faithful maid.

'Jenny made no attempt to help me,' he complained in July 1983, after sinking up to his knees in raw sewage that had been spread over a neighbouring field: '[and she] made it only too plain, as she did last summer, that I was a nuisance and not wanted.'

As a means of returning to Pamela he, in the same month, revealed to her, for the first time, the full extent of his wealth – or at least that he owned a share portfolio worth some £250,000 – and began making extravagant offers of financial assistance. While his former secretary may have felt these offers to be disingenuous, as well as self-serving, the sums advanced to the Duchess would suggest that he was less thrifty than in days of yore: by the middle of the year, the historian claimed that he had given her some £4,000 in gifts since their fairy-tale meeting in the Crystal Room.

There was, however, another woman to whom Sir Arthur began to feel himself indebted. Margaret Thatcher may not have shared his Dis-raelian Conservativism, but her premiership marked the revival in 'Vic-torian values' that he had, for so long, championed – at least in print. As the hangover of the 'Winter of Discontent' gave way to the triumphs of the Falklands War in the spring of 1982, Sir Arthur was among the first newspapermen to volunteer his services as her cheerleader. Forget-ting, like her, the long memorandum he had so recently written on the economy, he began to praise her unreservedly in both the columns of the *Illustrated London News* and via the flattering notes he generally slipped into signed copies of his books. When she received a copy of *The Spirit of England* upon its publication that November, the prime minister added her own scrawl to the foot of a rather generic note of thanks: 'I have already read the Introduction, which is wonderful ... A book like your own is a rare event today. So few people could write them.'

It was perhaps Thatcher's advocacy of Englishness and Britishness which gave Sir Arthur's final books their dying glow. Both *The Spirit of England* and *Set in a Silver Sea* were almost love letters to the country he so adored.

'There was a strange ferment in the air,' he wrote in a typical passage, 'of vague, vehement talk of justice and treason, not to the King but to the community; of friars preaching apocalyptical sermons in streets and on village greens; of cities arming their men and watching their gates; of the war in the Marches where the Prince of Gwynedd, Llywelyn ap Gruffydd, enraged by the encroachments of the English officials, was making a new nation of the Welsh and burning the lands and castles of the Marchers.'

Like a proselytiser, he sent out copies to every corner of the land and even subjected himself to one final publicity tour – albeit to places such as Harrow School and the Ruislip Literary Society rather than anywhere more 'fashionable'. If there was an element of toadyism in his decision to send signed copies of *Set in a Silver Sea* to every senior member of the Royal Family, there was at least a hint that his offerings were welcome. Although he did not receive his longed-for Garter honour, he was hardly less delighted by the response of the Queen Mother, who sent him a three-page handwritten letter stating that she was giving a copy to every one of her grandchildren – 'which should send the sales up quite a lot!' wrote Sir Arthur to Pamela.

But all this activity took its toll on the historian. Even before beginning work on these books, he had spoken darkly of having 'no time', and it was quite routine for him to allege that he was virtually at the point of death. Under the strain of his current projects, it seemed almost that he was losing his mind. This was something which Pamela had always feared. At the time of writing his biography, she had been told by one of the historian's oldest living relations – an elderly cousin called Dorothy – that a doctor had warned her, at the time of his bout of adolescent mumps, that his temperature had risen so high that it would be better for him to die, as if he survived he would 'never be quite the same'. Suddenly, as Sir Arthur's errors and mishaps proliferated, she feared that the worst was finally coming to pass. In November 1983 he spent an entire day looking for a lost pair of glasses; early the following year he began confusing the days of the week, and there were even more embarrassing mistakes, such as phoning up the wrong lady, or – as happened in the case of the Duchess – accidentally sending a present to a former 'doter' on the birthday of his ex-wife.

Partly as a result of these troubles, each of the women in Sir Arthur's life was beginning to find the situation unsustainable. As early as 29 April 1980 – under two weeks since the historic meeting in the Crystal Room – Lorelei had told Hugo Vickers at a publishing party that 'Laura's new beau' was 'an old philanderer, somewhat soft in the head ... an old man dreaming that he can put the world to rights and thinking himself a youthful Knight Errant.' Even Anne, the most unstinting of the fold, began to give way: in the middle of 1983 she announced that she was going on holiday, having first arranged for a young woman to come and make Sir Arthur his evening meals. Similarly, Duchess Laura paid two sisters living in the area to take turns typing the historian's final masterworks – an arrangement that lasted until they both departed in search of more restful employment. Pamela, meanwhile, continued to do what she could, hosting the elderly visitor whenever possible, but she was increasingly aware that she was now too busy with her own life and career to continue as before.

'He was always on about my being troubled, tired etc.,' she later wrote, 'seeming to project his own cares on to me. I was nothing of the sort, although I did explain that I had too much to do to be able to help him with his own work.'

The madness, isolation and loneliness of Sir Arthur's life was clear from nearly all the letters he sent to Pamela and the Duchess in the lead-up to his eighty-fifth birthday, which was also to coincide with the launch of *Set in a Silver Sea*. One typical example was the screed he sent his former secretary on 24 November, following her refusal to 'pester' the chairman of Collins, Ian Chapman, and his wife, Margery, with further invitations to dine with them at South Street:

> The reason why I want to meet them in this private and personal way … is that I've been trying with so much patience, and with such an appalling expenditure of time and money, to win them both [two of the editorial directors, Christopher MacLehose and Stuart Proffitt] to the realisation of the extreme importance of my book and of its ultimate purpose, which at first they failed to see. I can't blame them for that, for to them my book was only one among many and had, in their view, to wait its turn, and having at last, at least partly, won them to my view and with all their sudden changes of mind and plan, won their gradual and grudging admiration for what I'm trying to do and my book's – as you say – readability, I can only precipitate a major show-down with Ian Chapman, as you urged me on the telephone, at the expense of losing their hard won, if erratic, interest in my book and books for ever. And, as there seems to be no one else at No. 8 who could publish my books in their place – even

Michael Hyde, my one ally, is leaving at Christmas, I should not be better off but worse. Yet there are, with the necessary pressure from Ian, some very important things, particularly over [the] cheaper paperback (against which Christopher MacLehose is adamant, thinking only as he is of [the] £12 hardback edition which to him is the end of everything, however ultimately useless to me) things which Ian – who I know is sympathetic over this – could make all the difference if I can only have the opportunity of an unofficial and friendly talk with him.

When Pamela, on another occasion, suggested that she find him a room at the Nurses' Club, just across the road from her flat, so that they could both attend a party together without reliving the difficulties of past stays, Sir Arthur demurred.

'It would only really be to relieve Anne,' he wrote, 'for there is no point me going there for its own sake … I have enough lonely evenings here and in my life,' he added Eeyorishly, 'not to go out of my way to have more, merely in order to spent the night in London when you go back after the party to your flat to sleep.'

His resistance to compromise remained firm to the last.

After spending another gloomy Christmas in Salisbury with Anne, Alwynne and Pussums, the long-awaited publication of Sir Arthur's book finally arrived. Once again, the *Sunday Times* arranged a special lunch at the Vintners' Hall to mark this important occasion, and the historian was particularly keen that Pamela should be there too.

'I do so very much appreciate it,' she wrote back, 'especially as I am so out of your life now. I am sure it will be a wonderful affair and you will receive countless tributes.'

The guest list, as five years previously, lived up to this expectation. Nearly all Sir Arthur's admirers in public life turned out for one last bash: three former prime ministers (Macmillan, Wilson and Douglas-Home), newspaper editors, the leaders of City livery companies and corporations, as well as fellow writers, past and present. A wide-angle photograph of the event showed row upon row of grey, pale, male figures. 'The only person I can recognise in it (apart from my horrible shrunken little self!),' wrote Sir Arthur to Pamela, 'is you, by your lovely hat.'

Written tributes to Sir Arthur and his final work soon began to pour in. 'Your latest book is the most astonishing of all your achievements,' wrote A. J. P. Taylor. 'I read it with a mixture of wonder and admiration.' Similar encomiums arrived from the usual host of establishment figures, most notably the Lord Chancellor, Quintin Hogg, who declared that the author had 'done an incomparable service' to his country through his many books.

But the letters that were most treasured by the historian came from far less exalted persons. One of these came from an elderly lady who had, long ago, been a parlour maid in the house where Sir Arthur had proposed to his first wife, Sylvia Shakerley. 'I just felt that I would like you to know,' wrote Noreen Allison, 'how much pleasure I get from your books and I can escape from my unhappiness once I sit down to read them.'

In his delight, Sir Arthur sent this letter to each of his lady friends. But it was a letter from a twenty-year-old student at the London School of Economics – the bastion of 'trendy' intellectualism – which most gratified the historian.

'Dear Sir,' this admirer wrote. 'In your introduction to your fine and noble book, *Set in a Silver Sea*, you say that you address yourself chiefly to the young. I am a young man, and I feel as though I have a duty to confirm that your message is both heard and understood.' The correspondent went on to write:

> ... Mine is a generation that must be the most poorly-educated for a long time: we are those who have suffered for our elders' ideologies. They, not us, decided at some distant time that all men were the same, that learning had no value, that no man should seek to be wiser than any other but should try to sink effortlessly into the unthinking society of which he is a part. They, not us, have undermined respect for education and learning by the way they teach – forsaking self-discipline and dignity they lounge before us in their deliberately-cultivated untidiness, thinking they create a more comradely classroom atmosphere ... They are laughable and therefore we laugh at them. But having ignored them, we have no one else from whom to learn and the consequence is inevitable: we have no learning.
>
> I cannot emphasise this enough. Many are those who want to learn, who want to be taught by wise and civilised teachers, but have no opportunity. Instead of telling us of England's past as you have done so brilliantly, they give us 'Current Affairs', in other words a rehash of the garbled tricky lies of contemporary politicians. Instead of clarifying the glories of our language, they excuse any debasement of it on the grounds that no man's manner of speaking is less admirable than any other's.
>
> It is hardly surprising, then, that they have produced a sceptical generation, disillusioned with the egalitarian dream, but nevertheless unlearned. This is why your 'People's History' is so

timely. To learn we have to teach ourselves, and here is a book to help us do exactly that (though is the price not a little prohibitive?). You have opened up for me the history of the country I live in and love in a marvellous, almost poetic, way. I assure you that I am not the only one; I assure you that your book will be read, more by the young than anyone, for our 'radical' elders seem to care nothing about it.

Do not despair that you are not heard [*the author added by way of crescendo*] for there is a new people who hear you and will remember what you have said many years from now. We are those who care about our country and what it might do for the world. Having seen the many mistakes of our elders in our own time we are better placed to learn; the sort of examples we shall revere will be yours – your lessons are even now being learnt.

Sir Arthur could not have wished for a better ending.

5

It was almost a tragedy that Sir Arthur lived for a further year after the completion of *Set in a Silver Sea*. Had he died immediately after that triumph – as he often seemed to hope – then his relationships with Pamela, the Duchess and Anne would have closed with a certain degree of mutual respect and understanding. Sadly, however, the historian's last months were beset with arguments and recriminations as severe as ever before.

The Duchess was the first to pull the plug.

'Arthur was already ill,' she recalled of his eighty-fifth birthday celebrations. 'Anyway,' she went on, 'I stopped the writing to me; it was too much for him and me too!'

When he insisted on calling her up in spite of her strictures, she could be brutally unsympathetic: in the winter of 1984, she responded to his threat to throw himself from a window with characteristic nonchalance – 'Well there's plenty of snow. You wouldn't hurt yourself.' The relationship was certainly dead long before the historian finally departed the world on 22 January 1985.

In his final letter – a Christmas card with another cheque – he summed up his position. 'I am sending this little token,' he wrote, 'of my love and gratitude for your dear friendship to buy some little thing for Christmas with my unchanging love, Your devoted Jimmy.' At the foot of the card, the Duchess added, regretfully: 'He was worse in health than I realised.'

Pamela, too, would have liked to have put some distance between herself and the restless octogenarian. She could not understand how, just when he had every right to relax and forget his troubles, he seemed to become once again insatiable for work and worry. Most of this concerned the recasting of his interminable 'fan list'; a task that Pamela always felt to be somewhat pointless, not least because most of Sir Arthur's readers were as old as, or even older than, himself.

In May 1984 he wrote:

> I'm afraid in my search in the chaotic basement, I found far more foreign letters than the small number of 1981–4 ones I was looking for, including several hundred *ILN* ones from [the] US, S. America, Canada, Australia, N. Zealand etc. dating from the sixties [and] seventies, that is the last twenty years. And though a certain number of these may have died or changed their addresses, twenty years is not very long and the majority of them should still be extant.

When Pamela said that she could not possibly sort through such a mass of correspondence, there were further distressing scenes at South Street.

'It isn't right or kind of you,' wrote Sir Arthur after one such altercation, 'to insist on what is right or wrong for me, when you naturally don't know what my circumstances and problems are, and, least of all, to be so censorious and even abusive about them.'

Not even Pamela's quick decision to enlist the support of another former secretary, one Constance Clayton, entirely resolved their difficulties: Sir Arthur complained that he should have been consulted first, and soon Pamela was herself unhappy sharing her responsibilities with an ever growing assortment of women.

'I am so sorry these lists seem to be giving us so much altercation,' she wrote in July. 'I don't *mean* to get short-tempered about them, but it does seem incredibly difficult to complete when the task is being carried out in two places at once.'

As Sir Arthur had indicated, much of his behaviour during these final months related to his growing sense of impoverishment. Forgetting what he had so recently revealed about his share portfolio, he told Pamela that inflation had reduced the purchasing power of his earnings 'tenfold or even twenty-fold' since their first meeting. Back then, he continued, 'I was still a comparatively rich man with an income still at the top of the writer's profession and in excess of that earned … by … many Cabinet Ministers and businessmen.' He said that he now felt just as he did 'before literary success came to me … having to skimp and refrain from spending [on] all sorts of things in order that I might have enough for the things that were really essential.'

Even the Conservative government seemed to be against authors, an affront he took personally. His final article for a daily newspaper, written in his last weeks, raised the alarm to the dangers of proposals to introduce VAT for books. 'I can only pray [it] may achieve its object,' he wrote in a letter thanking Pamela for her assistance, 'for I am afraid if it doesn't books and their writers and publishers will be in for a bad time.'

Money, however, was only a part of the trouble.

'If he was prepared to sell one of his pictures,' wrote Pamela at the foot of one of his many jeremiads, 'it might have kept him in comfort for another year.'

Of far greater moment was the fact that few people – not even his publishers – continued to regard either him or his work with the importance he wanted. Throughout 1984 Sir Arthur continued to ask Pamela to arrange dinner parties with various literary executives and agents to ensure that his work was given more care and attention. When she suggested he make his own dining arrangement at one of his seven clubs, the historian replied: 'I can hardly talk finance with him [Ian Chapman] when there's no one to talk of something else to Margery.'

Yet somehow it was all useless. In one of his final letters to his long-suffering publishers – who had, a decade previously, offered to pay him £30,000 if only he would lay aside all work besides the *Story of England* – he complained that they seemed to care more about promoting the works of the late G. M. Trevelyan.

Deteriorating health did little to soothe these feelings of bitterness and neglect. Arthritis, backache, bronchitis, toothache, heart palpitations – the list of Sir Arthur's ailments was legion. By the end, even he was prepared to submit himself to the daily ministrations of the 'leeches'.

'The doctor,' he wrote in May 1984, 'when he examined me yesterday, has put me under a new and heavy course of Antibiotics for my bronchitis and at present I hardly know whether I am standing on my head or my feet, so muzzy am I.'

His principal trouble was that he did not realise that, by living his life as though still a much younger man, he was exacerbating his conditions.

'I suppose if one had not known Arthur Bryant,' wrote Pamela at the foot of another one of his long letters, 'one would have appeared a very heartless character to have taken all this lightly. But it was an accentuation of all that had gone before, and I still thought his way of life was quite unnecessary, that he seemed to create obstacles which, with a little bit of common sense and organisation, would never have arisen.'

When he came to her flat for 'rest' he often made matters worse, such as the occasion when he leapt from a stationary taxi and insisted on marching across Kensington Gardens, or the time he arrived from Salisbury only to eat a sandwich and then speed away to Collins. On this latter occasion, the stress of entertaining Sir Arthur was made worse by the fact that Pamela soon discovered that he had forgotten his dinner jacket, needed for a party he was attending that evening, and so had to travel to Anne's flat in a deluge to get his spare one.

Flattery remained the last bond.

'It was absolutely heroic of you,' he wrote after the case of the forgotten dinner jacket, 'to have done what you did to retrieve my own incompetence and carelessness, and I feel very ashamed to have put you to all that trouble – and for giving me what was the happiest, for all my dizziness and forgetfulness and senile incompetence, time I have had for a long time.'

Sometimes he could become almost incoherent in his paeans of praise, and on at least one occasion he felt compelled to tear up a letter because it was overly excessive. Knowing that Pamela's exasperation with him was largely a result of the pressure of her own literary work, he repeatedly told her that her latest novel, *The Millrace*, was a masterpiece.

'You are quite wrong,' he retorted to one of her protestations, 'in saying that I keep telling people this because I have an obsession about it simply because of my affection for you; it is entirely *the other way round.*'

Promising to write reviews in the *Salisbury Journal* and a quarterly magazine, *This England* – a telling indication of his shrinking platform – he told her that the book made her debut novels seem mere 'prentice works'. In one of his last letters he copied out an entire paragraph, the opening of Chapter 14, declaring: 'Only a great creative writer, linking the eternal to the ephemeral, can write like that – that is why *The Millrace* places you, however few may yet see it, among the immortals.'

Like his beloved Macaulay, Sir Arthur was still contemplating the vastness of history until the end. Not satisfied with his previous plan of simply reworking various chapters of his other books to complete his eight volume *Story of England*, the historian looked out longingly over huge vistas of the past about which he had written little – the rise of the British Empire; the Jacobite rebellion, and many more topics of sufficient complexity for any lifetime. It would be left to other hands to complete what became a condensed three-volume history of England, began with *Set in a Silver Sea*, and concluded with *Freedom's Own Island* and *The Search for Justice*, which were both published posthumously.

Fighting the forces of evil, and himself, until the end, Sir Arthur gave his lost Duchess one final glimpse into his darkening world.

'I find hope and courage in the words of the old fourteenth-century Scottish pirate, Sir Andrew Barton,' he scrawled on the back of his Christmas card; an image of *The Madonna of the Rabbit.* 'Fight on, my man,' he quoted: 'I am hurt but I am not slain/ I'll lie me down and bleed awhile/And then rise up and fight again.'

With a shaking hand, he added that she too – 'dear valiant and undefeatable soul, with your lovely face and body' – had also refused to submit to the 'ills of health and fortune'.

But it was his last letter to Pamela, written the same week, that gave the truest image of the historian at his end:

> I'm so sorry I was too late last night to ring you [*he wrote some-what more prosaically*]. It was nearly eleven pm before I got up from feeding and petting poor lonely Pussums and grappling with the central heating which I turned on for the first time for two years, having forgotten what to do – and I didn't dare ring you for fear of waking you. But I shall be doing so tonight.
>
> God bless you and again thank you.
>
> Yours,
>
> Boaz

The next time Pamela heard from Myles Place it was the voice of Anne. She told her that she should come and see Sir Arthur. Her tone was calm almost to the point of relief. Not recognising the urgency of the situation, the younger woman said she would try to come at the weekend. 'It might be too late,' came the gentle rebuke. Two hours later, Pamela was at his bedside, not unlike the closing scene of her first novel. As the historian struggled for breath, the two women decided to call for an ambulance. In her last and perhaps greatest act of love, Anne suggested that Pamela should go with him on her own – she said she 'wasn't feeling up to it'.

When the former lovers reached the hospital, Sir Arthur was given oxygen. In between rapid gasps he began to speak quite cheerfully and coherently. He talked of getting back to Myles Place in order to carry on with his books. Gently, he squeezed Pamela by the hand and told her how glad he was that she had come.

He died that night.

Epilogue

For nearly all the women involved in Sir Arthur Bryant's life, nothing would be quite the same after his death on 22 January 1985; but in the case of Pamela, this was particularly so. After a decade and a half of spending almost every waking hour 'dealing' with him in some capacity, her time and energy were now free to be allocated elsewhere. It was not going to be easy.

Certainly, she knew that she was to play some role in the winding up of his estate, but whenever they had discussed this in his lifetime, the historian had been at pains to emphasise that most of the work would be undertaken by solicitors and other professionals. Her main role, as she understood it, was to serve as his literary executor, responsible for the handling of all his published and unpublished works. Shortly before his death, however, he hinted that there was another person, Christopher Falkus, who actively courted this position, and Pamela was by no means opposed to passing on the responsibility to someone who clearly had more knowledge and experience in these matters. Only a small part of her felt, along with several other interested parties, that this substitution was a double betrayal: Mr Falkus worked for Weidenfeld and Nicolson, the chief rival of the publishing house which had, for over fifty years, brought out Sir Arthur's many books.

Nevertheless, there was undoubtedly a sense of relief in Pamela's mind immediately after Sir Arthur's passing. His few surviving relatives rallied round and assisted her with the necessary funeral arrangements. For a blissful few days it felt as if everything had worked out for the best. Pamela almost felt pleased that after years of never taking a proper break, 'dear Arthur' had finally been forced to stop for good.

When she soon began sorting through some of the clutter in Myles Place, she was surprised to see her own views reflected rather poignantly in a brief account the historian had written at the time of his mother's demise in the late 1950s.

'Her face in death was the most beautiful thing I have ever seen,' he wrote, 'with all the cares and infirmities of the past sixty years as though they had never been – like some exquisite medieval alabaster of faith, purity and serenity.'

At the foot of this loose fragment of autobiography, Pamela added: 'Arthur Bryant's own face in death seemed very similar. I have never seen him looking so happy and free from care.'

The reaction of Duchess Laura to Sir Arthur's death was somewhat more ambivalent. 'I was often infuriated by his late night calls,' she immediately wrote to Hugo Vickers, 'but I shall certainly miss them.' She confessed that he had 'screamed "Wolf! Wolf!"' so often about his health that she had ceased to believe him and now felt guilty for failing to make a final visit to Myles Place. Part of her did not really want to attend the funeral at Salisbury Cathedral owing to the probable cast of mourners. 'The Close will be packed with his captive audience,' she wrote, '[and] also [the] bitter faces of his ex-mistresses etc.'

Little persuasion, however, was required to bring Laura to the cathedral for the service on Saturday, 2 March. Her young friend, who drove her down from London, left a vivid account of proceedings in his diary:

> We arrived in the Close on a quite bright day and walked in. I carried the wreath and we placed it at the foot of the coffin ... Sir Arthur had a Union Jack on top – a huge sprig of rosemary, another little wreath – and some red, white and blue ribbons. There was a small congregation that included Alwynne Bardsley (next to me) – 'Little Alwynne', who minded very much about the whole thing – Sir Julian Paget ... the Teynhams ... and others, John Cordle ... (a [Reginald] Maudling character – used to be an MP) – then various publishers and Pam Street, his ex-secretary and girlfriend.
>
> The service was very beautiful – and the two solitary trumpets above the West Door played 'Sunset' so very beautifully – always the most poignant moment. Afterwards we watched the very smooth undertakers remove the coffin skilfully and without any fuss. It went down. We were then instructed to follow on down ...
>
> Outside we watched the coffin depart, surrounded by flowers – to be cremated. The ashes will be returned in due course to the Cathedral.
>
> We then ... went along to Myles Place for tea. I had never been inside before – and often wanted to go, but somehow I had always been out of favour or not there at the right time. It was magnificent with the book-lined library, the hall with its gallery, the little dining-room, the room that led down to the garden with its long lawned alley down to the river. There was a big spread of tea. There were lots of people – always a grim atmosphere ...

Laura and I escaped as soon as we could ... then we drove
back to London.

Pamela had, yet again, managed Sir Arthur's affairs without fault
or any desire for recognition. At her instigation, the editor of the
Illustrated London News, Ian Bishop – whom she also entertained for
lunch at the White Hart – delivered the eulogy. 'I felt A. B. would
have approved,' she wrote in her pocket-diary.

On the morning of the funeral she had even helped resolve a
final mini-crisis. 'There was much fuss,' recalls Anne's niece, Diana
O'Grady, 'about a locked safe [thought to contain love letters]. Eventually, someone managed to find the key – inside there was nothing
but a tin of sardines!'

Not everything, however, could be sorted out by Pamela. On the
Friday after the funeral, Sir Arthur's legal executor, Alan Macfadyen,
journeyed down to Salisbury from the offices of Messrs William
Charles Crocker of Farringdon Street to go through his last will and
testament. Each of the beneficiaries – Anne, Alwynne and Pamela –
had already received copies of this document, though it was not until
it was properly explained that its complexities were fully untangled.

The first surprise was that, contrary to the various promises he had
made, Sir Arthur had never actually redrafted the will he had lodged
with his solicitors in 1967 – a year before Pamela had first written
to him about her biography of her father. With so many changes in
his life since that time, this fact alone seemed almost unbelievable.
But it paled virtually into insignificance besides the codicil that he
had added in 1976. This revised the provisions of his existing will to
convert his estate into a kind of investment trust, making regular

payments to each beneficiary for the duration of their lifetime. Like the premise of an Agatha Christie murder mystery, the last survivor would then inherit the remaining capital – a fortune currently estimated to be in the region of £750,000.

Pamela's laconic diary entry for the day of this extraordinary meeting was apt: 'Such chaos.' A few years later she would articulate her precise feelings through the leading character of a novel, largely based on these events, suitably entitled *The Beneficiaries*:

> It was a damned silly will to have left ... but then ... her late
> mother Lady Rayner had always been capricious, the more so
> as she grew older. Joanna would not really have been surprised
> at anything she did; and Gloria would certainly have never
> brooked any advice over the way she bequeathed her estate,
> either from the now retired Percy Pemberton or his associates
> in the firm of Pemberton Stubbs in Chancery Lane.

To decode this text would require little more than the replacement of 'mother' with 'lover'; 'Lady (Gloria) Rayner' with 'Sir Arthur', and 'Joanna' with 'Pamela'. What the novel did not fully explore, however, was the crushing sense of guilt that Pamela felt as the youngest of the three beneficiaries. Were she to outlive both Anne and Alwynne, as seemed more than likely, then their entire families would receive absolutely nothing from a man who had, at various times, been either an uncle, a brother-in-law or a rather distant stepfather. Such a position would have been difficult for anyone, let alone a 'compulsive mental masochist' who repeatedly declared that she 'hated taking'.

These scruples do not appear to have been shared by many of the other people in Sir Arthur's life, particularly those who had been completely overlooked. No sooner had the details of the will been made public than Pamela was telephoned by Duchess Laura. She said that she could hardly believe that, after all Sir Arthur's promises, she had not been gifted a single memento – even the bust he had once promised her ended up going to Harrow School. Such entreaties predictably left Pamela unmoved.

'The chaos and *the greed*,' she hastily wrote in her pocket-diary: 'Laura ... furious re[garding] will not mentioned [*sic*].'

Then there were those who, albeit with less rancour, contacted Pamela about small items they believed to be theirs. The verger wanted to retrieve some valuable books he had, long ago, lent to the eminent historian. '*Success!*' he wrote after making his way into the master bedroom. 'I found my books immediately on the window-sill.'

More sadly, there were also letters from relations of Sir Arthur's first wife, Sylvia, who wanted to know if they could be reunited with various family portraits and artefacts which were supposedly lent to him in the 1920s.

'I fear I have no correspondence whatsoever,' wrote Sir Geoffrey Shakerley, 'concerning the loan of certain items ... to Sir Arthur ... [but] I gather Ian [Dunlop] has been granted two paintings ... and I wondered whether the same could apply in my case.'

Pamela could always be relied upon to do all that she could in such circumstances, and many of these heirlooms were eventually returned. She also, in the weeks and months after Sir Arthur's death, personally undertook the onerous task of responding to the many hundreds of letters, both of condolence and general correspondence, which arrived at Myles Place. The sheer range of these missives was prodigious. A representative sample included a letter from an elementary school pupil in America who said he wanted to become a 'great author like you'; a query about a passage in one of Sir Arthur's books from an attentive reader, and a communication from the former Leader of the Michigan House of Representatives, William R. Bryant, Jr., who wanted to know if he might be related to the famous historian.

Despite her anger about the way Sir Arthur had left his affairs, Pamela responded to each of these letters personally, without any hint of her true feelings. Most touchingly, she sent a long reply to the American schoolboy. After explaining about the intended recipient's death, and her own role as his secretary over the years, she wrote: 'I feel sure you have the determination to follow up your life's ambition to become a great author like Sir Arthur ... I do wish he could have seen your letter, as he would have been most impressed.'

This painstaking attention to detail inevitably proved too much. Alongside helping to organise a memorial service for Sir Arthur at Westminster Abbey – to say nothing of her own life and affairs – Pamela simply could not keep pace with the amount of labour required. The lawyers, too, were sensitive to this fact. Insisting that she stay for as long as required at her favourite hotel in Salisbury, the White Hart, they also provided her with the money required to engage a professional archivist and suitable administrative staff to catalogue the entire contents of Myles Place. The report subsequently drawn up gave a powerful summary of the full extent of Sir Arthur's dealings with the great and the good.

Alongside letters from the likes of P. G. Wodehouse and H. G. Wells from the early part of his writing career, there were packets of letters to and from a whole host of senior figures in the British establishment, including field marshals, cabinet ministers and innumerable members of the aristocracy. At the suggestion of another of Sir Arthur's old acquaintances, Sir Denis Hamilton, most of these documents eventually found their way to the Liddell Hart Centre for Military Archives at King's College, London.

The lawyers were less certain of what to do with the piles of documents said to be 'of no value'. These were the many thousands of letters the historian had exchanged over the years with his *inamoratas*.

'A. B. was a prolific letter-writer,' Pamela felt compelled to write to Mr Macfadyen, '... it seems to me that after the first few years we entered into a kind of paper war to the end as, sadly, I often disagreed with him.'

Initially it seemed likely that the entire consignment would be destroyed; but, following a request from Duchess Laura for the return of her correspondence, it was decided that it would be more proper to allow each of the ladies to come and collect their respective boxes.

The memorial service at Westminster Abbey was a far grander affair than the funeral in Salisbury. Due to the lengthy obituaries which had appeared in the newspapers, as well as his high reputation in 'establishment' circles, there were many hundreds of mourners, including: Denis Thatcher; Lord Denning; the Queen Mother's representative, her private secretary Lieutenant-Colonel Sir Martin Gilliat; John Profumo; Dame Barbara Cartland; Lord and Lady Longford, and innumerable politicians from both major parties. Sir John Gielgud read from one of Sir Arthur's wartime articles on the ennobling power of love, and a stirring eulogy was delivered by the historian Lord Blake, who remembered the deceased as 'a writer whose work gave more pleasure to more people than those of any other historian past or present'.

Afterwards, by arrangement with Anne, some thirty people were invited back to Pamela's flat at South Street for drinks. History does not record which – if any – of the other 'muses' were among their number, but it at least possible that Alwynne received a joint invitation with Gielgud, whom she had specifically asked to accompany herself and her son, Daniel, for the day. The two women continued to exchange letters and Christmas presents for the remainder of their lives.

Nor was this the only surviving link between Pamela and Sir Arthur's circle. Most obviously, the complexities of his will necessitated frequent contact with both Anne and Alwynne. This took the form not only of attending various storage depots and auction houses, but also trying to persuade them to allow the solicitors to break the trust arrangements, so that they could each part with equal shares of the estate. Pamela had already convinced them, in the weeks after Sir Arthur's death, to allow the most recent secretaries and neighbours to receive suitable monetary or sentimental gifts – predictably, none of them had been thought of, to say nothing of the cats, which were all found new homes by Pamela.

But breaking the trust proved especially difficult. Anne, in particular, felt that her ex-husband's posthumous wishes should be fully respected, even if she stood likely to lose out. Only through the assistance of both Alwynne and Mr Macfadyen was it eventually agreed, in 1988, to end the whole saga. So circuitous was the process that the solicitor felt compelled to apologise on several occasions for the excessive legal fees: the matter, he lamented, was of 'unusual complexity'.

Pamela's career as a novelist had, by this time, reached new heights. Between 1981 and 1996, she averaged one book a year, with titles such as *The Stepsisters, Doubtful Company* and *Hindsight* providing her with both a respectable additional source of income and a gratifying amount of public acclaim. A moment of especial pride came in July 1986, when her old friend Christina Foyle made her the guest of honour at one of her famous lunches – an event attended by many leading novelists of the day, including Jeffrey Archer. While several of Pamela's books were directly inspired by her time with Sir Arthur, only a handful of her readers could have realised this, and she had, in any case, long ceased to harbour resentment towards him. As long ago as March 1984, after rereading her typed correspondence with the historian, she wrote: 'I realise I owe him a lot, however ghastly it sometimes was. I gained so much experience and the added bonus of at last being able to stand on my own two feet.'

Freed from the corrosive influence of Sir Arthur's will, Pamela's friendship with Anne also blossomed. They saw one another most weeks for tea, either at Anne's flat or, more typically, South Street. Unlike at the time of their first meeting, it was now the older woman who was desperate to escape loneliness and isolation. Pamela, who often liaised with hospitals and care homes on her behalf, wrote scores of entries in her pocket-diaries such as: 'Anne to tea', 'oh dear, I fear for her memory' and, finally, on 1 May 1993: 'Anne Bryant has died. Poor thing. She gave up.' It was the end of an era.

The rest of the 'fold' likewise attempted to continue with life after their own fashion. While Lorelei Robinson never did meet 'Number Four' before her death in the early 2000s, she appears to have enjoyed a longer and more carefree dotage than Alwynne, who was diagnosed with dementia in the late 1980s and subsequently went to live with her elder son in South Africa, where she died just a few years later. No more is known of Barbara Longmate after the tragedy of her son killing his wife and children, but doubtless her final years, passed out in Rhodesia, were not particularly happy ones. Duchess Laura, meanwhile, continued to live in some style until her death in 1990, just one day after what would have been Sir Arthur's ninety-first birthday.

From time to time Pamela was contacted by people interested in the late historian. She always felt that he deserved a full-scale biography, but a suitable author never quite materialised. Her first choice was the young editorial assistant at Collins, Robin Baird-Smith, who had helped her with *Portrait of a Historian*, but he had carefully dodged the undertaking.

'It is an awe-inspiring idea,' he wrote after discussing the project at South Street, 'and I didn't say too much at the time for fear of embarrassing myself!'

Two of the archivists involved in cataloguing the Bryant Papers, Brigid Allen and Jennie Cotter, were also briefly in contention, and one William Seymour even obtained Anne Bryant's permission to author such a book. But either because of the unmanageable quantity of materials available, or the objections of other interested parties, no major biography was ever completed.

The task of composing a narrative of Sir Arthur's life fell instead to a young writer who had just made his name with a biography of Neville Chamberlain's Foreign Secretary, Lord Halifax. Andrew Roberts had been put in touch with Pamela by Christina Foyle, and he contacted her in October 1993 with a plea for assistance.

'As I said on the phone,' he subsequently wrote, 'I do hope you will not take offence at my treatment of Bryant's politics. I am fairly right-wing myself, but I think he was beyond the pale!'

It speaks volumes of Pamela's residual loyalty to the historian that she did not give Mr Roberts access to her vast private archive; nor did she give any real clue of her extraordinary relationship with him.

'I have a great deal of information about him,' she wrote back, cautiously, 'but aware of his desire for privacy, I have never attempted to write anything else about him [besides *Portrait of a Historian*] and have stuck to writing novels.'

Permission to quote from his works beyond statutory 'fair usage' was withheld.

When the biography – a chapter in *Eminent Churchillians* – appeared shortly afterwards, Sir Arthur's reputation received a blow from which it was never fully to recover. Focusing particularly on his work as an amateur diplomat in the lead-up to the Second World War, the author judged Sir Arthur to have been a 'Nazi sympathiser and a fascist fellow-traveller ... [as well as] a supreme toady, fraudulent scholar and humbug'. While later academic opinion would partially revise many of these judgements, few at the time risked defending the disgraced historian. Even Pamela, although shaken by the manner of the indictment, wondered in her pocket-diary whether there had not been some justification for 'put[ting] the boot in'.

Far more damaging for Pamela was the discovery that her revered father, A. G. Street, had, as a youth of eighteen, fathered an illegitimate child with one of the family's domestic servants. Certain that such a moral lapse could not have been possible, Pamela simply refused to believe the claims of her half-sibling's relations on the latter's death in 1992. Only when this lady's family subsequently sent her a copy of a legal agreement signed between their respective grandparents – to the effect that the child would be provided for so long as all contact ceased – did Pamela, almost, relent.

This well-meaning attempt by her new relations to 'let bygones by bygones' proved to be the beginning of the end for Pamela's mental health. Although her life had recently appeared to brighten both through her success as a novelist and her close relationship with her adored grandson, Rupert, she now sunk into her old state of depression and self-doubt. Following a final psychological breakdown in 1996, she spent the last eleven years of her life in and out of hospitals and care homes, a mere shadow of her former self.

At the time of her death in 2007, a family friend wrote to her daughter, Miranda McCormick, to say that he had hardly known such a 'genuinely sweet and lovely person ... always supportive in what one was doing and taking a keen interest in other people'.

'She was always so very kind and cheerful,' he wrote, 'putting on a wonderful front to keep up appearances.'

Similarly, in his eulogy at her funeral service at Mortlake Crematorium, South West London, her old friend at Collins, Robin Baird-Smith, remembered with gratitude her 'immense charm' and her winning gift of 'know[ing] how to listen'.

As such memories suggest, there had clearly been a lot more to Pamela's life than her involvement with Sir Arthur, however important that time had been. Miranda would later write a vivid account of her mother's wartime experiences in her book, *Farming, Fighting and Family*, and it seems that, in her old age, Pamela also began to view the whole period between 1970 and 1985 in broader perspective. One of her later pocket-diary entries, composed just a few years before her final collapse, may serve as a fitting endnote.

'How one changes as the years go by,' she wrote. 'Things one minded about passionately seem so stupid looking back. Was one the same person? Hard to believe.'

Acknowledgements

This book would simply not have been possible without the full support and cooperation of the owners of the letters and papers on which it is based. To each of them I can only inadequately convey my enormous gratitude: Miranda McCormick, Gillian and Daniel Bardsley, Jason Brooke, Rupert Davies, Diana O'Grady and Hugo Vickers. Their support has gone far beyond allowing me access to their letters: they have been a constant source of advice and support; often they have transcribed or photographed documents, and many times they have each extended to me their warm hospitality.

Others, too, have helped recreate the events narrated in this book in ways which I could never have anticipated. Adrian House and Nicolas Wright generously provided me with invaluable stories and anecdotes about their time working with Sir Arthur Bryant during the years covered in this book. Lady Antonia Fraser, Sir Ronald Harwood, Paul Johnson, Sir William Rees-Mogg, Kenneth Rose, Sir Roy Strong and Philip Ziegler gave up much of their time to respond to my queries. I am also extremely grateful to Susanna Hoe, who was kind enough to speak with me about her time working for the famous historian in the late 1960s, and how his support and encouragement helped launch her own writing career. It should be noted that she remained on good terms with him after she ceased working for him, and she also developed a lifelong friendship with Pamela Street.

For commenting on earlier drafts of this book, and general discussion and correspondence, I am particularly grateful to: Professor Jeremy Black, Ursula Buchan, Daniel Johnson, Professor Antony Lentin, Robert Low, Amy Ripley, Fletcher Robinson, Fleur Rossdale, Neville Bass and Professor Julia Stapleton. So many books have been of assistance to me that it would be invidious to attempt a comprehensive list – but the outstanding general histories of post-war Britain by Jeremy Black, Peter Hennessy, David Kynaston, Virginia Nicholson and Dominic Sandbrook have been particularly helpful to me. For details about Bryant's life, I remain indebted to the previous biographies of him by Andrew Roberts and Pamela Street, as well as Professor Julia Stapleton's *Sir Arthur Bryant and National History in Twentieth Century Britain*, which remains the most authoritative work on his public life. All errors in the present book are naturally my own.

As with my previous work on Bryant, I am grateful to the staff at the Liddell Hart Centre for Military Archives. Not many of their visitors, I would hazard to guess, have shown quite as much interest as I have in two boxes among the historian's papers labelled 'Secretaries', but those repositories shed unexpected light on my subject, and provided the ideal opening for this book.

For his incredible work in driving the whole project forwards and overcoming numerous difficulties, including the unprecedented disruption caused by the Covid-19 pandemic, I am enormously grateful to my publisher, Tom Perrin. From our first meeting in August 2018, he has been unstinting with his help and advice; the present book would have been very different without him. I would also like to express my thanks to George Tomsett and Laura Kincaid for their invaluable help with the editing process.

I would not like to forget those who played no knowing part in the writing of this book, notably my colleagues and students, who collectively remind me each day of the real value of scholarship.

Most of all, however, I am grateful to my wife, Rachel, whose insight into both history and human nature far surpasses my own. To her, this book is dedicated.

W. Sydney Robinson
January 2021